Adv

Pursuing Quality, Access, and Affordability

"Faculty members, deans, provosts, and presidents who want to improve their institutions can all find valuable food for thought in these pages. Ehrmann uses examples of several colleges and universities that have had notable success in improving the quality of education, affordability, and graduation rates while drawing on his own years of experience to present a wealth of useful ideas about how to bring about real reform."—*Derek Bok, 300th Anniversary University Research Professor and former president, Harvard University*

"Higher education has been headed toward a crisis of cost, quality, and equity for decades. Institutions often attend to one issue but not others, leaving the enterprise sorely lacking in a way forward. This book is one of the most important to be published in higher education in decades. It showcases institutions that have made progress on all three fronts. The book provides a beacon to lead other institutions into a sustainable and healthy future in which all students, faculty, and staff thrive. The vision for higher education outlined in this book is fundamentally different from how institutions have operated up until now. It requires institutional transformation that, although challenging, will ultimately give higher education the resiliency it needs to endure in coming decades. This book provides the principles, approaches, and case studies to help institutions in this difficult but worthy work of change."—*Adrianna Kezar, Wilbur Kieffer Endowed Professor and Dean's Professor of Leadership, Director of the Pullias Center for Higher Education, University of Southern California*

"Ehrmann's treatment of how to enhance student outcomes in higher education goes deep into the centrality of teaching and learning as a core function of the college. It also explores the emerging frontier of technology-enabled instruction and student services, data-driven decision-making, and remaking the academy for the next 100 years. It is a practical and thought-provoking work."—*Louis Soares, Chief Learning and Innovation Officer, American Council on Education*

"The problem: U.S. higher education is teeming with initiatives that seek to improve access, *or* quality, *or* affordability. But these efforts are typically siloed, fragmented, and under-performing, hindered as much by educators' own sense of what *can't* be done as by other impediments. The Ehrmann solution: An evidence-informed Integrative framework for campus change that knits all three priorities together and makes each a means to the other. Making superb use of case studies from broad access institutions, research evidence, and Ehrmann's own lifetime of leadership in the digital revolution, *Quality, Access,* and *Affordability* provides a persuasive, practical, and long-view guide to implementing transformative educational change across an entire institution and, ultimately, U.S. higher education as a whole. Every educator who wants to make higher education more responsive and more empowering for today's students will find this book both illuminating and immensely useful."—*Carol Geary Schneider; Consultant, Lumina Foundation; and President Emerita, Association of American Colleges & Universities*

"I plan to use this as a textbook in our graduate program on learning, design, and technology! It offers great insights into academic transformation and its implications for academic outcomes, culture, and professional roles. For example, as the book illustrates, future leaders must be skilled at working across organizational boundaries; Ehrmann shows how they will need to bridge hidden clashes in assumptions, culture, and even terminology (e.g., common terms with two or more widely used, clashing definitions, terms such as *teaching, online course*, and *transformation.*"—*Yianna Vovides; Director, Learning Design and Research, Center for New Designs in Learning and Scholarship (CNDLS); Curriculum Director and Professor, Learning, Design, and Technology, Graduate School of Arts and Sciences, Georgetown University*

"In *Pursuing Quality, Access,* and *Affordability,* Steve Ehrmann advances a compelling narrative on how higher education can be improved. Basing his analysis on six extensive institutional case studies, he outlines how it is possible for institutions to create what he terms *3fold gains* in educational quality, equitable access, and stakeholder affordability. These gains are achieved through Integrative learning-based constellations of mutually supportive educational strategies, organizational foundations, and interactions with the wider world. The book offers a cogent rationale for how such coordinated efforts can enhance quality, access, and affordability on an institutional scale. As higher education prepares for a post-COVID educational landscape much changed by current challenges, now is the time for forward-thinking institutions to imagine this future. Ehrmann's careful study, based on actual experiences of institutions that have achieved success in these areas at the core of higher education's mission and purpose, provides an excellent blueprint for success."—*David Eisler, President, Ferris State University*

PURSUING QUALITY, ACCESS, *AND* AFFORDABILITY

PURSUING QUALITY, ACCESS, *AND* AFFORDABILITY

A Field Guide to Improving Higher Education

Stephen C. Ehrmann

Foreword by Jillian Kinzie

STERLING, VIRGINIA

COPYRIGHT © 2021 BY STYLUS PUBLISHING, LLC

Published by Stylus Publishing, LLC.
22883 Quicksilver Drive
Sterling, Virginia 20166-2019

All rights reserved. No part of this book may be reprinted or reproduced in any form or by any electronic, mechanical, or other means, now known or hereafter invented, including photocopying, recording, and information storage and retrieval, without permission in writing from the publisher.

Library of Congress Cataloging-in-Publication Data
The CIP for this text has been applied for.

13-digit ISBN: 978-1-62036-990-6 (cloth)
13-digit ISBN: 978-1-62036-991-3 (paperback)
13-digit ISBN: 978-1-62036-992-0 (library networkable e-edition)
13-digit ISBN: 978-1-62036-993-7 (consumer e-edition)

Printed in the United States of America

All first editions printed on acid-free paper
that meets the American National Standards Institute
Z39-48 Standard.

Bulk Purchases
Quantity discounts are available for use in workshops and for staff development.
Call 1-800-232-0223

First Edition, 2021

To my mother, Dorothy Teach Ehrmann, who inspired me to write books, and to my patiently supportive family and friends who helped me get through 4 years of work on this one. Above all, to my wife and life partner, Leslie Berger Ehrmann, sine qua non.

That's a great idea but we don't have the money and no one has the time.
—Origin unknown

We already tried that here, and it doesn't work.
—Origin unknown

It takes a village . . .
—Possibly an African proverb

Know what to leave out.
—Dan Jenkins, sportswriter

CONTENTS

FOREWORD

Expanding and improving opportunities for more students to complete a high-quality undergraduate education is a national priority. Many institutions are implementing policies to accelerate completion through "15 credits to finish" campaigns, and states are investing in tuition-free college or dual enrollment programs to increase access and save students time and money. Other institutions are finding that activities such as first-year seminars, undergraduate research, and internships, collectively dubbed *high-impact practices* (HIPs), provide students with meaningful educational experiences that bolster completion rates (Kuh et al., 2013). Policies, models, and programs to increase student success are flourishing. Although the emphasis on increasing college quality, access, and affordability is high, real progress has been modest. The gloomy reality is that many students fail to complete degrees they start and debt levels are rising along with skepticism about the value of college. Consequently, when a book proclaims to address these challenges head-on and baldly promises 3fold gains, it deserves the attention of higher education policymakers, educators, and scholars.

As I eagerly started reading *Pursuing Quality, Access,* and *Affordability*, I immediately thought back to my work on a related publication, *Student Success in College* (Kuh et al., 2010), which described the practices of 20 institutions that engaged, retained, and graduated students at higher than expected levels. Using an intensive, mixed-method research design, we explored these institutions' practices and programs and outlined a set of six principles that explained the conditions that promote student success. The six institutional attributes—a living mission, unshakeable focus on student learning, environments adapted for educational enrichment, clearly marked pathways to student success, improvement-oriented ethos, and shared responsibility for educational quality—are necessary qualities for achieving higher rates of student success. The study documented effective educational strategies, but said little about affordability. Although many of the institutional practices are now somewhat dated, the book provided persuasive evidence that *institutions* shape student success.

Pursuing Quality, Access, and *Affordability,* I am happy to say, takes the study of effective colleges and universities to its necessary next level. Stephen C. Ehrmann expands our understanding about institutional change by explicating strategies and documenting the achievement of three challenging goals: quality, access, and affordability. The presentation of six institutions' experiences demonstrates how student success strategies imply changes in how higher education is organized. The cases suggest three contrasting ways to organize an institution—the Instruction Paradigm, Individualized Paradigm, and Integrative Paradigm—in the pursuit of 3fold gains in quality, equitable access, and affordability. Each paradigm makes different assumptions about learning and how to support it.

The goal of achieving 3fold gains in higher education is bold. Most leaders adhere to the "choose two" rule of the three constraints of the iron triangle. A restaurant's maxim that food can be cheap and tasty but not healthy, or tasty and healthy but not cheap, is about trading constraints. The adage allows for any combination of the elements involved, except the combination of all three. This book challenges the assumption of inevitable tradeoffs among quality, access, and affordability in higher education by illustrating how some institutions have made progress on all three fronts simultaneously. Breaking the constraints of the iron triangle requires the rejection of longstanding problematic beliefs, for example that increasing access with respect to both numbers and entering student performance levels will cost more and lead to reductions in quality. The institutions in this book offer fascinating illustrations of ways to break the rule of the iron triangle. For example, they demonstrate how scaled-up use of HIPs such as first-year seminars and internships can simultaneously improve quality, equity of access, and affordability for the student and the institution.

My sense of the higher education landscape today is that institutions, states, and higher education member organizations and foundations are leaning into the kinds of experimentation and new thinking that pursuing 3fold gains demands. Yet, as initiatives get underway, I think it is important to foreground the important ideas beyond the particulars of change. Five meta-lessons have emerged from my consultations with colleges and universities that are initiating change: assume institutional responsibility for change; commit to equity-mindedness; tailor "best practices"; connect initiatives; and assess for student success. These five meta-lessons are foundational to efforts to transform colleges and universities and achieve 3fold gains.

The first meta-lesson is that the institution must assume responsibility for change. All too often, I have encountered university administrators and educators who blame their low completion rates on poor student motivation or deficient preparation, yet eagerly attribute small improvements in student persistence to institutional policies and practices. Student persistence problems deserve more investigation than explaining them as something the student did or did not do. Even more, student impact research demonstrates that what students experience in college mediates student inputs and outcomes, which means it matters how institutions deploy their resources to ensure students are engaged in practices to promote learning and success.

The assumption of institutional responsibility is consistent with the inclusive principles and collaborative action of the Individualized and Integrative Paradigms described in this book. The adage of institutional responsibility is well illustrated by Guttman College, which was designed with needs of urban, first-generation students in mind. As such, Guttman took responsibility for designing structured experiences that require students to engage in HIPs such as service-learning and undergraduate research early in their academic journey. The lesson here is that it is not sufficient to explain why students cannot do something because of their background or demands on their time, rather the institution must recognize the barriers and then make engagement possible. This requires collaboration across the institution, among faculty, and in the case of Guttman, with the surrounding community.

Another approach to increasing institutional responsibility for student success is to flip the narrative by asking what the institution is doing to prepare for the students who are entering. Or, as McNair et al. (2016) put it: Is this a student-ready campus? Some of the beliefs of the Individualized Paradigm, which focus on engaging students who could not otherwise get an education, illustrate a commitment to developing a model that works for students. As related in this book, Governors State adopted the student-ready narrative by intentionally organizing its initiatives around the animating idea of identifying student strengths and building on them rather than simply providing remedies for weaknesses. The meta-lesson of taking responsibility means that assumptions about students' perceived deficits and beliefs about factors for student success must be questioned, myths must be busted, and the focus must be on what educators can, and must, do to change institutions for students.

The second meta-lesson is the adoption of a commitment to *equity-mindedness*. According to Bensimon et al. (2016), the pursuit of equity-mindedness, which emphasizes inclusive excellence through educational reform, "foregrounds the policies and practices contributing to differences in educational achievement and abstains from blaming students for those accumulated disparities" (p. 1). For example, feedback from historically underrepresented students about where Georgia State University was falling short, combined with disaggregated data showing that students who took three courses together in cohorts of freshman learning communities (FLCs) had higher GPAs and were more likely to retain their state merit scholarships and graduate on time, motivated the expansion of FLCs to all new students. This example of equity-minded practice—getting input from underrepresented students, disaggregating data, and committing to inclusive practice—demonstrates how equity-mindedness can motivate institutional action. Although the Instruction Paradigm described in this book has a vision of equality that demands teaching all students the same and assuming the good ones will succeed, the Individualized and Integrative Paradigms promote equity-mindedness by operating from the assumption that all students can achieve excellence in the right circumstances.

Enhancements in higher education have historically advanced through the adoption of "best practices" or by implementing "what works." However, it is my experience that such an approach is insufficient to make an appreciable difference in student success. My third meta-lesson is that practices and programs require significant contextualization, including tailoring based on the specific measurements of the institution to get a true fit. Institutional data, including enrolled student characteristics, program evaluation results, student engagement and learning outcomes results, campus climate studies, learning analytics, and other real-time signals must inform the continuous alteration of practices to the institution.

The effective adoption of best practices, or any of the educational strategies described in this book, requires tailoring and implementation with fidelity. For example, the implementation of meta-majors in the first year could appear to be a simple way to place students in courses. Yet implementation requires tailoring to the institution's majors. A commitment to fidelity requires curricular adjustments so that introductory courses provide adequate preparation for multiple majors, and that in turn relies on administrators and educators to build the knowledge and skill to make adjustments for their majors and their students' needs. Likewise, the replication of Governors State's clear pathways via the Dual Degree Program demands careful customizing to local needs and tailored collaboration with nearby community colleges to expand peer learning, cohort programs, and team projects.

A fourth meta-lesson is that improvement approaches must be integrated and connected to make a real difference. It is not enough to have an assortment of programs sponsored by different offices that engage many small groups of students and seem to be helpful. Rather, all efforts must be explicitly connected to the goal and to a theory of change and be thoughtfully coordinated to address student success goals. George Kuh and I (Kinzie & Kuh, 2017) suggested the use of "driver diagrams" to coordinate institutional efforts to increase student success. In this schema, the outcome "increased student success" is achieved by specifying the major causal explanations (drivers) to reach the goal and then identifying a variety of specific activities or interventions that align with the drivers and create conditions to realize the intended outcome.

This book shows how some institutions have assembled a set of coordinated, mutually supportive institutional changes in order to pursue gains in quality, access, and affordability. As the Georgia State case demonstrates, the recipe for success was an organized constellation of programs guided by common assumptions, including, for example, that institutional action should be guided by evidence, student abilities can be influenced by action, and action must be achieved through cross-campus collaboration. A series of changes can create the potential for 3fold gains, but it is only the thoughtful assembly of a constellation of initiatives that enables gains in quality, access, and costs to be realized.

Since I am an educational researcher and proponent of assessment to inform improvements in colleges and universities, it will probably come as no surprise that my final meta-lesson promotes the use of a combination of data about students' academic performance, learning outcomes, and student input on educationally purposeful activities to pursue 3fold gains. Assessment results and real-time analytics must be combined whenever possible to pinpoint needed action. Leaders at the University of Central Oklahoma used their National Survey of Student Engagement (NSSE) data to first expose high and low responses in relation to peer comparison institutions and then explore possible causes for these levels of performance. Then they shifted to identifying strategies for alleviating the root causes of low performance areas. These same items were then used as metrics as the institution worked through the root causes. Similarly, the first step in Georgia State's turnaround was to collect data around institutional problems that hindered student access and success.

National assessment projects like NSSE provide participating institutions with data while also offering a national portrait about aspects of the educational experience that matter to student success. The pursuit of an assessment plan for student success demands a complex approach that couples evidence of learning, student success (persistence and graduation rates), and access to investigate explanations and take action to improve. Assessment for student success is grounded in an explicit commitment to use data to change the conditions for educational quality and outcomes. Assessment activities must also provide feedback to the institution about how well it is achieving 3fold gains and to what extent educational strategies are contributing to improved outcomes.

This final point about assessment returns me to my recollections of the 20 colleges and universities profiled in *Student Success in College* (Kuh et al., 2010). One of the most inspiring attributes of these institutions was their commitment to using and acting on data about educational quality and assessing whether policies, programs, and practices had the desired effect on increased student success. These institutions were rarely satisfied with their performance, and they used data in ongoing efforts to tinker and improve. This condition, which we dubbed "positive restlessness," turned out to be a key factor in initiating and sustaining institutional effectiveness. This same commitment to assessing what contributes to 3fold gains and to their continuous improvement seems to undergird the approaches deployed among the case history institutions in this book.

The trinity of 3fold gains is achievable in higher education and is a concept worthy of more widespread consideration. Completion without quality is an empty promise, and access without affordability is a fraud. Now more than ever is the time for college and university leaders, educators, and higher education policymakers to dream and work collectively to transform higher education by designing effective educational strategies to achieve 3fold gains. The approaches and case histories featured in this book offer shining examples for higher education.

—Jillian Kinzie

Jillian Kinzie is associate director of the Indiana University Center for Postsecondary Research and the National Survey of Student Engagement (NSSE) Institute. She is also a senior scholar with the National Institute for Learning Outcomes Assessment (NILOA) project. She is coauthor of *Using Evidence of Student Learning to Improve Higher Education* (Jossey-Bass, 2015), *Student Success in College: Creating Conditions that Matter* (Jossey-Bass, 2005/2010), and *One Size Does Not Fit All: Traditional and Innovative Models of Student Affairs Practice* (Routledge, 2006/2013).

PREFACE

Higher education faces a triple challenge: compelling, urgent needs to improve what and how students learn; who can learn successfully; and what the student and other stakeholders need to invest in time and money in order for the process to work.

The thorny question is: In the real world, is making headway on all three of those umbrella goals—quality, access, and affordability—even possible? Spoiler alert: Some institutions are already doing it. But it took me four months of searching to find the first one. Perhaps that's partly because there was no word or phrase to ask about. What would you call a coherent set of academic and organizational reforms that simultaneously fostered improvements in the quality of learning, equitable access, and stakeholder affordability? (To be clear, I'm not talking about an aggregation of reforms, some intended to improve quality, others access, and still others affordability.) I realized early that the process of making progress was my primary interest and that progress seemed to take many years to unfold. Thus my descriptor: I was looking for institutions with a history of pursuing 3fold gains.

Where I'm Coming From

I was in my first academic position when Robert Pirsig's *Zen and the Art of Motorcycle Maintenance* was published in 1974. It's a quirky book, perhaps the most readable book on philosophy I've encountered. The gist of Pirsig's inquiry into "quality" was that quality could not ultimately be defined by something else. In the end, judging quality must be, at the start, deeply personal. Judgment can be trained but in the end it's still judgment.

In that sense, you may want to decide, before reading the rest of the book, whether I can be trusted to make good use of your time. The inquiry—how I decided what questions to ask and my assumptions about how best to carry out this research—all arise from personal experience. Here's how some of the major themes and assumptions in this volume emerged from my 5 decades of work on innovation in higher education. In the beginning, it was all coincidental.

As a sophomore at the Massachusetts Institute of Technology (MIT) in 1969, I became convinced, through conversations with friends, of the need for a student-authored guide for incoming students. To get material for "How to Get Around MIT" (pun intended), I interviewed many undergraduates. I realized that the students I'd interviewed seemed to fall into two categories. The first group tried to do everything their professors asked, or at least as much they could. They also tended to see the university as cold and demanding. Their motto, printed on T-shirts, was "I Hate This F— Place." They saw the central corridor through MIT's main building complex as an infinite series of closed doors. In contrast, the second group of students loved being at MIT. They set their own priorities, deciding which faculty requests to ignore or skimp in order to make time to pursue their own interests. Like me, many of them knocked on doors along that infinite corridor; they usually found a surprisingly warm welcome and offer of help. *What a university looks like to students depends to a surprising degree on their goals and how they manage their time.*

I wanted the book to be regularly updated after I'd graduated. So I found a stable student organization that was willing to take on annually updating the book. As of 2019, "How to Get Around MIT" is still edited and published annually. *To sustain an innovation, plan early for how to make that happen.*

In 1970, I had a small speaking part in a massive antiwar rally on campus. Apparently, I didn't have much memorable to say. As we streamed out of the auditorium, I was greeted by Arthur Steinberg, a young anthropology professor from whom I'd taken a course the previous year. Arthur asked, "What's happened to you? You used to have opinions about everything. Now, not so much." His question shamed me. Two years after that rally, still nagged by Arthur's question, I decided to do a little research, my first research on education. I closely read several editions of the MIT catalogue from the late 1960s. When describing an MIT education, the most common term was *analysis*. Not *advocacy*, nor *design*, nor *real world*, nor *creativity*. *I began to realize that a "hidden curriculum" (Snyder, 1970) had substantially influenced my education and not always for the better.*

In 1971, as a senior in engineering, I took a course that was interdisciplinary, problem-based, and team "taught." On the first day of the semester, faculty challenged us with the following statement: "Some people say that Maine is an environmental paradise, while others call it an economic disaster." They told us to organize ourselves into one or more teams to do something useful for the state. A few of us would go to Maine at the end of the semester and present the results of our work. Then they stepped away to let us work, watching and offering advice when asked. The Maine situation was a real-world challenge that could be framed in many ways, transcended any one discipline, and motivated us to work far harder than if only a grade had been at stake. It was my favorite course in college. *Students who work together on a real-world problem can be transformed by that experience.*

For my PhD dissertation, I studied the 30-year educational and research evolution of a single MIT department, the Department of Civil Engineering (CE). By better understanding how and why the program had changed in the past, I suspected lessons could be learned to help faculty and administrators adapt in the future. The method I adopted is similar to my approach to this book, halfway between applied history and journalism. When I interviewed older faculty about the department's history, their recollections usually took the form of, "First we did this and it worked, and then a few years later we did that and that worked, too." After a year or so of this research, I realized I was no longer using that narrative to explain the department's recent history to my friends. Instead, my narrative took the form of, "A change (in research funding priorities or job markets) occurred that had the potential to increase or decrease research (or enrollment). Sooner or later, the faculty noticed, adapted, and the hoped-for change occurred." Later on I realized that the narrative really continued this way: "When faculty first tried to adapt to the external change, they often misunderstood what was happening and for that reason their initial responses didn't work out." For example, after initially ignoring a slow decline in the number of undergraduate majors, faculty began blaming CE's lack of glamor compared with fields like aerospace engineering and physics. An attempt to remedy the problem by shifting to an environmentally responsible CE curriculum failed miserably. (With 20:20 hindsight, I realized that majors had actually been declining because the available jobs for civil engineering graduates paid less than jobs for other majors whose salaries were surging upward, thanks to federal spending.) The dean appointed as department head the only professor without a PhD, whose applications of computers had attracted the highest research funding in the department. His strong and stable leadership transformed the research and educational programs to work on developing software to do the math of engineering. The department began offering a programming course, the best at MIT. In combination with other changes, it made the difference, and student interest grew explosively (Ehrmann, 1978). *Though I didn't know it at the time, these findings were my first step toward the suggestions in chapters 12 and 15 about the importance of institutional interactions with the wider world.*

After leaving MIT, I became the program evaluator at The Evergreen State College, an interdisciplinary, project-based institution that used team teaching almost entirely while dispensing with academic departments and faculty ranks. As I was getting to know this unique institution, I'd ask colleagues to explain to me what was most important about the college and why it was organized in so many unusual ways. It seemed like no two people told me the same story. However, in sorting through all the elements of their stories, I could create a simple framework that would provide a rationale for Evergreen's many usual and unusual practices. The framework had three elements. First, educate students to work on real-world problems, combining tools and resources from two or more disciplines. Second, they'd learn by taking mostly team-taught academic programs (instead of courses), which would be the full-time responsibility for both its faculty and its students for at least one academic quarter. Third, full-time commitment maximized freedom for faculty to change plans. If, for example, a program on environmental issues taught by an ecologist and an economist decided to make a multiday field trip, they could do it with confidence that it wouldn't interfere with exams or projects in other courses.

These three fundamental principles helped explain many of Evergreen's other practices. For example, instead of grades, Evergreen programs relied on student essays and faculty responses about what the student had learned and what to address next. At many institutions, faculty don't know students well enough to write such an essay about each one. But when I was at Evergreen, each faculty member was responsible for only about 22 students each quarter and had many kinds of interaction with each of them. That experience revealed quite a lot about students' capabilities, achievements, and needs. That was especially important because, in our hypothetical program on the environment, the ecologist needed to assess what the student had accomplished with economics as well as with ecology. That cross-disciplinary faculty expertise wasn't automatic, so Evergreen devised a couple of practices to help faculty learn one another's fields well enough to moderate seminar discussions. *Evergreen was my first experience at what this book will call an* Integrative *institution. There I realized that, to achieve such goals, there needed to be some alignment between goals, educational strategies, and what I'll be calling* organizational foundations *(e.g., the narrative transcript; peer-to-peer faculty development over the summer).*

Evergreen's student numbers had been declining for some years; by 1977 almost all of its new students were from out of state and/or transfers from other institutions. Many legislators assumed that Evergreen's educational strategies were fundamentally unpopular and too expensive. A subsequent state study revealed that Evergreen's high per student cost was due to its small size, not to its educational strategies. A second state study revealed that Evergreen's unpopularity among students, parents, and guidance counselors was partly due to misconceptions. For example, they knew that Evergreen did not give letter grades, but they didn't know that narrative evaluations provided far more detail on student achievement than a GPA.

A new president, Dan Evans, a popular former governor who had helped create Evergreen, crisscrossed the state to present a more accurate view of Evergreen's educational strategies and outcomes. And in-state first year enrollments swung upward. *I learned from this story not to assume that most stakeholders understand what you're doing.*

I started hearing about the transformative potential of computing when I was in high school, around 1965. The example cited was how computer tools for analysis and design would enable students to work and learn at a higher level, with more attention to a problem or design made possible by reduced time spent on doing the math. Computers played just that kind of transformative role in the turnaround of the MIT CE Department. Later, as a grant maker, computer-focused proposals were routed in my direction. I've never written code; my decades-long engagement with digital technology has always been from the perspective of someone trying to aid transformative change in colleges and universities. For almost the next 20 years, I helped give grants for selected educational innovations in higher education, first with the Fund for the Improvement of Postsecondary Education (FIPSE) (1978–1985) and then with the Annenberg/CPB Projects at the Corporation for Public Broadcasting (1985–1996). Unless you've done it, it's hard to explain what an education it is to reason with wise and experienced colleagues about which proposals are most important and most feasible, and why. It was a fantastic postdoctoral education in innovations in higher education. In my first year at FIPSE, I was stunned by just how many new ideas were out there. However, within a few years, I began to realize that few of those ideas were actually new. Topics like collaborative learning, school-college partnerships, and visualization to help learning—they would rise in visibility, subside, and rise again over the decades. Meanwhile, the reasons for the failure of an old innovation in, say, school-college partnership initiatives predicted problems that faced a new implementation of similar ideas. For example, self-paced instruction on paper was succeeded by self-paced instruction on computers. The former didn't drive educational transformation for similar reasons as the latter didn't either, even though the technology was different. *The rare innovators who study past instantiations of their ideas are much more likely to anticipate and respond to risks that might otherwise disrupt their plans.*

In my sideline as an evaluation consultant, applicants often asked me, "How much money should our grant proposal allocate for evaluation?" I felt like responding, "How many hours does it take to write an article?" Both questions are unanswerable as framed. Instead I helped them figure out what they hoped the evaluation would influence and how much money they could allocate; then we talked about whether it was possible to attain their purposes within their proposed budget. *If you begin learning about an educational initiative by asking what it will cost, the reply should begin, "That all depends . . ."* That's not an evasion. (Chapter 1's investigation of affordability digs deep into this question.)

Some of the educational technology projects we funded were planned from day one to be sustained, and they sometimes continued their work for several decades. However, far too many flickered out rather than fueling the educational revolution that their champions had predicted. Some were doomed by "rapture of the technologies." We've mentioned the mistaken belief that when an innovative concept uses technology, there's no need to study to previous attempts to implement that concept. A related misconception is the belief that new technology should drive educational improvement. For example, one year's high-buzz innovation might use digital technology to help learners visualize abstract ideas. A wave of early adopters begins devising assignments and courses that can take advantage of this exciting breakthrough. But a year or two later, long before the new teaching approaches can benefit large numbers of students, a newer technology with an entirely different educational agenda (e.g., online learning communities) bursts on the scene. Early adopters and the information technology staff flip to the new agenda. In short, technology changes faster and more unpredictably than education can follow. The result is transient ripples of educational innovation across a largely stagnant pool of teaching and learning activities. *This is just one of several reasons why it's risky to assume that bleeding edge technology can stimulate bleeding edge education* (Ehrmann, 2000).

As a grant maker associated with educational technology, I was frequently asked whether research was proving (or disproving) that new technology improved learning. Eventually, I realized this was another unanswerable question. Computing doesn't directly improve learning, any more than sleeping with your head on a French-English dictionary helps you learn French. It's what people *do* with the technology that matters. For example, if faculty and students are eager to exchange questions and ideas, their educational activities can be enhanced with online communications. But, if they're not interested in conversing, even large investments in communications technology may have no effect on learning at all. So, in the late 1980s, I began asking faculty which teaching and learning activities were improving partly because of how students and their instructor were using technology. I especially wanted to know of activities that were spreading from faculty member to faculty member because of these technology uses. There seemed to be seven broad categories of such activities (e.g., faculty-student interaction, student-student collaboration, active learning). Then came an epiphany: Chickering and Gamson's (1987) list of "Seven Principles for Good Practice in Undergraduate Education." These were categories of teaching and learning activities that, research demonstrated, could improve student learning. Their seven principles almost matched my list of seven spreading, technology-enhanced activities: if, say, technology was enabling an increase in active learning, educational research suggested that learning outcomes were improving too. *That insight, that technology can be a lever for learning, had implications for how to evaluate the educational outcomes of institutional, student, and faculty uses of technology* (Chickering & Ehrmann, 1996). It also fit with something else I'd observed: *The most educationally influential uses of technology were rarely the headline; instead, familiar, affordable technological tools and resources played an essential supporting role in improving learning.* For example, the process approach to writing (rewriting and rethinking) wouldn't have spread in the 1980s without the widening use of word processors.

During the 1990s, I noticed something new in conference presentations and grant proposals concerning educational uses of technology. Some dealt with technology applications that could improve both quality and access. That was a surprise because during the prior two decades, some grant proposals wanted to use technology to improve quality (and were reflexively attacked by some reviewers for helping the rich get richer). Another set proposed using technology to open access (and were reflexively accused by some of their reviewers of lowering standards). *These "quality + access" proposals and conference sessions hinted at a new way in which technology could benefit students* (Ehrmann, 1995, 1999).

In 1996, Steve Gilbert and I created a nonprofit consulting firm called the Teaching, Learning, and Technology Group (TLT Group). When planning campus visits, Steve would ask to speak to a wide range of people at the institution, from the provost to the manager of the bookstore (which sold software). What the people on his list had in common was their collective influence on what technology was available and how it might benefit students. It was simplest, he realized, to bring all these people together in a room, rather than meeting each separately. Surprisingly, even in small institutions, some of these people had never even met each other, let alone worked together on the challenges of technology; many of them hadn't wandered far from their own silos. That was the beginning of our work on TLT Roundtables (TLTRs), cross-silo councils that could advise provosts on budget requests and plans to improve education with technology. The use of TLTRs spread to many institutions in the 1990s (Gilbert, 2016). Over the years, we realized that TLTRs succeeded to the extent that the provost took an active interest, plying the TLTR with recommendations for advice and action. But if that provost left and was replaced with someone with different priorities, the TLTR could wither. That was a significant risk because few institutions included educational uses of technology in their provosts' job descriptions. *This book's attention to cross-silo collaboration emerged from that TLT Group work on TLTRs.*

In 2011, I became vice provost for teaching and learning at The George Washington University. Perhaps our biggest priority was to help scale up undergraduate research while making it a more visible part of GW's identity. I'll share more about that when we discuss the organizational foundations needed to scale and sustain educational innovations (chapter 11).

My last position before retiring was associate director of what is now the Kirwan Center for Academic Innovation at the University System of Maryland. I studied the impacts of 8 previous years of course redesign across the system. Among other benefits, these 57 courses had improved quality (students earning A, B, or C grades, and in some cases, higher scores on the same tests) while reducing costs per student (Ehrmann & Bishop, 2015). We'll have a lot more to say about course redesign and why it worked in a later chapter (chapter 10) on educational strategies. The Kirwan Center's mission was to nurture system-wide improvements in effectiveness, access, and efficiency. As I prepared to retire in 2016, I wondered whether there might be an elegantly simple way to achieve all three. I'd seen practices that improved quality and affordability, or that improved quality and access. *It seemed there ought to be a single way to achieve gains in all three areas.* But I had no idea how this might be accomplished. Perhaps some institutions were already doing this, and I could learn from them. And that is where my journey to this book began.

Warning! Dangerously Ambiguous Language Ahead

Access, active learning, affordability, competence-based education, quality, teaching, technology: All of these terms, each used repeatedly in this volume, are *confusors.*

> A *confusor* is a term with at least two widely accepted, conflicting definitions. For example, some people use *active learning* to describe what a learner does physically (e.g., writes a paper; uses online courseware) while others use the same phrase to describe what the learner does mentally (e.g., listens quietly to a lecture while continually questioning how the message fits with what they already know). Unrecognized confusors can deceive readers and listeners. A mirage of agreement, or of disagreement, can conceal conflict that may burst out later, fostering a sense of betrayal on both sides and destroying a team that might otherwise have succeeded. Confusors and other specialized terms used in this book are identified in boxed text.

What This Book Is Not

This book is not a top-down recipe, nor a panacea. Its goal is to prepare readers to improvise their own ways to improve selected elements of quality, access, and affordability at their institutions.

This book is not a representative sample of institutions. Each case was chosen solely because it showcases different facets of the pursuit of 3fold gains. As a group they are quite unrepresentative of higher education: Only one (University of Southern New Hampshire) is private; none is for-profit. Only one (Guttman) is a community college. All are in the same country. Most are in the southern and eastern United States; the furthest west is in Oklahoma.

This book is not comprehensive. When we talk about educational strategies, for example, we'll look at just enough examples to understand the role played by educational strategies in the effort to improve quality, access, and affordability.

This book is not a history of what individuals did but of what institutions did. In researching the case histories, I've not tried to decide which people were responsible for this or that. Rather, the goal of the case histories is to explain just enough about what each institution changed to help readers imagine a conceptual framework that any institution could use to improve quality, access, and affordability.

Audience for This Book

This book has been written for academic leaders. Some will have formal responsibilities—president, provost, dean, department chair, chief information officer, dean of student affairs, dean of libraries. Some might be leaders of accrediting agencies or funding agencies. Others will have taken on leadership: faculty, staff and others who act as "statesmen," that is, put the institution's welfare at least on a par with the welfare of their own piece of the institution.

Note for international readers: Perhaps you will find that lessons from this research can be applied with minimal adaptation in your own context. I'd guess that this international relevance is more likely in countries in which institutions have considerable autonomy to shape their own futures. I hope you'll let me know what fits, and what doesn't.

The Book in Outline

Part One is titled "Why Improve Quality, Equitable Access, and Affordability? And How?" Chapter 1 summarizes many different lines of research that strongly suggest that institutions of higher education fall short with respect to all three goals. Chapter 2 describes the most common remedial approach: separate aggregations of sometimes clashing initiatives to improve (separately) quality, access, and affordability. Many leaders of such institutions believe that pursuing all three gains at once will be doomed by an "iron triangle." But the chapter concludes by sketching three different ways in which quality, access, and affordability can be improved by a single constellation of initiatives.

Part Two, "3Fold Gains Guided by a Single Paradigm," begins with the Georgia State University (chapter 3) case history. It illustrates how, over many years, a university can assemble a set of mutually supportive, sustainable initiatives that, together, foster 3fold gains. Governors State University (chapter 4) is improving due in part to a carefully aligned 4-year design for undergraduate education. Governors State's and Georgia State's educational programs both rely on evidence-based practices such as peer interaction, learning communities, team projects, and service-learning. In contrast, Southern New Hampshire University's College for America (chapter 5) is competency-based and individualized, so that each student can progress toward mastery and graduation as quickly as possible. Chapter 6 describes three clashing approaches for pursuing 3fold gains. Each approach aligns with a different, coherent set of beliefs about education, a different paradigm. The most promising, the Integrative learning paradigm, already influences recent initiatives at Georgia State, Governors State, and many other institutions. Integrative assumptions provide a rationale for high-impact practices such as undergraduate research, internships, service-learning, and learning communities. The remainder of the book describes different ways that Integrative assumptions and practices can be used to pursue 3fold gains.

Part Two, with the first three case histories, illustrates how different learning paradigms can provide a rationale for very different educational strategies. Part Three adds a focus on the institutional and environmental factors influencing whether learning-centered strategies can be scaled and sustained. "Sustaining the Integrative Approach of 3Fold Gains," begins with the final three case histories. Guttman Community College (chapter 7) is a system-created college specifically created to improve quality and equitable access with Integrative educational strategies. The case showcases how Guttman's founders pursued 3fold gains by creating a constellation of mutually supportive Integrative educational strategies, organizational foundations, and wider-world interactions. The University of Central Oklahoma (chapter 8) has bought into ambitious learning goals that transcend the boundaries of formal and informal learning. Assessment activities and students' academic records are aligned with those goals; the results, over 15 years, have been transformational. The University of Central Florida (chapter 9) has been praised for "breaking the iron triangle"; its blended and online courses are partly responsible for UCF attaining 3fold gains.

Part Four, "Aligning Initiatives Across Three Domains," distills the lessons from the case history institutions that are successfully pursuing 3fold gains. Chapter 10 describes some of the most common and powerful Integrative educational strategies. Chapter 11 delves into several organizational foundations that can make or break Integrative educational strategies. Interactions with the wider world are integral to the success of Integrative strategies, and that's the topic of Chapter 12.

Part Five, "Doing It," is oriented toward action at the individual, institutional, and national levels. Chapter 13 summarizes the conceptual framework for attaining 3fold gains and chapter 14 suggests several principles for implementing the framework, both at the institutional level. To make a dent in the national-scale challenges that were outlined in chapter 1, hundreds and ultimately thousands of institutions ought to begin pursuing 3fold gains. Such large-scale change will require large-scale encouragement and support in the form of changes to the world in which the nation's institutions operate (e.g., research into institutions pursuing 3fold gains, accreditation, grantmaking). These national scale-changes are the subject of chapter 15. The chapter and book conclude by asking whether or not these changes are likely to occur and then summarizing some takeaways.

ACKNOWLEDGMENTS

I'm especially grateful to the 100-plus people who generously allowed me to interview them, sometimes for as much as 5 hours across several sessions. Without them, there would be no findings and no book.

My thinking as a researcher and author has been influenced by more people than I can count. A few have had major impacts on the thinking that led to this book, including:

- Carol Geary Schneider, president emerita, Association of American Colleges & Universities. Carol and I have been discussing and debating many of the issues in this book for over 40 years. Our discussions have utterly transformed the way I once thought about both quality and access.
- Tim Renick, vice president and vice provost at Georgia State University. Tim's talk at the University of Maryland helped me see that 3fold gains could be achieved and that a historical narrative would be the best way to share their experience with others.
- Richard Guarasci and his colleagues at Wagner College. Wagner was one of the earlier traditional institutions to begin a transition to the Integrative pursuit of 3fold gains. A campus visit and numerous telephone interviews helped me better understand many issues later developed in this book. Wagner was not ultimately chosen for this volume, but my thinking benefited from learning how service-learning and community engagement contribute to a practical liberal arts education.
- Arthur Levine, Woodrow Wilson Foundation, whose book *Why Innovation Fails* (1980) demonstrated the value of studying the economics of educational initiatives to explain why some persisted while others withered.
- Jack Wilson, whose development of studio courses at Rennselaer Polytechnic Institute demonstrated the possibility of 2fold gains (improved quality with lower operating costs) (Wilson & Jennings, 2000).
- Carol Twigg, National Center for Academic Transformation, who led a national effort to encourage course redesign for what I've termed *3fold gains* (Twigg, 2015).

- Jack Mudd, former dean of the University of Montana Law School. In the early 1980s, he surveyed the state's judges and lawyers, asking for their judgments about where newly graduated lawyers were satisfactorily competent and where they were not. His recommendations sparked reform, first at Montana and ultimately nationally. It was the first example I'd seen of assessing the competencies of graduating students in order to rethink and reform the program from which they'd graduated.
- Steven W. Gilbert who, in countless ways, influenced my ideas about educational uses of technology, cross-silo coalitions, evaluation, program improvement, and faculty development.
- The late Diane Pelkus Balestri, my writing partner for two earlier books. Her insights, intelligence, writing style, and grace still inspire me.
- MJ Bishop, director of the Kirwan Center for Academic Innovation at the University System of Maryland. My thinking about 3fold gains began while I worked with her at the Kirwan Center. Since I retired and began this research, MJ has been consistently supportive.
- David Brightman at Stylus Publishing, who championed this book while giving me invaluable feedback on how its argument could be organized.
- Judith Miller, my patient and encouraging editor, who helped me narrow the gap between what I'd written and what I actually wanted to say.

I interviewed a number of people at each of these six institutions but relied especially on one or two contacts at each: Don Betz and Jeff King at the University of Central Oklahoma, Tom Cavanagh and Kelvin Thompson at the University of Central Oklahoma, Lauren Keene and Paul LeBlanc at Southern New Hampshire University, Elaine Maimon at Governors State University, Tim Renick at Georgia State University, and Howard Wach at Guttman Community College.

The following individuals have been especially helpful in providing feedback on ideas and drafts of this book: Tonya Amankwatia, Tom Angelo, Phil Berger Jr., Steve Bindeman, Gary Brown, Malcolm Brown, Donald Carter, Tom Cavanagh, Helen Chen, Laurie Dodge, Ann Ferren, Jeff Galle, Joel Hartman, Natasha Jankowski, Richard Katz, Lauren Keene, Jeff King, Vijay Kumar, Phil Long, Bill Massy, Phil Mierzwa, Bonnie Mullinix, Phil Piety, Ginny Redish, Tim Renick, Terry Rhodes, Scott Roberts, Bror Saxberg, Carol Geary Schneider, Joellen Shendy, Tiffany-Rose Sikorski, Kelvin Thompson, Carolyn Toscano, Karen Vignare, Yianna Vovides, Howard Wach, Eddie Watson, Fred Winter, and Ralph Wolff.

PART ONE

WHY IMPROVE QUALITY, EQUITABLE ACCESS, AND AFFORDABILITY? AND HOW?

We're going to be taking an inside look at just how colleges and universities could improve what and how students learn, the equity of access to a college degree, and how affordable that education is for students, for the institutions educating them, and their benefactors. Before we start on that journey, however, chapter 1 makes the case for urgency. Chapter 2 then describes three different ways to approach these three goals. The first approach says, "Don't bother. It's impossible." A second approach is quite common but over the years it doesn't seem to have accomplished much. The third approach may seem counterintuitive, but several institutions have been using it and it seems to work. Briefly, each institution has, over a period of years, been developing a constellation of mutually supportive initiatives. It's the constellation more than any of its elements alone that enable institutions to improve quality, access, *and* affordability.

I

WHAT'S SO URGENT?

For reasons we'll discuss in this chapter, it's likely that most or all colleges and universities urgently need to make specific *gains* within *three broad goals*: quality of learning, equitable access, and stakeholder affordability. We'll define each of those three terms in the following sections. To begin let's define *broad goals* and *gain*.

Terms like *quality* and *quality of learning* are umbrella terms. *Broad goals* describes the kind of focused goals that can influence action. For example, the intention to improve education in mathematics so that graduates can make better use of it is a goal to improve the quality of learning. The title of this book uses the phrase "quality, access, and affordability." That's shorthand for "focused goals that fall under the broad umbrellas of quality of learning, access and equity, and stakeholder affordability."

In this book *gain* refers to improvements compared to what otherwise would probably have happened. If enrollments were likely to plummet by 10%, but new initiatives cut the decrease to only 5%, that's a gain.

Quality: The Importance of Making Additional Gains

Quality is invoked far more often than it is defined.

Quality is a confusor (see preface). When it's used to describe academic institutions or programs, the term has at least three widely used definitions.

Results or hoped-for results: the nature and value of student capabilities, achievements, and attributes by the time they complete their course of study. These are sometimes called "(essential) student learning outcomes."

Activities: teaching and learning activities that, evidence suggests, are likely to produce improve learning outcomes; or

Ingredients: selectivity of admissions, attributes of admitted students, qualifications of faculty, and/or excellence of facilities. Institutional and program accreditors and rating systems have often relied on this ingredient definition of *quality*.

When this book uses *quality*, assume we're using the first definition. If we're using either of the other two definitions, the text will say so.

As Michael Roth (2014) points out, higher education should strengthen students' development in three overlapping spheres of life: as participants in the economy; as people, often transforming their vision of themselves and their potential; and as responsible and active citizens in their political, social, economic, and familial communities. I've listed those three spheres in the order that people currently seem to prioritize them. But that order has changed many times over the last century. For example, in the years after World War II, the Truman Commission recommended greater access to college because the country needed educated and active citizens (Hutcheson, 2007). When I went to college in the late 1960s, personal transformation was often seen as a major goal for higher learning.

No matter in what order work, personal development, and responsible citizenry are ranked, success and fulfilment in each requires some of the same capabilities, such as being able to frame questions, find information from many sources, sift and analyze that information, and then use the analysis to take action. The development of these capabilities, through what we will call a *liberal education*, is far more difficult and time-consuming than memorizing facts.

Liberal education, also referred to as *liberal learning*, is a confusor. Some people assume *liberal* must mean politically liberal. Others use the term as a synonym for education in the humanities, equating liberal learning with some or all of the liberal arts and sciences. Still others assume that liberal learning is the opposite of education for good jobs. As used in this book, a liberal education prepares students to use information from many sources to think and take action in their work and in their civic and community lives; in the process students are likely to transform their visions of the world, who they are, and what they are capable of doing.

First, the good news. Since the beginning of the 21st century there has been growing agreement across colleges and universities about the necessary capabilities and *attributes* of a college graduate.

In this book, students' *attributes* reflect who they are and what qualities they possess—for example curiosity, a desire to act in an ethical way, a passion for service, or a commitment to racial justice.

The Association of American Colleges & Universities (AAC&U) has framed the following set of Essential Learning Outcomes (ELOs) by synthesizing the academic goals of hundreds of their member institutions (AAC&U, 2018a):

- Knowledge of human cultures and the physical and natural world through study across many disciplines that is focused by engagement with big questions, both contemporary and enduring
- Intellectual and practical skills (including inquiry and analysis, critical and creative thinking, teamwork, and problem-solving) that are developed through extensive practice on progressively more challenging problems, projects, and standards of performance
- The capability for personal and social responsibility, enabled by civic knowledge, intercultural knowledge and competence, ethical reasoning, and lifelong learning, all developed through active involvement with diverse communities and real-world challenges
- Integrative and applied learning, in the form of synthesis and advanced accomplishment across general and specialized studies, demonstrated through the application of knowledge, skills, and responsibilities to new settings and complex problems

The Lumina Foundation's Degree Qualifications Profile (DQP) asserts a set of outcomes for what undergraduates should learn that are similar to AAC&U's ELOs (Adelman et al., 2011).

Employers agree that AAC&U's ELOs and Lumina's DQP describe important goals. A survey by Hart Research Associates (2015) found that employers identify effective verbal and written communication, teamwork, ethical decision-making, critical thinking, and the ability to apply knowledge and skills in real-world settings as among the most important college learning outcomes that define high-quality job candidates. I'd say that these same capabilities are as important for civic engagement and personal development as they are for the working world. So rather than looking at the adequacy of outcomes within each of those three spheres of liberal education, we'll focus on the outcomes important to all spheres.

Now, the bad news. AAC&U regularly surveys executives and hiring managers at for-profit and nonprofit companies of more than 25 employees who frequently hire graduates with 2- and 4-year degrees. Executives and hiring managers gave pretty much the same responses, and the results haven't changed much over the years of the survey. Respondents widely agreed on the value of a college education, but they were largely dissatisfied with the actual graduates (Figure 1.1). In 2018, about 40% had doubts about the capability of recent graduates to work in entry-level positions, and only 30% were confident that the educations of new hires prepared them adequately for advancement. For example, they judged that only 39% of recent graduates were well prepared to apply what they've been taught in real-world settings; that's a quality that 87% of hiring managers saw as "very important." The same was true for self-motivation, which hiring managers saw in only 39% of recent graduates (Hart Research Associates, 2018). Hart's "Falling Short?" report 3 years earlier had revealed similar gaps between the educational preparation employers wanted from new hires and what the new hires could do; then, as later, the gap between content-specific knowledge and preparation was much smaller (Hart Research Associates, 2015).

It costs an employer significant money to replace a new employee within a year or two of hiring. Too many recent graduates lose their jobs because of lack of those abilities identified by the employer survey. For example, a human resources company did a 3-year study of 5,247 hiring managers from 312 public and private business and health-care organizations. Collectively these managers hired more than 20,000 employees during the study period. Almost half those hires (46%) failed. Respondents reported that, of the new hires that failed, 26% did so because they couldn't accept feedback, 23% because they were unable to understand and manage emotions, 17% because they lacked the necessary motivation to excel, 15% because they had the wrong temperament for the job, and only 11% because they lacked the necessary technical skills (LeadershipIQ, 2019). Employers know what they need, and when new employees come up short, they often lose their jobs.

So far we've looked only at employer judgments about graduates' abilities. The evidence also suggests that a substantial fraction of college graduates haven't developed capabilities that many colleges and universities see as primary goals. Critical thinking is essential in all of the liberal learning spheres, development for work, personhood, and active citizenry. In both 2004 and 2010, over 85% of seniors believed that, during college, they personally learned to think critically "very much" or at least "quite a bit" (National Survey of Student Engagement [NSSE] finding, cited in Finley, 2012).

Figure 1.1. Hiring managers identify major gaps in the education of recent hires.

Among hiring managers:	Recent college grads well prepared*	Very important quality*	Prepared Gap
Apply knowledge/skills to real world	39%	87%	–48
Self-motivated	39%	85%	–46
Communicate effectively orally	47%	90%	–43
Critical thinking/analytical reasoning	41%	84%	–43
Able to work independently	42%	85%	–43
Ethical judgment/decision-making	47%	87%	–40
Able to work effectively in teams	50%	87%	–37
Able to analyze/solve complex problems	38%	75%	–37
Communicate effectively in writing	45%	78%	–33
Find, organize, evaluate info: multiple sources	46%	79%	–33
Solve problems with people of diff. backgrounds	43%	73%	–30
Able to innovate/be creative	41%	66%	–25
Stay current on changing tech	57%	73%	–16
Able to work with numbers/stats	43%	55%	–12
Proficiency in foreign language	23%	25%	–2

0% 20% 40% 60% 80% 100%

* 8–10 ratings on a 0- to- 10 scale

Source: Hart Research Associates (2018). Reproduced with permission of AAC&U.

Arum and Roksa's *Academically Adrift* (2011a) cited empirical evidence suggesting that the seniors in the NSSE survey overestimated their capabilities (as employers believe). They analyzed data from the standardized student writing assignments in the Collegiate Learning Assessment (CLA). The authors wrote in a *New York Times* op-ed:

> We found that large numbers of the students were making their way through college with minimal exposure to rigorous coursework, only a modest investment of effort and little or no meaningful improvement in skills like writing and reasoning.
>
> In a typical semester, for instance, 32% of the students did not take a single course with more than 40 pages of reading per week, and 50% did not take any course requiring more than 20 pages of writing over the semester. The average student spent only about 12 to 13 hours per week studying—about half the time a full-time college student in 1960 spent studying, according to the labor economists Philip S. Babcock and Mindy S. Marks.
>
> Not surprisingly, a large number of the students showed no significant progress on tests of critical thinking, complex reasoning, and writing that were administered when they began college and then again at the ends of their sophomore and senior years. If the test that we used, the Collegiate Learning Assessment, were scaled on a traditional 0-to-100 point range, 45% of the students would not have demonstrated gains of even 1 point over the first 2 years of college, and 36% would not have shown such gains over 4 years of college. (Arum & Roksa, 2011b, paras. 2–4)

Another corroboration of the hypothesis of declining quality in U.S. higher education comes from a literature review in 2014 that agreed that the capabilities of graduating students may have declined in many ways since the mid-1960s (Stewart & Kilmartin, 2014). Similarly, the Organisation for Economic Cooperation and Development (OECD) Survey of Adult Skills, conducted through the Programme for the International Assessment of Adult Competencies, found that the average literacy, numeracy, and problem-solving skill levels of 16- to 24-year-olds in the United States is significantly below the average of OECD member countries (Desjardins & Colleagues, 2013).

Let's focus on reflective judgment, a crucial component of all three spheres of liberal education: education for work, for personal development, and for living in communities. A team of researchers interviewed students while they considered open-ended problems such as whether the Egyptians could possibly have built the pyramids (King & Kitchener, 1993, 2004). Over 1,300 students from high school through graduate school were asked to describe what they knew and why they believed it. The model was used to classify how students interpret their world and think about what they know. Using redacted copies of student responses, raters decided where each student response fit in a seven-stage model of how reflective judgment develops. Most undergraduate and graduate students were found to be somewhere between stages 3 and 6:

- Stage 3 signature statement: "When there is evidence that people can give to convince everybody one way or another, then it will be knowledge; until then it's just a guess." To put it another way, knowledge is either absolutely certain or else temporarily uncertain.
- Stage 4 signature statement: "I'd be more inclined to believe evolution if they had proof. . . . Who are you going to ask? No one was there." For Stage 4 respondents, knowing always involves an element of ambiguity. To prove something, begin with what you believe and then find evidence that supports it.
- Stage 5 signature statement: "People think differently and so they attack the problem differently. Other theories could be as true as my own, but based on different evidence." Only interpretations of evidence can be known.
- Stage 6 signature statement: "There are degrees of sureness. You come to a point at which you are sure enough for a personal stance on the subject." Beliefs are justified by comparing evidence and opinion from different sources and across different contexts.

It's a safe guess that most faculty want seniors to have developed to at least stage 6. But most undergraduates in the sample didn't make it past stage 4. About two-thirds of first-year college students were between stages 3 and 4. The seniors averaged only about half a stage higher than first-year students. Apparently only a small fraction of college graduates in the late 1990s were prepared to work on ill-structured, open-ended problems and, using evidence, to explain their actions to others who disagree.

So far, all of these findings are based on student work done outside normal academic assignments. Perhaps student scores were low because they saw no reason to think hard about their responses. That's why an AAC&U study focused on taking a second look at course assignments students had already finished (Finley, 2017). The study, done in collaboration with Indiana University's Center for Postsecondary Research, engaged faculty from many institutions who wanted to see how their students' work measured up. Each faculty member contributed an assignment plus several relevant graded pieces of student work on that assignment. Institutional, faculty, and student names were redacted, as was the original grade. Faculty from other institutions then reviewed each piece of student work using AAC&U Valid Assessment of Learning in Undergraduate Education (VALUE) rubrics (AAC&U, 2018b) to assess the capabilities revealed by that piece of work. Since 2008, faculty working with VALUE have developed and validated rubrics for 16 ELOs. Each rubric corresponds to an ELO that is espoused by a large number of 2- and 4-year institutions. Each rubric is separated into 4 or 5 dimensions. For example, the dimensions of critical thinking are

- explanation of issues,
- evidence (selecting and using evidence to investigate a point of view or conclusion),
- influence of context and assumptions,
- student's position (perspective, thesis/hypothesis), and
- conclusions and related outcomes (implications and consequences).

For each dimension, the faculty reviewer rated the student's work at one of four levels. For rating the dimension "student's position (perspective, thesis/hypothesis)," for example, the following are the four levels:

1. Benchmark (lowest level): Specific position is stated but is simplistic and obvious.
2. Milestone 2: Specific position (perspective, thesis/hypothesis) acknowledges different sides of an issue.
3. Milestone 3: Specific position (perspective, thesis/hypothesis) takes into account the complexities of an issue. Others' points of view are acknowledged within the position.
4. Capstone (highest level): Specific position (perspective, thesis/hypothesis) is imaginative, taking into account the complexities of the issue. Limits of position are acknowledged. Others' points of view are synthesized within the position.

The faculty assessors could not see the grades assigned nor did they know whether the students were in second-year or fourth-year courses, or in 2- or 4-year institutions. Their findings aligned with the research we've already reported. To illustrate, let's look at students at 4-year institutions who had finished at least 75% of the credits needed for graduation. We'll stick with the dimension "student's position (perspective, thesis/hypothesis)." Only 7% of those seniors' work was judged to be at the capstone level. In contrast, 58% of the seniors were rated at milestone 2 or lower. Other single-digit percentages of capstone competency were found for virtually every dimension of critical thinking, quantitative literacy, and written communications.

Each of these study methodologies—Hart's employer research, Arum and Roksa's analysis of the CLA, Stewart and Kilmartin's literature review, OECD's Survey of Adult Skills, King and Kitchener's reflective judgment, and AAC&U's VALUE rubrics—used a different methodology and each has its limitations. What's striking, however, is how much their findings agree: Dangerously high numbers of soon-to-graduate students have not yet developed the capabilities that faculty and employers believe college graduates should have. Because of the centrality of capabilities such as reflective judgment, it's likely that graduates fall short of expectations in personal development and community and civic engagement capabilities as well.

Although the data cited here come from undergraduate programs, the findings have critical implications for graduate schools as well. Many graduate and professional programs are designed as though ELOs have been mastered during bachelor's degree programs, capabilities such as critical thinking or the ability to work with people from different cultures. As we've just seen, that's seems unlikely. Graduate and professional programs might consider strengthening the liberal education side of their academic programs.

The studies cited so far have focused on what students have learned. Another devastating critique of current quality zeroes in on low graduation rates. What do you think a satisfactory graduation rate should be? What's the graduation rate at your favorite institution? As Figure 1.2 depicts, graduation rates differ greatly across institutions, from less than 10% to 100%. However, at more than half of 2- and 4-year institutions, graduation rates are lower than 50%. About 10% of 4-year institutions graduate fewer than

Figure 1.2. Graduation rates of U.S. colleges.

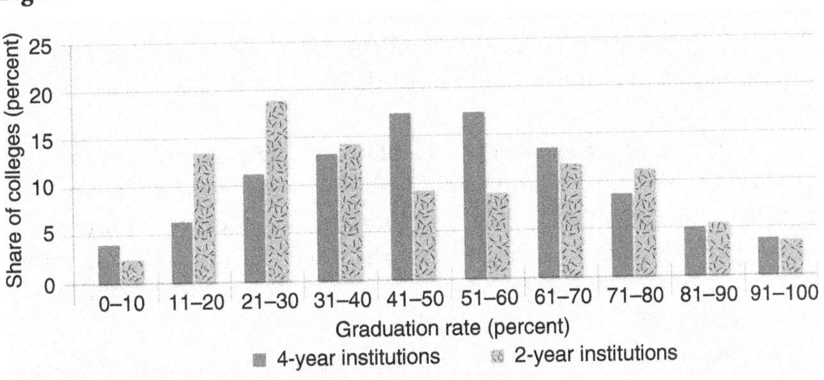

Note. Graduation rates reflect first-time, full-time degree or certificate-seeking students who completed their degree within 6 years for 4-year institutions and 3 years for 2-year institutions. Data are based on institutions in the United States that participate in federal financial aid programs.
Source. Erickson, 2020. Reprinted by permission of *Education Next*, EducationNext.org

20% of their admitted students within 6 years (that percentage doesn't count students who transferred and graduated elsewhere). About 17% of community colleges graduate fewer than 20% of their admitted students within 3 years.

Many faculty and administrators will say that quality at their own institution is acceptable, though it should be better. But what is your definition of *acceptable*? What does evidence suggest about whether graduation rates or other quality measures are acceptable?

Equitable Access: The Importance of Making Additional Gains

All six of our case history institutions share a mission to serve students who are often shortchanged because of their race or ethnicity, economic background, or role in life. In this book, this goal is called *equitable access*, or, for brevity, *access*.

> *Access* is a confusor. Sometimes *access* means enrolling and graduating more students to help an institution grow or to meet public targets for how many citizens should have a degree. Some people use *access* to refer to the number of people admitted to college. But when students enter and then fail to graduate, in some ways they may be worse off than when they entered, having lost some or all of their options to borrow money for their education (Goldrick-Raab, 2016). Although some people assume that college dropouts have only themselves to blame, there is strong evidence that dropout rates also depend substantially on what colleges do and don't do. So the fact that about 28% of all students who enroll in college fail to get even an associate degree means that colleges as well as their dropouts are falling short (Ryan & Bauman, 2016).
>
> In this book, *access* refers to enrolling, educating, and eventually graduating groups who have traditionally been under- or ill-served by the institution or by all of higher education. We occasionally use the term *equitable access* as a reminder of the kind of access we're discussing. In this vein the speaker may have just one such group in mind, for example, a racial or ethnic group, those who need physical or intellectual accommodations, working adults, or some combination of these and other categories. For us, *access* refers to the number and categories of underserved students who not only enter but also complete a degree or certificate, either at the original institution or another.

TABLE 1.1
Bachelor's Degree Attainment by Household Income

Quartile of household income	*Highest (≥ $133,299)*	*Second ($74,904–$133,299)*	*Third ($42,056–$74,904)*	*Lowest (< $42,056)*
% of dependent young adults who earn a bachelor's degree before age 24	62%	47%	20%	18%

Note. Cahalan et al., 2019. Data from 2017

Earlier we mentioned that about 28% of all students who enter college never get a degree. That figure is 39% for all African Americans, rich and poor (Ryan & Bauman, 2016). For dependent students from the lowest quartile of family incomes, only 18% earn a bachelor's degree before age 24, less than one-third the rate of students from the highest quartile (Table 1.1).

This alarming relationship between household income and educational success is an issue of equitable access, not of affordability per se. Household income influences students in many ways, including quality of early schooling, parenting presence, health, and experience in using modern technologies. The deck is stacked in multiple ways against young people with the bad luck to come from poor backgrounds. Worse, income equality has grown in recent decades, while pathways upward have been narrowed. This inequality of opportunity is even worse for victims of racial discrimination who happen to live in lower quartile households.

Stakeholder Affordability: The Importance of Making Additional Gains

In this book, *stakeholder affordability* refers to the likelihood that students and other relevant stakeholders can and will invest enough time and money to sustain the program's methods of educating students and to help students succeed in that program. Costs in higher education increase for many reasons, some unrelated to the instruction program. In recent years, the downward pressure on college prices has been getting stronger. Some alternative models (e.g., see College for America in chapter 5) were designed to reduce costs. Demographic changes are shrinking the numbers of 18-year-olds graduating from high school, which increases competitive pressure on the price of institutions that are striving to get a big enough piece of a shrinking pie.

Stakeholders are people or entities who may gain or lose if a program or institution changes. For institutions of higher education, students, parents, faculty, staff, organizational units within the institution, accreditors, taxpayers, benefactors, and the legislature are all stakeholders. Stakeholders have some expectations about the performance of the institution or a program within it; they may take action if performance drops below, or exceeds, those expectations. Initiatives to advance gains in quality, access, and affordability virtually always require backing or active engagement from a coalition of stakeholders.

Affordability is a confusor. For most people, most of the time, *affordability* refers to the capacity of students (one set of stakeholders) to pay for tuition, room, and board. However, that's not how this book uses *affordability* and *stakeholder affordability*. First, our definition includes not only students but also other stakeholders. For example, students and the institution (as an organization with staff, budgets, and policies) are both stakeholders in the institution's academic program. Second, our definition of *affordability* refers to stakeholders' time as well as their money. Are students making use of their time in ways that encourage them to invest even more time and thought in their studies? Can faculty afford the time to teach in collaborative, problem-focused ways? Third, our definition of *affordability* refers to whether stakeholders are both willing and able to sustain a regular investment of time and money. Specifically, how much of a stakeholder group's time or money could conceivably be allocated to the educational activities in question? Are they able, willing, and motivated enough to actually make that reallocation of their time or money? To say that a program is affordable means that its stakeholders are both able and willing to sustain their own participation in the program.

This book describes changes in institutionalized *educational strategies* that can influence quality, access, and affordability. We're not going to discuss why academic prices or costs are so high (that relates to many factors unconnected with institutions' academic programs). What we do ask is, "How can colleges and universities alter their ways of working in order to improve quality and access within the constraints of affordability?"

How often have you heard statements like these?

- "They said they accomplish that in how little time??! Impossible! It takes us twice that much time."
- "Their budget is how big??! They must be wasting some of it; we don't spend nearly that amount of money to do the same thing!"

- "Sorry, your idea has promise, but we can't do it. We don't have enough money or time."

They all rest on a fallacy: that a certain practice, old or new, has a more or less fixed price tag of money and time. For example, many people believe that teaching online is fundamentally more (or less) time-consuming for faculty compared with teaching the same course on campus. So let's begin by talking about faculty time.

There was some debate a few decades ago about whether faculty needed more time to teach students online than they did to teach students on campus. If an institution were going to shift more faculty effort to online teaching, would that ease faculty workloads or intensify them? If 5,000 student enrollments would shift from campus to online, would more faculty be needed or fewer? Aren't those answerable questions?

C. Northcote Parkinson (Parkinson & Osborn, 1957) asserted that "Work expands to fill the time available." Some people take Parkinson's law to be a sarcastic critique of bureaucracy. It's more than that. Think about what that statement means for budgeting time.

Christine Geith and Michele Cometa (2003), in a small-scale research project at one college, revealed what Parkinson's law means for affordability in time. They wanted to know which was more time-consuming, to teach a certain number of students online or on campus. Obviously, when faculty or anyone else tries out a new way of doing things, it takes more time on the first attempt. So the researchers interviewed only faculty who were experienced in both modes of teaching. Nine faculty were chosen for this pilot test, seven in science, technology, engineering, and mathematics (STEM) fields; each was currently teaching sections in both modes.

First, the interviewees were asked the question directly: Which mode is more time-consuming? They responded unanimously that teaching a distant learner took more faculty time. Each interviewee was asked to estimate how many hours over the semester they spent on each category of activity for teaching a course in each mode: preparation, presentation, interaction, assessment, practice, application (special projects, papers, and labs), and evaluation. Each interviewee's total time teaching the course was then divided by the number of students. It turned out that, roughly speaking, each faculty member spent about the same amount of time per student in both modes. My guess is that, over several offerings of the course, faculty altered what they were doing until their work fit more comfortably with their needs. That's why, eventually, they were spending about the same number of hours per students in both modes. (It's worth repeating that this study involved only nine experienced faculty from STEM fields at one institution.)

But here's the stunner: For the campus sections, time per student varied among faculty by a factor of three. For distant sections, some faculty were spending seven times more hours per student than their colleagues (Geith & Cometa, 2003). The differences in time investment among faculty varied far more than the difference in time investment by campus versus distance.

Before we draw any conclusions, let's ask the same question about budgets. Is there a normal price for using any particular educational strategy? For example, are high-impact practices necessarily more expensive than lectures? The evidence here is more indirect, but what information we have lines up with the research on time.

Howard Bowen (1980) was interested in instructional budgets at colleges and universities. He studied instructional budgets from hundreds of institutions with similar character, size, and setting. Within groups of similar institutions, there were major variations in instructional cost per student. Were similar institutions spending similar amounts for similar things (e.g., salaries)? No. One institution might spend more on faculty salaries and less on space, while another institution might allocate its dollars in the opposite way. Bowen concluded that a *revenue theory of costs* was the best way to account for short-term variations in the diverse ways in which institutions spend money. An institution's instructional budget is not primarily influenced by the nature of its academic programs, the size of the institution, or its location. Instead, each institution raises all the money it can, spends all the money it gets, and spends it this year in pretty much the way as last year. In other words, a major determinant of how many dollars are spent on instruction, and how, is the institution's revenue history.

So statements like "we don't have the money or the time" appear in a new light. Big crash programs may arouse backlash. Slow, committed implementations may accomplish more. "Can we allocate $90,000 annually for this, starting right now?" "This is very important but I just can't find the money." "Then about ramping up to $90,000/year over the next 3 years?" "Yes, I can do that. What could you do with $30K this year, $60K next year, and then $90K?" We'll return to this idea of gradual change in the discussion of implementation in chapter 14.

So, is there a relationship between budgets and learning? It's not surprising to discover that the answer is "not much." Many studies have shown that there is hardly any relationship between an institution's wealth and selectivity, the dollars it spends per student, how those dollars are allocated, and its educational effectiveness, estimated using evidence about outcomes and use of good practices. Ewell (2008) summarized studies that sought to find a relationship between budgets and learning and didn't find much. For example, the highly selective, usually expensive institutions in the top 100 in the

US News & World report rankings are apparently no more instructionally effective than institutions in the middle of those rankings. Also, of 30 public institutions that spent between $10,000 and $11,000 per student, four had 6-year graduation rates over 70%, and another four had graduation rates below 35%. Ewell concluded that institutional budgets and educational performance were only loosely related.

The most important conclusions to draw from this may be the following:

- There are probably always ways to improve affordability while improving quality and equitable access.
- Even comparatively poor institutions can potentially improve quality, access, and affordability if other factors are favorable. (For example, later on we'll see examples of the importance of transformative leaders; faculty dedicated to improving student learning; and powerful educational strategies in improving quality, access, and affordability.)

Turning the Page

Issues such as those discussed in this chapter are urgent because colleges and universities get only one shot at educating most students. When students have finished their first year, it makes no difference to them if a year later, the first-year experience is improved so that students go into their second year better prepared. If attrition rates are high this year at this institution for African American males, next year's quality enhancements won't repay them for the time and money they've lost. As for costs, each year's choices about time and money constrain the options for the next year. It's trite but true: We really can't afford to wait.

So let's assume that it's important to get started on improving quality, access, and affordability. Chapter 2 compares three approaches: a bad one, a comparatively ineffective one, and a better one.

2

IRON TRIANGLES, THREE GAINS, AND 3FOLD GAINS

Is there a way to (re)organize an institution's educational strategies to create the potential for simultaneous gains in quality, access, and affordability? Choose one:

1. *Iron triangle*: No, it's impossible. Gains in access water down standards. Changes in quality require more resources per student, which makes education less affordable.
2. *Three gains, bit by bit*: Yes, with a balanced portfolio of initiatives, some of which improve the quality of learning, some equitable access, and some affordability. Faculty usually lead quality initiatives, starting with making improvements to their courses. Access initiatives (e.g., scholarships for low-income students; disability support services) are usually the responsibility of staff. Affordability usually equates to budget cutting.
3. *3fold gains*: Yes, by building a set of mutually supportive initiatives that collectively foster all three kinds of gain.

This chapter addresses each of these choices in turn.

The Fallacy of the Iron Triangle

Chapter 1 asserted that quality, equitable access, and affordability need to improve substantially, probably at all institutions. What do college presidents think of that proposition? In 2008, the National Center for Public Policy and Higher Education asked dozens of college and university presidents about quality, access, and costs. In the view of many presidents, the three main factors in higher education—cost, quality, and access—exist in what has been called an iron triangle. These factors, it was claimed, are linked in an unbreakable tradeoff relationship, such that any improvement in one can only be accomplished by making sacrifices in at least one of the other two. Most of the college presidents believed that to improve the quality of higher education, one must either put more money into the system or be prepared to see higher education become less accessible to students. Conversely, cutting costs in higher education must eventually lead to cuts either in quality or access (Immerwahr et al., 2008).

The iron triangle hypothesis implies that quality is determined by dividing the quantity of academic resources by the number of students; for example, that quality is determined to a substantial degree by institutional student–faculty ratio or average class size. If that were true, any increase in student numbers must necessarily divide available resources, including personal attention, into smaller portions per student unless the number of faculty increases proportionally. Though many institutional presidents believed in the iron triangle, their institutions are peppered with efforts to improve quality, to improve access, and to improve affordability, as though the three were unrelated.

Three Gains, Bit by Bit

In my experience, all institutions implement isolated initiatives to improve facets of quality, access, *or* affordability. Such initiatives are often undertaken by people and units who are unaware of one another's activities. The result is an almost random gaggle of initiatives. For example:

- Faculty, individually and collectively, often see institutional quality as their responsibility. Quality (i.e., academic resources) is sometimes improved by hiring faculty who can expand the teaching and research capabilities of their departments. Updates to courses are usually made by individual faculty, and such changes may or may not leave students better prepared for later courses or for life. The teaching center offers workshops on disparate topics that seem likely to attract faculty participants. Library acquisitions are more likely to be influenced by individual faculty preferences than by programmatic priorities.
- Broadening access is often considered the province of units such as remedial programs, financial aid, and advising. These efforts are often uncoordinated. Disability support services may have different goals and strategies than a unit concerned with racial diversity.

- From the institutional perspective, affordability is often seen as the responsibility of those who make budgets and manage spending. Tuition changes influence affordability for students, while a host of independent choices by faculty have some influence on whether students feel they can afford the time to complete a course or a program. Time affordability for students can also be affected by online courses and programs that reduce student time spent commuting to campus.

The following is an example of this bit by bit approach as it was articulated in a national study. An American Academy of Arts and Sciences Commission on the Future of Undergraduate Education listed a variety of separate recommendations for quality, for access, and for affordability (Table 2.1).

TABLE 2.1
Example Recommendations for (Separately) Improving Quality, Access, and Affordability

	Example recommendations from the report
Improve the quality of the student experience	• Master's and doctoral programs should integrate meaningful teacher training opportunities • All college credentials—certificates and associate and bachelor's degrees—should incorporate academic, career, and civic knowledge and skills • Researchers should develop more reliable measures of student learning gains
Increase completion and reduce inequities (access)	• Data collection and nuanced analyses should enable institution-specific insights and support rigorous evaluation and careful assessment of completion-related student interventions • Expand experimentation with and research on guided pathways designs, which already help many institutions increase completion and reduce time-to-degree and excess credits • Work toward a new national understanding of and approach to student transfer
Control costs and increase affordability	• Design a single income-driven repayment plan • Track student progress across institutions and provide access to continued aid based on satisfactory academic progress across multiple institutions • Direct scarce resources to the students for whom they will have the greatest impact

Source. Commission on the Future of Undergraduate Education, 2017.

Take a look at the action recommendations (bullets) in the quality row of Table 2.1. They are completely separate organizational activities that each relate to quality. Meanwhile the access recommendations have no relationship to quality, and neither relates to the goal or recommendations for affordability. That doesn't make them bad recommendations. But it does pit each action recommendation against all the others in the competition for attention and resources.

Using Constellations of Institutional Attributes and Initiatives to Foster 3Fold Gains

Thanks to some personal history described in the preface, I was convinced that there must be a conceptually simple way to simultaneously improve quality, access, and affordability. But I wasn't sure what it would look like, and I didn't know how to describe clearly to others what I had in mind.

My research shifted into high gear after hearing a talk by Tim Renick of Georgia State University in which he described just such an effort. For a decade Georgia State had been assembling a collection of long-time institutional attributes and recent initiatives that reinforced and sustained one another. And Georgia State had gathered evidence to help explain how its work was improving graduation rates, equity of access, *and* affordability. (We'll describe Georgia State's efforts in chapter 3.) Eventually, I identified five additional U.S. institutions that had also, over the years, been assembling such *constellations* to pursue *3fold gains.*

> An institution's *constellation* is not a coincidental gaggle of institutional attributes and initiatives. Instead, as the right side of Figure 2.1 suggests, the constellation's elements, in concert, help sustain and scale one another's contributions to related, cumulative gains in quality of learning, equitable access, and stakeholder affordability, that is, *3fold gains.* One reason the attributes and initiatives work together is that each is guided by similar assumptions about how learning works. For example, many institutions today assume that lasting, usable learning depends partly on students looking critically at their own thinking so that they become conscious of and test their own assumptions. That's an assumption about learning. That same institution may rely partly on writing-intensive courses and partly on electronic portfolios to help students develop this self-aware, self-critical approach to thinking and learning.

Figure 2.1. Three gains versus 3fold gains.

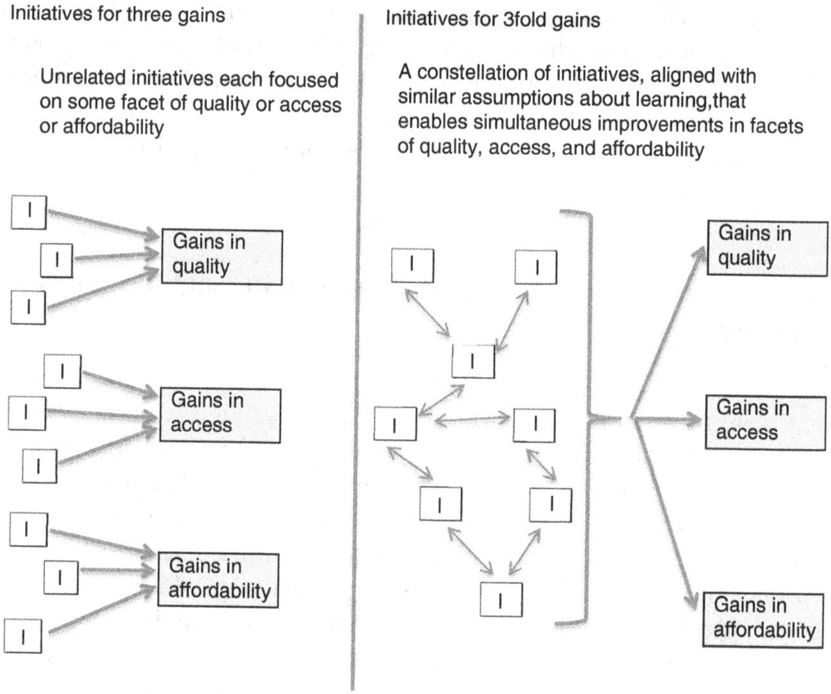

Initiatives for three gains

Unrelated initiatives each focused on some facet of quality or access or affordability

Gains in quality

Gains in access

Gains in affordability

Initiatives for 3fold gains

A constellation of initiatives, aligned with similar assumptions about learning,that enables simultaneous improvements in facets of quality, access, and affordability

Gains in quality

Gains in access

Gains in affordability

The purpose of this book is to shed light on those institutional strengths and initiatives that, together, can create 3fold gains in quality, equitable access, *and* stakeholder affordability. More on this in later chapters.

Gains Always Entail Losses

The iron triangle isn't made of iron, but there is still some truth in it. There are always tradeoffs, even steps backward, when any change is implemented. Imagine education in the time of Socrates: It was limited to dialogue with other people, complemented by occasional hands-on demonstrations. Around that time, reading and writing triggered a transformational change in learning. Eventually, each student read Plato's recreations of Socratic dialogue and then returned to discuss with a master and their peers. The result was 3fold gains:

- Quality: The combination of close reading and dialogue about the reading is better for developing insight and critical thinking than either activity alone.
- Access: Students can learn from distant, even dead, authors.

- Affordability: The combination of writing, reading, and dialogue should enable both students and their teacher to get more value and greater fulfillment from their time.

But there were losses as well.

- Quality: According to Plato's *Phaedrus*, Socrates condemned the use of written sources because students might well repeat what they'd read without necessarily understanding the ideas, and neither they nor the author would realize that no real learning had occurred. This can happen even when reading is followed by dialogue.
- Access: Illiterate students and teachers were barred, no matter how thoughtful they might be.
- Affordability: Eventually people could read faster than experts could talk, a time-saver. But learning to read well enough to engage in higher learning—that's quite time-consuming.

Those gains and losses can be opposite sides of the same coin. Consider the shift from learners being guided only by their "Socrates" to also being able to read the writings of many authorities. For some, that experience can be transformational. But those conflicting authorities can leave other learners floundering and perhaps repulsed by the lack of single authoritative answers. On the access front, huge numbers of literate learners, even today, learn from Plato's writings about Socrates. But in societies where literacy is not widespread, many people did and do lose access because of this new kind of higher learning.

The losses resulting from the addition of reading and writing are real and substantial. So why do we use reading and writing in higher education? Because, from the perspective of students, teachers, and other stakeholders, the gains outweigh the losses. The gains and losses resulting from the introduction of reading and writing are similar to those resulting from the creation of universities on campuses, and from the introduction of the internet (Ehrmann, 1999).

Turning the Page

Now that we've described pursuit of 3fold gains conceptually, it's time to examine the history of three institutions' efforts to improve quality, access, and affordability. We'll return to 3fold gains in chapter 6, where we will explore at least three mutually exclusive ways to pursue 3fold gains, each with somewhat different goals and conflicting strategies.

PART TWO

3FOLD GAINS GUIDED BY A SINGLE PARADIGM

My interest in 3fold gains turned from hunch to organized research in 2016 when I first heard of Georgia State University's decade of successful efforts to improve graduation rates and thereby improve quality, equitable access, and affordability.

Our first case history institution, Georgia State University (chapter 3), stands out for several reasons. First is their methodical and determined use of evidence to take one improvement initiative after another. Second, all the initiatives are consistent with similar assumptions about learning and how to support it. Third, Georgia State is also the only case history institution in which degree programs were redesigned as programs (not just as collections of courses).

Governors State University (chapter 4) managed to increase both enrollment and access while improving quality, all while enduring suffocating state budget cuts. We'll focus on their design for the 4-year curriculum and their creative approach to reallocating resources during a period of dramatically declining state support.

Southern New Hampshire University's College for America (CfA) (chapter 5) is the only *competency-based academic program* in our six case histories. From its conception, CfA was intended to be unusually effective in fostering quality, access, and affordability. For example, one of the first design decisions was to keep operating costs per student dramatically low; planners then designed an academic program that could achieve those levels of quality and access while staying within the constraint of low costs.

Competency-based education (CBE) is a confusor. Outside this book, the term sometimes denotes what we would call "good instructional design" or "backward design": to oversimplify, define goals, create assessments of student progress toward those goals, plan teaching and learning activities to stimulate development toward the goals, and then flesh out the program by selecting or creating materials and tools needed to engage in the activity. Some CBE is used to refer to courseware designed in that way; in this book we use the term *adaptive courseware* to refer to such courseware.

In this book, we use the definition of *CBE* created by the Competency-Based Education Network (2017):

> Competency-based education combines an intentional and transparent approach to curricular design with an academic model in which the time it takes to demonstrate competencies varies and the expectations about learning are held constant. Students acquire and demonstrate their knowledge and skills by engaging in learning exercises, activities and experiences that align with clearly defined programmatic outcomes. Students receive proactive guidance and support from faculty and staff. Learners earn credentials by demonstrating mastery through multiple forms of assessment, often at a personalized pace. (para. I)

Unless a CBE program has very large numbers of students, it is likely to incorporate less academic peer interaction than in some other models of organizing higher learning.

These first three case studies (chapters 3, 4, and 5) hint that there might be more than one way to pursue 3fold gains. In fact, there appear to be at least three ways to do it. Chapter 6 describes three general paradigms for organizing higher education and pursuing 3fold gains. The assumptions of the Instruction Paradigm provide a rationale for the way higher education often works today and also for why it's so hard to transform institutions. The assumptions of the Individualized Learning Paradigm underlie some competency-based programs, especially those using direct assessment. The Integrative Learning Paradigm aligns with the kind of transformation that many of today's colleges and universities are talking about today: experiential learning and authentic assessment, for example. The more an institution is aligned with one of these approaches, the harder it is to lean on either of the other two. For example, each approach needs a different kind of instructional staff and a different reward system for those people. In chapter 6, we'll look into how each of three approaches works. As we'll explain, the Integrative Paradigm seems most promising and has been attracting the most interest. The rest of the book will develop a sustainable framework for the Integrative pursuit of 3fold gains.

3

GEORGIA STATE UNIVERSITY

Assembling a Constellation for 3Fold Gains

In 2003, Georgia State University was a growing public, research-intensive institution with over 20,000 undergraduates as well as several thousand graduate students. In that year, according to a later university report, "underserved populations were foundering. Graduation rates were 22% for Latinos, 29% for African Americans, and 18% for African American males. Pell students were graduating at rates far below those of non-Pell students" (Georgia State University, 2017, pp. 1–2). In fact, in that same year, only 50% of African American Pell grant students even made it to their sophomore year. In 2003, only about one in three Georgia State students were graduating within 6 years with a bachelor's degree. Rates were even lower for students who were poor, first generation, or African American.

By 2018, enrollment for bachelor's degrees had grown by over 20%, to over 24,000 students. During that same period, the percentages of undergraduates who were Pell-eligible increased from less than 35% in fall 2008 to 55% in fall 2018, and those from underrepresented groups from 54% to over 70%. In 2016, the five campuses of Atlanta's 2-year Perimeter College were consolidated into Georgia State, making it the largest university in Georgia, with over 51,000 2-year, 4-year, and graduate students by fall 2018. Georgia State University is one of only two universities to rank in the top 15 in the nation for both its racial/ethnic diversity and the percent of low-income students enrolled (Georgia State University, 2017).

Suppose someone explained all those facts to you about Georgia State. And suppose they added that the institution became significantly more research-oriented between 2008 and 2018. Would you assume that 4-year retention and graduation rates would have dropped even lower? Actually, graduation rates improved over that period of growth as Georgia State implemented a growing constellation of initiatives (Figure 3.1).

Figure 3.1. Georgia State innovations and graduation rates.

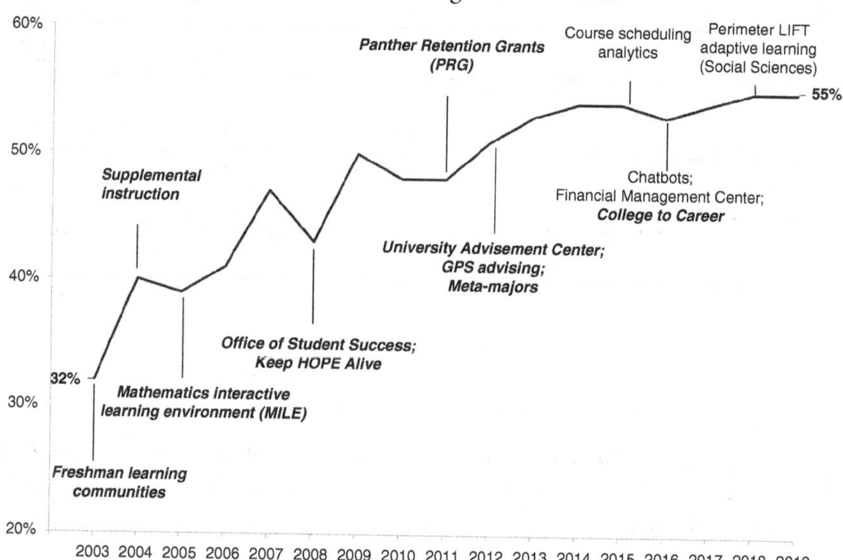

Note. As Georgia State assembled a constellation of sustained initiatives, graduation rates rose. ***Boldfaced and italicized*** initiatives are described in this chapter.

Kurzweil and Wu (2015) accounted for this remarkable improvement in graduation rate: "The university's improvement represents the accumulated impact of a dozen or more relatively modest programs. As it turns out, the recipe for [Georgia State]'s success is not a particular solution, but rather a particular approach to problem-solving" (p. 3). Before we delve into the individual "modest programs," it's important to understand Georgia State's "particular approach to problem-solving," that is, how it has learned to use evidence to guide and manage its initiatives.

Organizational Capacity to Analyze and Improve Student Progress

Challenge: Students encountered many stumbling blocks on their way from admission to graduation, especially to graduation by the time their eligibility for financial aid was exhausted.

Response: Georgia State began creating the organizational infrastructure needed to identify, analyze, and respond to barriers to student success. In 2008, the chair of religious studies, Tim Renick, applied for the position of associate provost, which carried responsibility for admissions, financial aid, and the registrar. During his interview with the provost, Renick suggested that the position be responsible for coordinating additional offices that influenced student success, such as freshman advising. The provost approved his idea and appointed him.

Renick believed deeply in using evidence to guide, evaluate, and defend change. The first step was to make sure that evidence was valid and easily collected from many sources. He began to work with the offices of the registrar and institutional research on "cleaning" Georgia State data. For example, previously, administrative users had filled in a blank space to indicate a student's major. When statistics were collected, "BioSci," "biological science," and "biological sciences" were counted as different majors because they were spelled differently. The first step toward creating gold standard information was to create a lexicon: "Every evening we would check to make sure that day's entries of majors conformed to the lexicon and would immediately correct errors" (Renick, personal communication). Ultimately the data warehouse became the most valid and dependable way to analyze a huge amount of Georgia State data from many sources and about many topics. In 2009, President Mark Becker declared that *only* warehouse data could be used in institutional reports. With that mandate, the warehouse grew to include all data concerning student, faculty, and courses (including, for example, the ability to extract grade distribution by course section); human resources; housing; and more (Georgia State University, 2019). As the warehouse grew, it became increasingly useful for spotlighting where and how many students were being derailed on their journey toward a degree (Kurzweil & Wu, 2015).

Renick's team also developed a standard approach for making incremental improvements in student success (Georgia State University, 2017):

1. *Collect data identifying an institutional issue hindering student success.* The university starts by analyzing problems that may particularly plague students of a certain race, ethnicity, first-generation status, or income level. Ultimately, the university looks for problems that affect many students.
2. Create *a strategy for addressing the problem* that could, if successful, be scaled and sustained for many years to come, usually benefiting most or all students. By designing initiatives that could be scaled and then sustained, the university assembled what ultimately became a mutually reinforcing constellation of initiatives by adding one or two new ones at a time.
3. Test the new strategy on a *small scale* first, if necessary. Use information from that pilot test to *improve the strategy*. Keep revising the strategy until it's ready to be scaled up.

4. *Scale and sustain the initiative* to handle sufficiently large numbers of students. By relying on sustainable initiatives, Georgia State could develop an increasingly comprehensive approach to student success while adding a new initiative only every couple years.
5. Use evidence of gains in quality, access, and/or affordability to *inform internal and external stakeholders and attract support* to carry out the next round of improvements.

Repeated gains in graduation rates demonstrated the power of cross-silo integration. By 2019, the Office of Enrollment and Student Success had grown to include

- units that deal primarily with bringing in new students (undergraduate admissions, graduate admissions, welcome center);
- units that support students in the routines of their work at Georgia State (academic advisement, student success, registrar, financial aid, scholarships, military outreach, international student and scholar services); and
- units that support high-impact experiential learning and preparation for life after graduation (signature experience, co-ops and internships, and university career services).

A Growing Constellation of Large-Scale Initiatives

From 2003 to 2018, Georgia State gradually assembled a number of initiatives that, together, led to substantial 3fold gains. Many were created under the aegis of the enrollment and student success programs and were intended from the start to become permanent features of the university if they were demonstrably effective. Typically, each initiative was designed to aid most or all undergraduates. Here a few of those initiatives, each illustrating a different facet of Georgia State's approach.

Freshman Learning Communities and Meta-Majors

Challenge: Reduce high D/F/Withdrawal (DFW) rates and achievement gaps in the freshman year.

Response: In 1999 Georgia State began a small freshman learning community (FLC) program. Research elsewhere had shown this strategy could improve student learning and retention; later research on learning communities as a high-impact practice (HIP) showed that, especially in combination with other HIPs, they could enhance learning for all students while reducing achievement gaps that plague students from underserved groups. (For more on HIPs, see chapter 10.) At Georgia State, cohorts of 25 students took five or six of their first-year courses together, multiplying their opportunities to get to know and support one another. The courses were scheduled one after the other in large time blocks, making scheduling easier for first-year commuting students. In 2003, the FLC program was expanded to all first-year students.

The FLC effort was sustained but not static. A decade later, the Office of Student Success gathered evidence showing that, when students changed majors, their progress toward a degree was slowed because coursework in their prior major no longer counted toward graduation. So in 2013, Georgia State began organizing every FLC around a group of related majors (a meta-major). This strategy was intended to motivate students as soon as they entered the university, make it easier for departments to connect with potential future majors, and smooth the process of changing majors, because all the majors in a meta-major had similar early requirements. Meta-majors are an element of Georgia State's constellation that is intended to reduce the time and costs of getting a degree. Earlier I talked about the importance of sustaining initiatives so that, over the years, the constellation could grow. As we've just seen, sustaining an initiative does not mean that it is unchanging. Georgia State's use of evidence helps generate ideas for continual improvement of an initiative and then, once the improvement is in place, to see whether it's really working.

Outcomes: Students are automatically enrolled in an FLC unless they opt out. In 2017–2018, more than 70% of bachelor's-degree and 92% of associate-degree freshmen participated in FLCs. In the 2016–2017 academic year, enrollment in an FLC by meta-major was found to increase a student's likelihood of being retained to the following year by 5% (Georgia State University, 2019). At the newly added 2-year Perimeter College campuses, participation in an FLC was associated with an 8% gain in retention. By relying on FLCs organized around meta-majors, the university has reduced the number of students changing majors after their freshman year by 32%. By finding a good-fitting major earlier, students now earn their bachelor's degrees more than half a semester earlier (Renick, personal communication, September 19, 2016). Acceleration toward graduation improves affordability for both the student and for the institution.

Redesign of Large Enrollment Courses With Chronically High DFW Rates

Challenge: Nationally, certain high-enrollment courses, especially introductory math, are notorious for high DFW rates. At Georgia State, math students met for 4 hours a week of lecture-centric instruction in traditional classrooms. In 2006, fully 43% of Georgia State students who registered for introductory math courses withdrew or received D's and F's.

Response: Research in the field suggested that more active and individualized forms of study could improve learning outcomes. So, in 2006, Georgia State math faculty decided to apply such approaches to precalculus, college algebra, and later statistics. The faculty–staff team devised a specialized lab facility, the mathematics interactive learning environment (MILE) that relied heavily on computer tutorials. There students work through guided online tutorials (*adaptive courseware*) that personalize instruction, customizing content and assessment procedures while adapting to student preferences for acquiring information. Step by step, evidence about the student, especially their earlier responses, influences what the student is asked to do next. In the MILE lab, graduate teaching assistants (GTAs), prepared undergraduate assistants, and faculty all provide on-demand help during business hours.

MILE courses generally employ a mixture of traditional classroom activities, adaptive software, and homework. Initially the math faculty tried a course design that combined 2 hours of traditional work with 2 hours of lab. But learning gains were disappointingly small. Based on some research about how math labs were performing elsewhere, the format was shifted in 2008 to 1 hour of classroom time and 3 unscheduled hours in the lab.

In 2008, 900 to 1,000 students per year took these courses. Those numbers climbed to 1,600 to 1,700 students, leading the faculty to tweak the format yet again. Giving students free choice of when to do lab work produced crowding far beyond the lab's capacity at certain times. So, beginning in 2014, students were scheduled for two 75-minute sessions in the lab each week plus 1 hour of classroom work. This is yet another example of a Georgia State innovation that has been sustained but not static.

In order for these new teaching strategies to work, some changes in organizational infrastructure were needed. A second 80-seat MILE Lab was created. In 2017, Georgia State tweaked how credit and teaching load were allocated among instructional staff. A course coordinator leads both the courseware evolution and the planning for classroom sessions. Because the course coordinator designs activities for all classroom sessions, the GTA for a MILE course doesn't need to spend much time on preparation. Therefore, each GTA is assigned four sections of 40 students (4 hours of leading classroom sessions) each week. Georgia State decided these 4 hours should count as one "course" when calculating the GTA's teaching load. (We'll have more to discuss about organizational foundations that support educational strategies in chapter 11.)

Outcomes: The MILE approach fostered 3fold gains.

- Quality: When the pilot versions of MILE-based course were compared with randomized control groups taught in the traditional way, employing the same midterm and final examinations, the MILE students did better. Even more importantly, MILE students also earned higher grades in courses for which MILE math courses are prerequisites (Patterson et al., 2006). As of 2017, DFW rates in MILE-based sections were hovering around 28%, compared with the pre-MILE rate of 43%. In 2018, all 8,500 seats of Introduction to Statistics, College Algebra, and Precalculus offered at the Atlanta campus were taught using adaptive, hybrid pedagogies. Since the launch of the program, nonpass rates for these courses have been reduced by 35%. In all, 1,300 more bachelor's students annually pass math courses on first attempt than was the case before the launch of the initiative (Georgia State University, 2019).
- Equitable access: Students from underserved groups benefitted more than average. DFW rates for minority and Pell-eligible students declined by up to 11% compared with nonminority, non-Pell students (Boston Consulting Group & Arizona State University, 2018). Recent evidence suggests that hybrid courses such as those taught in MILE labs in English and psychology are reducing achievement gaps between minority and nonminority, as well as Pell and non-Pell, students. To illustrate, in English 1101, DFW rates were 8% for minority students in sections using adaptive courseware versus 19% for students in traditional sections. Similarly, in Psychology 1101, minority student DFW rates were 11% versus 19% for minority students in traditional sections (Renick, personal communication).
- Affordability: The MILE design enables the university to reduce per-student costs compared with the traditional classroom format. MILE's increased percentage of students with passing grades eventually contributes to significant savings for students (who don't need to take and perhaps retake the same math course before going on to more advanced subjects) and for the university (which doesn't need to add class sections to accommodate students who must retake the course). About a half million dollars of one-time money was spent developing the MILE labs. Renick reports that the redesign has paid for itself through increased pass rates and likely decreases in the number of students dropping out of the university because they failed math.

The early successes of MILE-based courses encouraged Georgia State to create a second MILE classroom and invest in wider use of adaptive courseware.

The university now uses adaptive courseware to offer 15 different courses across 9 departments, including English, economics, and social sciences.

Data-Driven Advising

Challenge: As part of its string of investigations into retention and graduation rates, Georgia State staff gathered evidence from its professional advisers about how they invested their time in students. The primary finding was that these advisers spent most of their time responding to those students who most urgently demanded their help: honors students and students who were already on probation. Very few of the latter graduated, even after help from advisers—those students had asked for assistance too late. Meanwhile, most undergraduates did not engage with their overworked advisers, whose average load was 750 students (within Arts & Sciences, the load per adviser was 1,200).

Response: Georgia State sought vendor assistance to develop models and services that are now marketed as the EAB student success collaborative; within Georgia State they are called the graduation and progression system (GPS). The system went fully live in 2012. Georgia State already had a decade of data, including 140,000 student records and 2.5 million course grades. Analysis of this evidence with EAB enabled the development of over 800 different analytics-based alerts for undergraduates. Meanwhile retention and graduation rates were already increasing due to earlier initiatives. Some of the resulting revenue gains were allocated to multiply the number of advisers, each able to do more than before by using this new tool. Student activities such as midterm exam grades and their work online are monitored daily; if any activity (or lack thereof) triggers an alert, a message is sent to the student's adviser describing possible actions that the adviser might take. For example, to help assure that students graduate before exhausting their financial aid, the student and adviser are both notified when the student signs up for a course that does not meet any graduation requirement. Many students had been unaware of this issue and, as a result of such alerts, 90% of students responded by dropping the course. Another alert trigger is getting a poor grade in the first quiz of the semester. In Introduction to Chemistry, 67% of students who get a B on the first quiz pass the course, compared to fewer than 40% of students who get a C and 8% of students who get a D. The relationship between grade on the first quiz and likelihood of passing the course is even more dramatic for political science majors taking Comparative Politics and music majors taking Music Theory I. Previously these connections had gone unnoticed by the university; now advisers meet immediately with students to discuss how the student might respond. Faculty feared that this kind of early alert might channel students toward the easiest majors. Quite the contrary, as it turned out, according to Renick; GPS seems to have encouraged growth of majors such as computer science and biology.

Outcomes: It would be inappropriate to separate the benefits of GPS from related elements of Georgia State's constellation; they were intended to work in combination. But one good sign is that student visits with advisers have increased.

Keep HOPE Alive and Panther Retention Grants

"Helping Outstanding Pupils Educationally" (HOPE) is a statewide program of largely merit-based financial aid for Georgia residents. Around 2008, the Offices of Student Success Programs identified a population of students who were dropping out after their academic performance inched just below the HOPE standards and who then lost their scholarships. "Keep HOPE Alive" gave up to $1,000 to these students, offering them a second chance to raise their academic performance back to HOPE scholarship eligibility. The money comes with strings attached. Recipients must

- pursue a minimum of 30 credit hours within the next academic year,
- attend student success workshops hosted by the Office of Undergraduate Studies,
- regularly with an academic coach, and
- attend mandatory advisement sessions offered by the University Advisement Center.

For this group of "Keep HOPE Alive" students, the 6-year graduation rate grew from 21% in 2008 (just before the program was introduced) to 38% in 2017.

Panther Retention Grants (PRGs): In 2011, another needlessly at-risk population was identified: students in good academic standing who didn't have quite enough money to pay for their final semester of academic work. PRGs of about $500 were intended to help them over this final financial hump. For each student who was enabled to take a final semester of courses, GSU revenue increased by a net $1,600. This grant program thus helped make college affordable to students who couldn't afford to complete their degree otherwise, while also contributing to a net increase in university revenues, and it further increased graduation rates by enabling these students to complete their last semester. More than 11,000 PRGs have been awarded since the program's inception in 2011. Of the students who received the grant, 86.5% have graduated, most within two semesters (Georgia State University, 2019).

College to Career

Challenge: The organization of many academic programs does little to help students to think about how their activities, formal and informal, are preparing them for life after graduation until their senior year. One of the effects is that students who are less prepared may find themselves shunted into lower-paying jobs with less of a future.

Response: College to Career (CTC) is a university-wide initiative to help students begin thinking about their lives after graduation beginning before they even arrive in fall of their first year. CTC is also the centerpiece of Georgia State's Quality Enhancement Plan (QEP), required as part of the university's Southern Association of Colleges and Schools (SACS) reaccreditation process.

As a result of this multiyear initiative (2016–2020), a learning pathway from arrival to graduation guides Georgia State undergraduates through steps such as the following:

- Even before arrival students can begin using a portal that presents data on current job opportunities in the region for graduates from various majors.
- During orientation, students get more opportunities to use that portal. They receive their own ePortfolios and post their first artifacts—evidence of job- and life-relevant achievements drawn from their formal schooling and life experience. At this time, students choose a meta-major (described earlier) and are assigned to an FLC.
- Throughout their course of study, students encounter course assignments that help them see the relevance of the course for their later lives. CTC offers faculty small grants to develop such assignments.
- Career planning, including personalized guidance to help students understand the relationship of their academic choices to their career goals, is integrated into academic advisement.

To fund CTC, Georgia State obtained a $2 million grant from the Goizueta Foundation, based in Atlanta. Their proposal was persuasive for several reasons. The university had already committed $2 million of its own funds to support the work and was able to document earlier, contributing initiatives and their outcomes. Several key elements of the overall plan were already in place, including FLCs organized around meta-majors and provision of ePortfolios to every student. The proposal was organized around a compelling vision of how to improve student learning outcomes.

Outcomes: Early results from the CTC program are encouraging. For example, in 2018, students posted more than 700,000 artifacts as evidence of advances in their career competencies. Visits by first- and second-year students to University Career Services have increased by more than 100% since 2015.

Other Initiatives of Interest

In addition to these initiatives, Georgia State has created a Student Success Academy as a bridge program for students who may be particularly at risk. Chatbots, which interpret the most frequently texted plain language questions and respond with text messages in an average of 7 seconds, are available to all students. For a more complete list and analysis of Georgia State's initiatives, look online for the university's reports to Complete College Georgia (Georgia State University, 2019).

Hallmarks of Georgia State's Constellation of Initiatives

The initiatives I've described all align with certain assumptions about learning and how best to support it:

- An institution's quality should be measured in part by what fraction of its students graduate.
- Depending on their experiences in college, students' capabilities and talents can be changed substantially.
- Lasting learning benefits from a variety of human interactions, such as communities of shared understanding and support among students; opportunities to explain a point to a peer and get feedback (sometimes just a puzzled look); providing feedback in such a conversation; role playing; team projects; competitions; seminar dialogues; and brainstorming.
- Students' learning results solely from what they do. If, for example, assignments and activities don't challenge them to apply what they're being taught in unfamiliar contexts, they won't learn as much.

- Many Georgia State initiatives are intended to increase student motivation to study thoughtfully and energetically. The CTC program is the most obvious example; other programs that enhance interpersonal interaction (e.g., FLC and GPS) have that potential, too. Students are likely to gain more value from their educational opportunities when they're intrinsically motivated.

Evidence for 3Fold Gains by Georgia State

Evidence for quality gains: At many universities and colleges, evaluation of discrete innovations is focused only on usage and user reactions. For example, a new advising service might be evaluated by how many students used it and how well they reported liking it. That sort of assessment goes on at Georgia State as well. But an unusual amount of effort is put into analyzing the outcomes of its constellation of initiatives, especially retention and graduation rates, which affect access and affordability as well. That attention to graduation rates is emblematic of Georgia State's pursuit of 3fold gains.

Obviously, graduation rates are not a sole sufficient measure of quality gains: They say nothing about the nature and value of what students are learning. However, Georgia State's evaluations of MILE courses did attend to learning, comparing grades in sections taught differently. CTC's use of ePortfolios will provide even more direct evidence of learning over time.

Evidence for equitable access gains. Thanks to more than a dozen carefully targeted strategic initiatives, several of which are described in this chapter, Georgia State's achievement gap has shrunk dramatically. As Figure 3.2 illustrates, the achievement gap has flipped, with African American and Hispanic students graduating from Georgia State within 6 years at a slightly *higher* rate than White students.

This progress was made despite the fact that the odds were getting worse: the numbers of Pell-eligible students at Georgia State had soared during this period. Yet by 2012, Pell-eligible undergraduates were (and are) graduating at rates, on average, equal to those of non-Pell students. Evidence suggests that these gains were also achieved while more students turned to majors in science, technology, engineering, and mathematics (STEM) fields. For example, compared with 2010, total enrollment of African American students had grown by 50% by 2017; during that period the percentage of African Americans earning STEM degrees grew by 167%. (The number of African American males earning STEM degrees grew by 221%.) During that 7-year period, Hispanic student enrollment grew by 118% while the number of Hispanic students earning STEM degrees grew by 388%.

Figure 3.2. Georgia State 6-year graduation rates by race.

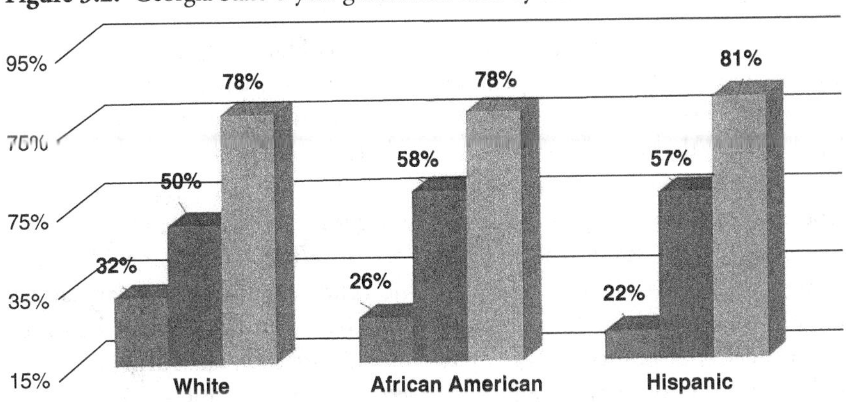

Note. "Today" represents students who entered 6 years before 2017. The right-hand bar in each cluster refers to National Student Clearinghouse data that includes students who began at Georgia State but graduated either from Georgia State or from another institution, or who were still in college (so these bars do not represent a 6-year graduation rate).
Source: Georgia State University, 2019, p. 26. Reprinted with permission.

Evidence for affordability gains. This same constellation of initiatives has economic benefits for students and for the university. Each percentage point gain in graduation rate represents over $3 million in additional revenue for Georgia State. But the changes mean that students are more likely to find education affordable, too. For example, students in the class of 2016 took eight fewer credit hours to graduate, on average, than did the class of 2013. This change alone represents a savings for students of $12 million in tuition and fees. Also, students who graduate sooner spend less time in school and more time working, so that college-level earnings start earlier; over a lifetime, that makes a difference. Affordability gains are greatest for students who wouldn't have graduated without these initiatives. A lifetime of college level earnings versus a lifetime of earning far less—that's a significant motivator.

Other evidence of progress: Finally, Georgia State's pursuit of 3fold gains has been validated by not only major grants for new work but also prizes. In 2013, the Association of Public and Land-Grant Universities awarded its first-ever MVP award to Georgia State University, declaring that it had made greater strides improving student success than any other public institution in the country. In 2015, the American Council on Education awarded the university its Institutional Transformation Award, only the second time that honor had been given. In 2017, *U.S. News & World Report* rated Georgia State the fourth most innovative university in the country.

Turning the Page

From the first time I heard about what Georgia State had been doing, what struck me was how patient, persistent, and dogged their pursuit of student success had been. Year after year, they would try to identify a serious, fixable barrier. They'd study it, take action, and study what happened. In almost every case, they were right to expect that, if the initiative were successful, it would be sustained. If you didn't know or guess their shared purpose, these initiatives would seem wholly disconnected. What do freshman learning communities have to do with small emergency injections of financial aid for students who could be graduating soon? It's like looking up at the starry night. Scattered points of light may suddenly take on the form of a constellation, an understandable picture. Georgia State continues to develop its constellation.

At first glance, Governors State University in Illinois might seem to have a wholly different story from Georgia State. But if you look at it from the right angle, you might see a similar constellation.

4

GOVERNORS STATE UNIVERSITY

A 4-Year Educational Strategy

As I've mentioned, Governors State University caught my eye because of its elegant end-to-end design of bachelor's degree programs and its effective integration of graduates of partnering community colleges into its upper division undergraduate program.

Governors State in Illinois was created in 1969 with an unusual design. It offered degree programs for upper-division undergraduate, master's, and starting in 2007, doctoral students. Within 4 years, the head count had grown to 1,147 undergraduate and 1,069 graduate students. It was designed from the start to be an experimenting university for students graduating from Chicago-area community colleges. Early on, it was competency based. Its faculty were organized into interdisciplinary areas rather than traditional academic departments. In those days, all faculty had the rank of university professor (no reference to either rank or discipline). In the 1990s the university was known for its extensive use of live video to reach students.

However, by the time Elaine Maimon took over as Governors State's fifth president in 2007, the university had reverted almost completely to traditional academic norms. Its undergraduate program, with a headcount enrollment of perhaps 3,500 students, still served only upper-division students, many of whom were transfers from regional community colleges. Governors State had always been at the bottom of the funding hierarchy for 4-year public institutions in Illinois. Because the budgeting process was guided by the previous year's budget rather than formulae for equitable funding across state institutions, the state budget allocation had been low for many years. Then things got worse. From FY2008 through FY2015, state appropriations for Illinois public universities were cut every year. In FY2016, the legislature failed to pass a budget at all.

Fortunately, President Maimon brought considerable experience and energy to the university. She cofounded the Writing Across the Curriculum (WAC) movement in the late 1970s, led Arizona State University's distinctive West Campus, and most recently served as chancellor of the University of Alaska at Anchorage.

By 2019, the university had what I'd call a "mission sentence": "Governors State University is committed to offering an exceptional and accessible education that prepares students with the knowledge, skills, and confidence to succeed in a global society" (Governors State University, 2020c, para. 1). That mission is complemented by a one-sentence vision, "GSU will create an intellectually stimulating public square, serve as an economic catalyst for the region, and lead as a model of academic excellence, innovation, diversity, and responsible citizenship" (para. 2). Several things in those two sentences struck me. First, education must be both exceptional—a model of academic quality—and also accessible. Second, education is conceived as more than content delivery ("skills, confidence"). Third, continual innovation is still at the heart of Governors State's vision.

Under President Maimon, the university's access mission focuses on what they call *first generation (!) students*, that is, potential students who have no one in their immediate or extended family (aunts, uncles, cousins) or even in their neighborhoods who have ever graduated from college. When they enter, first generation (!) students are oriented to their neighborhoods, not the globe. The mission sentence asserts that the university is responsible for changing that, to help all its students understand and excel in a global context. Quality and access are explicit goals. The third goal is unspoken but just as important: to succeed within the constraints of declining state support.

Since 2007, Governors State has undertaken major initiatives to pursue those quality, access, and affordability goals, including

- implementing a dual degree program in collaboration with regional community colleges;
- adding a lower division and organizing the resulting 4-year degree program around essential learning outcomes and high-impact practices (HIPs);
- adding infrastructure such as the Center for the Junior Year to support learning;
- coordinating planning and collaborative action across organizational silos;
- transparent budgeting and continual reallocation.

Dual Degree Program

For an upper-division-only university, productive relationships with feeder community colleges can leverage increasing enrollment while also improving students' 4-year educational experience. The four most recent presidents of the university had already tried to accelerate the flow of community college graduates into its upper division undergraduate programs, but with little success.

When President Maimon met with community college leaders, she heard that the university hadn't always been a good listener: for example, the university and the 2-year colleges had not developed strategies for cooperation among faculty or administrators at all levels. "After a few missteps, I began to hear what the community college leaders were saying about the conditions for breaking down hierarchies and establishing game-changing cooperation" (Maimon, 2018, p. 85).

After two-and-a-half years of consultation and planning, Governors State established a dual degree program (DDP) in 2010 that now engages 17 Chicago area community colleges. Creating these partnerships required that the presidents learn to trust one another to deliver on institutional commitments. Maimon viewed each community college relationship as unique, founded on personal relationships at the top. To run the DDP, Maimon hired a retiring community college provost who was known to be skeptical about prior attempts to get 2- and 4-year institutions to work together.

The institutions' faculty worked together to improve pathways to a baccalaureate degree, starting from entry in a 2-year college. The 2-year college faculty had more experience working with Governors State's target students than the university's own faculty. At the same time, Governors State faculty had specialized knowledge and experience in their fields to share with their community college colleagues. One goal of the cross-faculty discussions was to assure that community college transfer courses aligned learning outcomes with Governors State upper-division courses so that all credits would meet Governors State requirements. Faculty from the university and the community colleges conferred about educational strategies such as WAC.

Nationally, research indicates that students with associate degrees are more likely to earn undergraduate degrees than students without degrees who transfer credits from a community college (Doyle, 2006; Rosenbaum et al., 2006). DDP provided a plan for all community college students to earn an appropriate 4-year degree, including students who had earned associate degrees from technical programs.

Following "15 to finish" policies suggested by Complete College America (Complete College America, n.d.), DDP students were advised to earn at least 30 credits each year and to finish their associate degrees within

5 semesters. DDP worked in many other ways to facilitate the students' academic journey through their two degrees. For instance, while still registered at their 2-year institutions, DDP students had privileges on the Governors State campus including use of its library. Governors State transfer specialists spent 4 days a week on DDP campuses working with counselors there. Maimon's first fund-raising drive after becoming president was to raise $1 million to provide financial aid for community college transfers.

Symbols have meaning in a cultural context and changing symbols can contribute to changing culture. Maimon (2018) wrote:

> [Entering DDP students] receive cap and gown cords in the school colors of their community colleges. Before their GSU graduation, these community college colors are braided with GSU's base colors of black and white, signifying the cooperation of the community college and the university in students' success. These braided cords are presented at a special ceremony during graduation week, and the DDP students wear the cords proudly during Commencement. Community college presidents are invited to sit on the GSU Commencement stage to share in the celebration of students' accomplishments through two institutions of higher education. (p. 90)

At the end of the first 6 years of DDP, an average of 91% of DDP students who transferred to Governors State either graduated or were on track to graduate. As one student remarked during a focus group, "Before I discovered the DDP, I was on a dark and winding road without a flashlight" (Maimon, 2018, p. 92)

Adding a Lower Division While Reconceiving the 4-Year Course of Study

In 2011, the Illinois Board of Higher Education approved Governors State's proposal to create a lower division. The university already had a strong commitment to learning-centered general education in the upper division; adding a lower division would give Governors State a rare opportunity to develop a coherent 4-year strategy for quality and access. Community colleges could have viewed Governors State's expansion into the lower division as problematic competition. But Governors State had already assured them it would not recruit community college students who hadn't yet finished their associate degrees. Lower division admissions were limited to fewer than 300 per year. And of course the dual degree lower division program at all these community colleges had to prepare students for a smooth transition to upper division work at the university.

Governors State's Faculty Senate was actively involved in the task force planning for the lower division. Curriculum development was organized as a scholarly dialogue, first among Governors State faculty and then expanding to all interested members of the campus community. The development process included two symposia in 2012, featuring invited speakers and open to the community, which have continued since then, supporting continuing efforts to improve student learning. Their final design was also influenced by Association of American Colleges & Universities (AAC&U) Liberal Education and America's Promise (LEAP) Program, Complete College America, and the John N. Gardner Institute for Excellence in Undergraduate Education.

Several animating ideas influenced how Governors State designed its new integrated 4-year academic program (Maimon, 2018, p. 99), principles such as:

- Design the curriculum so that students see the connections between their learning in various courses from their general education, degree programs, and other academic requirements.
- Identify student strengths (including life experiences) and build on them, rather than searching for student weaknesses in order to remedy them.
- Organize around *inquiry-led, integrative, and applied liberal learning* to meet the needs of career-minded students so that students learn to make sense of what they're learning from many disciplines.
- Differences between the students and those with whom they interact should *enlarge students' understanding of people from different cultures and backgrounds* and help them respectfully use these differences as learning resources.

Guided by those principles, the 4 years of undergraduate work were reorganized, starting with freshman year. Here are a few features of that design; for more detail, look at chapter 8 of Maimon's book (2018).

One of those animating ideas was to build on students' strengths. Conditionally admitted students must take a 2-week summer course called Smart Start; it's been called a fun boot camp on writing and math. Smart Start expresses the university's philosophy that people generally achieve more when they build upward and outward from their strengths. When President Maimon visited a Smart Start class session and asked how things were going, she was surprised that several students raised their hands and sounded excited. Said one, "This class is great because the professor is showing me I know things!"

The 4-year program is organized around HIPs, including learning communities (LCs) for first-year students, internships, cornerstone courses in majors for juniors, and capstone courses that involve considerable research and reflection for seniors.

As at Georgia State, incoming students are each assigned to an LC. Each cohort of students takes the same three courses together. The LCs were initially oriented to one of three themes—civic engagement, global citizenship, or sustainability—all of which helped undergraduates begin to attain "the knowledge, skills, and confidence to succeed in a global society" (Governors State University, 2020c). More recently, the LCs were each aligned with a meta-major, helping first-year students explore a family of careers and related degree programs. Each LC is supported by a success team of peer mentors, cohort advisers, career specialists, writing consultants, library liaisons, digital learning experts, psychological counselors, and staff from the Center for the Junior Year (described in the next section). The success team integrates support into the mainstream experience rather than diverting some students to a slower, remedial pathway. These same success team services support DDP students in area community colleges.

An HIP for juniors is a cornerstone course in every major that helps students to begin using, and questioning, their majors. About half of the junior cornerstone courses explore discipline-based research questions, while the other half pose ethical questions in their fields. In addition to integrating homegrown and transfer students, the junior cornerstone seminar has 2 goals: transition (connecting broad intellectual concepts from the general education course work of the first 2 years to the focused study of a particular discipline) and conceptual development (exploration of significant ideas and reflection on the nature of inquiry in the field). Another HIP that helps students see connections across their learning: the internships that are encouraged throughout the students' program.

The HIP for seniors is an interdisciplinary research-based capstone course in their field, a climax to a 4-year pathway that connects academic studies with careers. In addition to research on interdisciplinary challenges, students interrogate their own experiences in internships. The reflection goes the other way, too: for example, what specifically does their sociology course illuminate about their experiences in the internship?

Infrastructure to Support Learning

A major theme of this book is the need for appropriate organizational foundations to support an institution's evolving educational strategies. To sustain and support its new practices, Governors State's organizational infrastructure needed to change. In 2015 Governors State began developing the Center for the Junior Year (CJY) to support the third year of study (the first year for transfers with associate degrees) as students take ownership of their majors. Now, CJY works on not only the junior year but also preparation during the first and second years. For example, in Governors State's first-year LCs, CJY staff help students identify their personal mission—what they want to achieve in life—and then look for appropriate internships and relevant on-campus employment. They also help develop this sense among students at the DDP community colleges.

Governors State also looks for evidence that candidates for faculty positions have demonstrated commitment to learning-centered practices in previous appointments or as doctoral students. The university supports, including with small grants, faculty doing scholarly research into student learning. Such scholarship of teaching and learning is considered to be research in promotion decisions. President Maimon commented, "In hiring, and promotion, we encourage praxis—connecting scholarship and teaching" (Maimon, personal communication, March 15, 2019). Another way in which incentives were modified was through changes in the faculty union contract. The teaching credit allocation in the old contract incentivized faculty to teach small graduate courses (4 credits) rather than larger undergraduate courses (3 credits). The union recognized the importance of undergraduate teaching and agreed to alter the contract so that all courses were valued at 3 credits.

Cross-Silo Problem-Solving

By 2017, lapses in state funding had been a threat to operations and morale for several years running. That was the bad news. But challenges that serious and widely felt can also stimulate creativity, attract resources, and drive collaborative action. For example, when no academic unit has enough money or staff to fully accomplish its goals on its own, they're motivated to work together. Marco Krcatovich II, director of institutional research and effectiveness (IR), called this a shift of perspective from "my job" to "our job." (That shift toward "our job" is something I noticed at all six institutions in this book.)

Here's an example of cross-silo problem-solving. It began when one Governors State academic department noticed that, inexplicably, six full-time students in their program were reported as taking only a part-time load. Errors in data entry? That how it seemed at first. However, when the department worked closely with IR, they discovered that six "full-time" students had indeed dropped down to a part-time load for what seemed to the students like compelling reasons. For example, some of those students hadn't realized that they could add as well as drop courses early in the semester. Of course, dropping back to part-time loads could slow their progress to degree and make it more likely that they would drop out later. Motivated by this finding, departments worked with IR to redesign enrollment reporting. With those improved tools, advisers can now help students understand why and how to register for a full-time load.

Ironically, another such cross-silo investigation revealed that some full-time students had registered for programs designed only for part-time students. Once program administrators were alerted, a pathway to a degree was devised that helped these full-time students advance more quickly. For example, the scheduling of courses was reviewed to assure that courses a full-time student might need were not scheduled opposite one another. The full-time students were profiled to help align recruitment strategies to attract more of them.

This problem-solving cycle at Governors State begins with staff who are prepared to notice patterns in what might otherwise have been identified as random errors in data. It also requires training of administrators and campus leaders to not only read reports but also understand and interpret data. To respond, the appropriate offices and departments have to regard student success as their collective responsibility.

Cultural change is necessary, too. Krcatovich remarked, "I need to approach other offices with the attitude of 'what can I learn from you,' rather than 'I'm going to tell you what you need to do'" (Krcatovich, personal communication, December 12, 2016). He continued that this approach to problem-solving requires more time and patience up front. But it saves significant time in the long haul because the participating units have developed a response that they can implement effectively and efficiently, even though they are probably understaffed.

Transparent Budgeting for Reallocation

President Maimon realized that for Governors State to change, money and time had to be reallocated. This is almost always the case; a change in an institution's ways of doing things can't and shouldn't be funded by new money from outside, unless that new money is guaranteed to remain in the base budget. The act of reallocation should engage everyone in considering relative priorities rather than always simply defending their own turf. This imperative was even more urgent because of the perpetual cuts in state funding. And for reallocation to be sustainable it needed to be transparent and the decision-making process inclusive (Maimon, 2018).

Working with the faculty senate, Maimon appointed a 17-member planning and budget advisory council (PBAC) cochaired, across silos, by the provost and the vice president for administration and finance. Budget and all major financial decisions are open for PBAC review. As state budgets were cut each year, the PBAC made recommendations for how funds should be cut and, to some degree, reallocated. For example, money was shifted to student affairs so that the advising staff for the new lower-division students could be expanded. Program review sought to separate programs of highest quality from those that were only average compared with the competition. Some programs were eliminated, freeing up money for new programs for emerging needs such as health informatics, and for online programming geared to returning adult learners. Another reallocation stemmed from the decision to rely more on full-time faculty carrying full-time teaching loads; some of the budget for adjunct faculty could then be cut. During this period, no new faculty slots were added. I was struck by what President Maimon told me:

> As people retired or departed, the university did not automatically replace the position. Instead, we developed job descriptions that fit the university's new directions. All departments were alerted that any new hire had to be interested in undergraduate education, even if the larger portion of responsibility might be in graduate programs. In the context of strategic plans that emphasize quality, we tightened up the implementation of criteria for faculty retention, promotion, and tenure. We hired outstanding deans for the four colleges. All of this has led to, on the whole, a more productive, creative, and mission-driven faculty than we had in 2007. (Maimon, personal communication, August 16, 2019)

By working hard to keep expenditures in check, the university was able to invest substantially in areas of need. The administration encouraged faculty to deal creatively with cuts, figuring out ways to cope while making courses and programs more student centered and up to date. Not all changes had to be paid for totally through cuts in other areas: despite the cuts, the university invested in new programs and markets. For example, the addition of the lower division program was partly motivated by the need to tap new markets in order to expand tuition revenues while maintaining the university's comparatively low tuition.

Evidence for 3Fold Gains by Governors State

Evidence for quality gains: Like some other institutions in our study, Governors State has made use of student evidence collected through administrations of the National Survey of Student Engagement (NSSE), which surveys students about their engagement in activities that are known from prior research to improve learning outcomes. These evidence-based activities range from the nature of students' interaction with faculty to how frequently their work is assessed. The more extensive the students' engagement in these evidence-based activities, says the research, the more likely the students are learning at a high level. Governors State periodically analyzes NSSE reports that compare the percentage of its students engaging in HIPs with data from a pool of participating Illinois public universities. The 2018 survey found that 80% of Governors State's first-year students engaged in at least two HIPs, versus 57% at comparison institutions. HIP use is more common in the upper division at most institutions, but still Governors State rated well: 89% of Governors State graduating seniors took part in two HIPs or more, compared with 82% for graduating seniors at comparison institutions. (For much more on HIPs, see chapter 10). Governors State's effort to improve learning caught other eyes as well. A visiting team from their regional accreditor commented, "Such deep and significant change with such a high level of quality control and in such a short timeframe is rare in higher education" (Maimon, 2018, p. 24).

Evidence for equitable access gains: President Maimon's highest priority was to increase enrollment. By fall 2015, undergraduate head count had increased to 3,526, up from 2,554 in 2006.

To judge equity of access, the university needed to analyze outcomes for different categories of students. In 2019, Krcatovich provided some encouraging evidence on equitable access, a priority for this minority-serving institution, for students who entered in fall 2017:

- Latino students earned on average three more credit hours in the first year compared to the overall population, a level nearly equivalent to that of White students (23.40 Latino, 24.90 White, 20.68 overall). African American students earned 19.20 credit hours (an improvement over the prior 2 years).
- The gap between all first-year students and Pell-grant-receiving first-year students was only one credit hour (20.68 for all students, 19.52 for Pell recipients).
- Latino freshmen had a first to second semester persistence rate of 80%, compared to 67% for White students, 47% for African American students, and 53% overall.

Evidence for affordability gains: Governors State uses a low-tuition, low-aid strategy to attract a more economically diverse student body. In 2018–2019,

Governors State's tuition and fee bill for a full academic year was $11,646, the lowest of the public 4-year institutions in Illinois, despite its new programs and despite receiving the lowest state appropriation of any Illinois public 4-year institution. For comparison, the Illinois average for 4-year institutions was $13,970 in 2018–2019 (College Board, 2019).

Turning the Page

I originally looked into Governors State because I knew Elaine Maimon and her record of pioneering educational improvement on an institutional scale: (e.g., WAC). I was convinced to select it for a case history when I learned about the well-crafted 4-year approach to achieving essential student outcomes. Eventually I realized that DDP was an integral part of Governors State's larger strategy for achieving 3fold gains: the smooth articulation with community colleges and a powerful upper division design could improve both quality and access. A variety of factors, including the lower tuition that is common at community colleges, could advance affordability. (And in writing this chapter I was helped enormously by Maimon's [2018] fine book, *Leading Academic Change*, which describes how some grounded assumptions about learning guided her transformative work throughout her career.)

You have probably noticed some parallels between Georgia State's and Governors State's approaches to achieving 3fold gains. Before we draw too much from these examples, however, we go on to something almost completely different: a competency-based, individualized academic program with an altogether different approach.

5

COLLEGE FOR AMERICA

Project-Based, Individualized Learning

The world equally distributes talent, but it does not equally distribute opportunity. We seek to change that inequality. (Southern New Hampshire University, n.d., p. 3)

Is it possible to create a program with dramatically low tuition that gives adult working students plenty of human support while simultaneously improving learning with high-impact practices (HIPs) like project-based learning? Is it possible for a university to think outside its own box when developing such a program? Southern New Hampshire University (SNHU) took on these challenges and more when it created its College for America (CfA).

Founded in 1932 as a for-profit business college, New Hampshire College became a nonprofit private college in 1968 and offered its first online courses in 1995. In 2003 Paul LeBlanc became president of what was by then called SNHU, a private nonprofit university. Enrollments in online and continuing education grew strongly during LeBlanc's first decade, so those programs were organized into the College of Online and Continuing Education (COCE). Online programs became popular in part because, in an unusual move, SNHU charged only about half as much for online as for comparable programs on campus. COCE offerings were similar in design to many online programs: Course materials were designed up front, and instructors, often part time, did the teaching. Online programs required far less in the way of physical campus facilities, so they cost far less to offer than campus programs. The price, publicized through extensive advertising, helped COCE enrollments increase to the point where they dwarfed campus enrollments. The annual surge in revenue, fueled by the ongoing increase in online enrollments for the COCE, gave SNHU the money and confidence to develop a second strategy for educating working people.

Creating SNHU's College for America

In 2011, LeBlanc conceived of a new SNHU college that could improve the career prospects of working adults by developing their work-related competencies. It would offer degree programs that were totally online but independent of COCE and would cost even less than COCE's online courses. Influenced by the work of Clayton Christensen on disruptive innovations, the president created an insulated incubator for experimentation: The planning team could follow or ignore existing policies, practices, job descriptions, and services. After developing the plan, the team was to pilot test it so they could evaluate its educational effectiveness and appeal to target audiences. LeBlanc told me that he omitted one important element from this initial charge to the team: All elements of the design must be scalable in an efficient way. In other words, avoid expedient solutions that work well only when enrollments are still small.

Before we delve further into the creation of CfA, its unique pedagogy, and what is known so far about its outcomes, we're going to explore a key element of institutional transformation: finding the right people to run such a program.

Leadership for Academic Transformation

Reflecting on the 15 years of his presidency, LeBlanc (2018) described what he looks for in candidates for leadership roles at the university:

- *Mission*: "We have an innate belief in the power of education to transform lives and to create opportunity as a tool of social mobility and source of hope. If that mission does not fire someone up, they probably should work elsewhere" (para. 6).
- *Work Ethic*: "A lot of success comes with showing up and putting in the time and effort. I often ask job candidates what their parents did for work and what they carry with them in their own professional lives. . . . One candidate was uncomfortable about the fact that his father was a janitor and mother worked as a cashier in a convenience store, quickly shifting the topic to his own sophisticated lifestyle. Not a guy for us" (para. 7).
- *Curiosity*: "[What] I often ask is 'What books are you reading?' or some variation. My intent is . . . to see (a) that they like to learn and are curious and (b) what ideas and questions inspire them. . . . Beware those who have no good questions" (para. 8).

- *Empathy*: "Because of where I sit in the organization, I hire people into leadership roles. They invariably manage people and work closely with colleagues, especially as we become a more interdependent organization in which teamwork and building consensus are prized traits. Those who lack empathy almost always fail.... [Hiring people with empathy] helps you motivate and develop your people, to build win-win solutions and manage team projects, to... treat people with more kindness when things do not work out" (para. 9).

Goals for the New College

SNHU's mission statement explicitly asserts goals of quality, access, and affordability. LeBlanc refers to them as the Holy Triad of higher education:

> Southern New Hampshire University transforms the lives of students. Our success is defined by our students' success. By relentlessly challenging the status quo and providing the best support in higher education, Southern New Hampshire University expands access to education by creating high quality, affordable and innovative pathways to meet the unique needs of each and every learner. (Southern New Hampshire University, 2020)

New programs are expensive to create and rarely make money in their first few years. Therefore, they require expensive patience for those first few years. If that innovation is not understood or appreciated by stakeholders in the larger institution or if it's seen as an implicit rebuke of institutional practices, that patience is likely to soon run out (Levine, 1980). In its first 5 years CfA didn't generate surplus revenue, but its survival was assured because the university's president had conceived it as a test ground for practices that could spread to other parts of the university.

Doctoral student Sarah Hansen studied the nativity and early development of the program, interviewing many of the founding staff. All of her nine interviewees who described CfA's goals mentioned access and affordability. As one person put it,

> We all have one common mission at the university, and that is to provide access to higher education for as many people as we can. That's a huge general kind of mission. I would say that CfA's mission . . . is basically to do the same, but to provide it to adult learners in the workplace—and really for learners who never saw themselves as ever acquiring a college degree—and to do it at an extremely low price point. (Hansen, 2016, pp. 76–77)

Educational Strategies for the New College

The planning team chose several educational strategies that were consistent with each other and with the goals of CfA.

Organize the academic program around broad competencies that have obvious relevance to workplace success (quality): The resulting CfA goals also drew upon the broad competencies of the Association of American Colleges & Universities's (AAC&U) Liberal Education and America's Promise (LEAP) Essential Learning Outcomes (AAC&U, 2018a) and Lumina Foundation's Degree Qualifications Profile (DQP) (Adelman et al., 2011). These CfA goals were also influenced by extensive collaboration with employers, especially those who had partnered with the university.

Develop and demonstrate competencies through project-based learning: Projects often parallel workplace tasks; others prepare students for such tasks. Students can choose which project to work on next. Here's a project description from 2016:

> Because training and advising employees will be central to your role, you want to prepare thoroughly and thoughtfully before engaging in the work. As a communications specialist, you know that being effective isn't just about knowing the material. You also need strong self-awareness as a communicator. That is why you plan to reflect on your own interpersonal communications experience by repeating a Self-Reflection worksheet. Familiarize yourself with the Foundations in Interpersonal Communication resource and then complete the Self-Reflection worksheet, which is the deliverable for this project.

Materials such as this resource and worksheet are, by plan, free for students; the program developers find some free online educational resources and then fill in remaining gaps by developing new material. For this project, those resources included a link to an open educational resource (OER, described in detail in chapter 12) textbook, a blog post about a model of managing conflict, and a video interview about functional perspective theory. From the start of the project, students have access to the rubric that will be used to assess whether their deliverable does, or doesn't yet, demonstrate mastery of several competencies.

Competencies are typically developed and refined across several projects. For an example, let's look at writing. Depending on the specific projects they choose, by the time they graduate, general studies students with a concentration in business need to demonstrate mastery of writing through a minimum of

- 10 essays of 500–1,500 words, in APA or MLA format;
- 15 shorter writing pieces;

- at least 7 videos; and
- multiple PowerPoint presentations, posters, lab reports, agendas, audio recordings, spreadsheets, game boards, and menus.

All of these tasks are integral elements of projects set in the context of a simulated organization.

Require all students to master every competency in their program: Each project gives the student the opportunity to demonstrate mastery of several competencies. Once the student is satisfied with a project, subject matter experts (SMEs) assess it. Along with their comments and suggestions, the assessor judges decide whether the deliverable demonstrates mastery of the competency; the two possible ratings are "mastery" and "not yet." Each time a student resubmits a project to demonstrate mastery, the same assessor rates it while also providing substantive advice. For the next project and its incorporated competencies, different assessor(s) do the rating (Kazin, 2014).

For each project, provide an array of materials to help students develop needed capabilities: These materials are always free—OERs developed either elsewhere or by the CfA program team. Only a fraction of the materials are interactive software that guide the individual with feedback and suggestions; that kind of courseware can be comparatively expensive to develop and maintain. The lion's share of CfA materials consists of text, images, and videos.

Organizational Infrastructure of the New College

Planners decided that the new college had to be organized differently than the rest of SNHU, partly in order to drop the price to students to a more affordable level. These organizational innovations included:

Virtual facilities and services: For students, everything would be online, student services as well as educational resources, tutoring, and assessment. Thus, CfA's staff need not all live locally. Online programs can hire people with unusual skills who live anywhere in the world.

Redistributing "faculty" functions: In conventional colleges, faculty, especially full-time, are jacks-of-all-trades: designing courses and degree programs, creating and organizing course materials, presenting instruction, assessing student work, providing feedback, participating in university governance, and more. Instead of faculty, CfA employs a variety of specialists, such as full-time and part-time developers of curriculum and assessment, learning coaches, assessors, and advisers.

Employer and community partners: The majority of CfA students are employees of business partners. Tuition costs for business partners' employees are covered mostly by employers' existing programs of tuition support. The rest of the students are affiliated with SNHU public community partners such as the Peace Corps, community-based agencies, and experimental high schools. The community partners programs are aimed specifically at low-income youth, ages 18 to 25, in communities where the partner provides on-site services that often begin during public schooling. These community partners usually help pay for their students' tuition. By 2016, CfA had about 120 partners, the majority of whom were employers. Because of this partner structure, and in contrast to COCE, which grew rapidly because of a sophisticated and expensive international marketing effort to recruit individual learners, CfA does no mass marketing to potential students; they recruit through their employer and community partners instead.

Some partners advise on formulating competencies for each program. The recruiting model means that students often know one another from their workplace or community affiliation, so that local study and support groups are both possible and encouraged.

Dramatically low prices: The planners wanted CfA to be as close to free as possible, a price low enough that employee benefits might pay for 100% of tuition. The tuition also needed to be low enough to allow CfA to appeal to employers partly because its low price compared to the competition, including SNHU's other online programs. CfA's initial tuition for associate of arts (AA) and bachelor of arts (BA) students was $4,000/year.

CfA 2.0: Mainstreamed

By 2015, 2 years after CfA admitted its first students, the continuing but slow pace of growth prompted SNHU to question whether or not CfA should continue as a separate business unit and consider what could be learned from its founding years. The resulting transformation included improving economic scalability, converting some CfA services into university resources, reworking CfA curricular resources, and changing bits of CfA terminology to improve communication with the wider world.

Remember that President LeBlanc said he regretted not including scalability in his charge to CfA planners. CfA 1.0 had been built partly upon some systems and practices that could not be scaled without unacceptable increases in costs. CfA 2.0 moved to a commercial learning management system rather than continuing to rely on a locally adapted product. Eventually, CfA's degree programs were incorporated into the global campus (GC, formerly COCE), enabling the elimination of most CfA-specific staff positions; since the GC was far larger than CfA, incorporating CfA was quite feasible. CfA's office of business and community partnerships, as well as its academic coaching infrastructure, were transformed into a service for all of SNHU.

CfA 1.0's competency-based, SNHU-specific terminology seemed to discourage some potential students whose first impression was that CfA was both not "normal" and hard to comprehend. A particular problem was that students expect *courses*, but that term wasn't used in CfA 1.0. So CfA 2.0 adapted the word *course* to denote one goal and three competencies along with its associated projects and academic materials; completing a CfA course earns students three credits toward graduation. Obviously, CfA courses are in most ways completely unlike the traditional college three-credit course. For example, each student can start and complete a CfA course at any time. Because students are working at their own pace and through course materials in different orders, there can be no class meetings. Instead, as students work through course materials, their guidance and encouragement come from a learning coach, an adviser, and the SMEs assessing their projects. Yet, as different as CfA goals are from the courses taught on the SNHU campus, making the two terms synonymous has helped prospective and incoming students feel more comfortable. Other accommodations to the language of the wider world were also made. For example, President LeBlanc told me:

> As one of the tweaks in 2.0, we changed the competency definitions so that one competency would equate to 1 credit hour. [In CfA 1.0], students might have earned a half-credit for certain competencies. But growing experience showed us that it made no sense for transcripts to include fractions of a credit. We had to [align projects and competencies with credits] for our regional accreditor and for the Government. (Paul LeBlanc, personal communication, September 20, 2018).

To sum up, a CfA 2.0 AA program now consists of 20 goals (courses), each earning 3 credits. Here, for example, are 3 of the 20 goals for all associates in arts degrees in general studies:

- *Perspectives on People and Society*: Analyze how stories shape our society and investigate how varying interpretations of history influence how we see today's issues.
- *Leadership and Group Dynamics*: Identify leadership skills for engaging in teamwork in your career and practice communication strategies for addressing feedback.
- *Science, Technology, and Society*: Discover how scientific evidence can inform decision-making and examine the ethical considerations of pursuing scientific advancement.

As we described earlier in this chapter, each CfA goal (course) consists of three projects, mastery of three competencies, and the award of three credits.

For CfA 2.0, SNHU wanted to make it easier to quickly create competency-based programs tailored to the needs of particular populations, including shorter programs, rather than forcing students to choose among existing degree programs. The new curriculum map was designed to be easy to break into discrete chunks that could be mixed and matched for specific needs of specific populations. CfA 1.0's curricular elements had been so interconnected that such tailoring would have created unacceptable expenses.

By 2018, CfA programs enrolled 9,859 students; 966 graduated that year, 658 with bachelor's degrees, 306 with a AAs, and 2 with certificates. (The full-time/part-time dichotomy does not apply to CfA. All students pay the same tuition for a 6-month term. One of the strengths of the individualized program is flexibility in time; students can advance at any speed they can handle, investing as much time as they can afford.)

Evidence for 3Fold Gains by CfA

Evidence for quality gains: Evidence from employers is a crucial component of CfA's quality assessment. For example, managers at the Veterans Administration New England Health Care System assessed workplace-relevant characteristics of employees who were about to enter the CfA program and then reevaluated those same learners after 6 months in CfA studies. Managers observed improvements in skills such as decision-making (from 68% rated "moderately above average" or "far above average" before enrolling to 90% after 6 months) and critical thinking (from 82.5% to 100%). Anthem, Inc. found that over 30% of their CfA graduates had been promoted, nearly a 50% higher rate than nongraduates in similar roles (Lauren Keene, personal communication, August 19, 2019).

Evidence for equitable access gains: CfA was designed for students who might not otherwise have access to a college education. Enrollments have grown about 25% a year, as more partners join. That suggests that CfA may be filling an important niche.

Community partners help open access to CfA programs for more students from underserved groups. For example, in 2018, more than 80% of community partner students were eligible for Pell grants. Approximately 90% of students who enrolled via community partners identified as students of color (as compared with almost 50% of business partners' students.)

These community partner students do well at CfA. Although community partner students generally require more submissions per project to reach mastery, they complete degrees faster than do students enrolled through employer partners. According to FY18 data, community partner students also have higher rates of year-to-year retention (64.2%) than students enrolled in employer partner programs (42.2%) (Keene, personal communication).

Evidence for affordability gains: In 2018–2019, tuition for CfA programs was $5,000 per year. In comparison,

- an online degree from SNHU's Global Campus was priced at $9,600 per year, still frozen at its 2012 rate;
- an SNHU degree from its physical campus was priced at $31,136 in 2018–2019;
- neighboring Manchester Community College charged $6,880/year in 2019–2020; and
- Keene State University's annual tuition for students studying on campus was $11,468 in 2019–2020.

Even though CfA tuition is already comparatively low, about three-quarters of CfA student-employees use some form of tuition assistance. In fact, about half of all students have so much assistance that they pay no tuition at all. That helps explain how, by 2018, 60% of CfA graduates had incurred no student debt (Keene, personal communication, August 19, 2019).

Another measure of affordability is time to degree. On campus, SNHU students take an average of 1.8 years to graduate, but CfA students average only 1.3 years to complete a 2-year program. Similarly, it takes upper-division campus students 2.6 more years to graduate with a bachelor's degree at SNHU, while CfA students with 2-year degrees average only 1.5 more years to earn a baccalaureate. The ability of students to demonstrate mastery at the beginning of a course makes it possible for adult learners to progress more swiftly.

Affordability is also a concern for SNHU as an institution. In 2019, SNHU's enormous GC online programs are still subsidizing CfA degree programs. CfA expects to begin breaking even when its enrollments exceed 10,000.

Turning the Page

So far, all indications suggest that CfA is achieving 3fold gains by means of an innovative online program that uses projects to motivate, organize, and assess student learning. The evidence for quality of CfA offerings is encouraging, and better than that of many campus-based or online degree programs. CfA's use of business partners as intermediaries for many of its students offers an almost unique opportunity for a college to study its graduates at work. Its steady growth rate suggests that SNHU has identified a niche where CfA programs can do some good. Although the program is not yet breaking even for SNHU, it's expected to go into the black while remaining unusually affordable for its targeted students.

The three case histories provide some hints about a possible generalized framework for achieving 3fold gains. The next chapter takes a first step toward assembling this framework.

6

THREE COMPETING PARADIGMS FOR PURSUING 3FOLD GAINS

"But we don't want to teach 'em," replied the Badger. "We want to learn 'em—learn 'em, learn 'em! And what's more, we're going to do it, too!" (Grahame Greene, The Wind in the Willows, *1908)*

This book aims to develop a widely adaptable framework for institutions to follow to make 3fold gains of their choosing. As I tried to distill my observations into one or more general approaches to the pursuit of 3fold gains, the biggest difference I found was not among the six case history institutions, but between those six institutions and my own undergraduate experience. At MIT in the late 1960s, classroom learning was mostly passive, especially in science, technology, engineering, and mathematics (STEM) fields (I majored in aerospace engineering). During most of each class session, only one person talked—the instructor. Students quietly took notes; when the instructor paused to ask if we had questions, one or two hands might go up. We studied textbooks and worked out abstract problems set by our faculty. We took challenging, specialized courses, but faculty rarely illustrated how working engineers used information from our course of study. No one said much about how learning works, other than warning that "getting an education at MIT is like drinking from a fire hydrant." Our first three case history institutions are not identical but they are all certainly different from MIT in the late 1960s.

What Is a Paradigm?

Table 6.1 hints that that the MIT of the late 1960s may represent one *paradigm* about learning, Georgia State University (chapter 3) and Governors State

TABLE 6.1

Standout Features of Four Undergraduate Programs

	MIT (1967)	*Georgia State*	*Governors State*	*College for America*
Beliefs about entering students	Smart entering students will do well and graduate at the top	Entering students' capabilities can be developed, depending on how the institution helps them learn		
Pedagogy	Deliver content through lectures, textbooks, problem-solving	Help students develop essential learning outcomes (capabilities such as critical thinking) for applying content		
Required learning communities	No	Yes		No
Collaborative assignments and projects	Rare	More common	More common	Not applicable
Some large enrollment courses redesigned to foster active learning	No	Yes		Not applicable
Proactive advising	Little to none	Yes		
Faculty role	Jack of all trades (participate in design of degree programs; design courses and their materials and assessments; lecture; facilitate classroom learning activities; coach and advise individual students)			Faculty role split among specialists (subject matter specialists who develop degree programs and assess student deliverables; learning coaches; advisers)

University (chapter 4) (the two GSUs) a second, and College for America (CfA) (chapter 5) a third.

An institution's *paradigm*, as used in this book, is its theory in use, a set of assumptions about learning that can inferred by examining the institution's routine patterns of teaching and learning activity. Assumptions within a paradigm should explain what most people do most of the time. For example, "learning is mainly driven by how faculty organize and explain content" provides a partial rationale for why most classrooms are filled with rows of seats facing forward. At The Evergreen State College where I once worked, the assumption that "learning is mainly driven and deepened by students' discussions with one another, prompted by faculty" helped explain why, in most classrooms, the furniture was usually arranged in a circle or around a table.

Now, let's return to the late 1960s.

The Instruction Paradigm and Its Approach to Pursuing 3fold Gains

The MIT I remember aligned pretty closely with a set of assumptions about teaching and learning that Barr and Tagg (1995) called the *Instruction Paradigm.*

Instruction Paradigm (capitalized, in this book) assumptions about education include:

- *Student capabilities are largely fixed* by the time they enroll and are the biggest determinant of how well students will do at a university. During my first week on campus, in almost all my first conversations with other new students, we'd introduce ourselves by comparing SAT scores. (My 18-year-old self saw that I had no hope of being at the top of the class with any reasonable amount of effort, so I didn't try.)
- *Good students will almost inevitably learn well while lesser students won't learn as much.* Students who did poorly in introductory-level courses

in a major ought to change majors. Another way to put this is to assume that instruction is the faculty member's responsibility while learning results from unchangeable student aptitudes. A corollary is that faculty can't influence student learning but they can filter out students who don't have the needed aptitudes to succeed in a field. Modest failure rates are inevitable, unless the faculty member panders to students through grade inflation.

- *Learning is driven mostly by a faculty member explaining content in a classroom while students sit quietly and take notes.* Homework prepares students for class. Education, it's assumed, is content delivery; lecturing is the most motivating, efficient way to deliver content.
- *An institution's quality results from its wealth of academic resources*, including the research achievements of its faculty, the modernity and expense of its facilities, and the academic strength of its incoming students (signaled by its selectivity).
- *Courses are described by the content they cover*, not by the capabilities they help students develop, capabilities such as resilience or "thinking like an engineer."
- *Teaching is time-consuming for faculty but not intellectually challenging.* That's a corollary of the beliefs that student talents are fixed and that the best way to teach is to explain the content. This belief helps explain why most future faculty invest many years mastering their content specialty, but little or no time studying how to teach.
- *Within most courses, faculty should have great autonomy.* Individual instructors have the right to decide content, create quizzes, crack jokes, criticize absent colleagues, set the pace, and grade in whatever ways they prefer.
- *Education is organized and scheduled around seat time* (and not, for instance, around how much students have learned). Regardless of how students are doing or what they might need, class meetings are usually 50 minutes long. Bachelor's degrees require eight semesters of full-time study.
- *Education is (and should be) organized so that the actions of one program or person don't usually have consequences for other programs or people.* Karl Weick (1976) used universities as an example of what he termed *loosely coupled systems*. For example, faculty roles are defined in terms of the content they deliver to students and their expertise (authority) to do so. That helps explain the cultural norm that faculty should leave each other alone, almost entirely, when it comes to teaching. Because

it doesn't focus on learning outcomes, the Instruction Paradigm offers no rationale for faculty coordinating their courses in order to cumulatively develop student capabilities.

Instruction-aligned institutions have long known that the way to improve quality, access, and affordability is to increase class sizes. Remember that the Instruction Paradigm defines *quality* by inputs (e.g., faculty qualification, selectivity of admissions) rather than by what students actually learn. So if the same faculty member teaches a larger class than before, quality remains the same.

There's empirical evidence to support this class size assumption. In their oft-cited summary of the research on student learning, Pascarella and Terenzini (1991) wrote, "Class size is not a particularly important factor when the goal of instruction is the acquisition of subject matter knowledge and academic skills" (p. 87). To put it in our terms, where lectures rule, quality and class size are virtually unrelated.

Here's the Instruction-aligned recipe for making 3fold gains. Imagine that an institution's 20-person class sections are taught by expert instructors who are each paid $5,000 for teaching that course. Let's say students each pay $1,500 to take this course. Therefore, this section earns its institution $30,000 in revenue (20 students at $1,500 apiece). Some years pass. Now our imaginary institution wants to improve quality, access, and affordability. The institution identifies a bigger classroom for this course and fills it with triple the number of seats, 60 instead of 20. To recruit students to fill those seats by making education more affordable, let's imagine that the course tuition is *reduced* from $1,500 to $1,000. Even though the price has been cut by one third, the course now earns far more for the institution—$60,000 in revenue (60 students x $1000). As a result, the following occurs:

- *Quality can improve*: With some of that extra revenue, the institution can now afford to pay an instructor $10,000 to teach the course, which should help the institution hire and retain faculty with even more expertise in their field.
- *Access improves*: There are 60 students now learning instead of 20. And some of the 40 additional students may come from poorer backgrounds since price made a difference.
- *Affordability improves*: Each student now has to pay only $1,000 instead of $1,500. For the institution, the cost of faculty per student is cut from $250 per student ($5,000/20 students) to $167 per student ($10,000/60 students).

The Instruction Paradigm provided a consistent rationale for institutional decisions about facilities and pedagogy in the 1960s. This kind of calculation continues to guide the pursuit of 3fold gains at more than a few institutions. But in recent decades, research findings and the rising price of higher education has caused many to question the Instruction assumption that students' capabilities can't be improved during college by altering how they learn. (Chapter 10's section on active and collaborative learning summarizes several powerful studies that directly contradict that Instruction assumption.) When faculty believe that students' capabilities are fixed, all students suffer, especially those from underserved groups. A university studied 150 of its science, technology, engineering, and mathematics (STEM) professors and more than 15,000 students. Racial achievement gaps in courses taught by faculty with a fixed mind-set were twice as large as those in courses taught by faculty with a growth mind-set. Student evaluations revealed that, in courses taught by fixed-mind-set faculty, *all* students were more likely to lose interest in the content and report negative experiences than in courses taught by growth mind-set faculty. Of all the faculty characteristics studied, mind-set beliefs were the best way to predict student achievement and motivation (Canning et al., 2019). For these and other reasons, accreditors and regulators have been shifting away from just judging quality in terms of inputs and toward more reliance on evidence of learning outcomes (Wergin, 2005). The Instruction assumption of fixed student capabilities is giving way to evidence that institutions, faculty, and the students can together develop students' capabilities.

Barr and Tagg's Learning Paradigm

As a counterpoint to the Instruction Paradigm, Barr and Tagg (1995) defined a *learning paradigm,* a set of assumptions that today provide a rationale for what the GSUs' and CfA's programs are doing.

As defined by Barr and Tagg, a *learning paradigm* (the Barr and Tagg version is not capitalized in this book) is a set of assumptions that I'd summarize this way:

- *An institution's quality is defined in large part by the quality (defined as capabilities) of its graduating students,* more so than by the quality (defined by entrance exams) of its entering students. I'd add that the quality of graduating students necessarily includes the quality of students from underserved minorities and poor households.

- Even after they enter college, *students' capabilities and talents can be changed substantially,* depending on what happens to them in college. All aspects of a college or university can potentially contribute to changes in students' capabilities, as we saw at Georgia State. Extensive literature (see especially Ambrose et al., 2010) supports this view of the potentially powerful university. Can students become good at math during college? The Instruction Paradigm says "no" but learning paradigms say "yes."
- *Institutional outcomes are easier to improve by altering the cumulative development of outcomes.* Barr and Tagg asserted that, in the learning paradigm, the whole should be considered before the parts. In contrast, the Instruction Paradigm is atomistic, planning the parts before considering the whole.

Although Barr and Tagg didn't mention the following assumptions, they are a smooth fit with the learning paradigm

- To understand something, *students need plenty of practice trying it out, with appropriate coaching.* In contrast to the Instruction Paradigm's focus on what faculty do, learning paradigms pay attention to what students do, inside and outside the classroom.
- Because we still have so much to learn about learning, *teaching is intellectually challenging* as well as time-consuming.
- Important capabilities in students are developed over many experiences, formal and informal, to constitute *cumulative gains.* Something similar is true for attaining goals for equitable access and for stakeholder affordability; they require initiatives that help attain goals by program's end. *Cumulative* does not imply *additive,* however. To greatly oversimplify, students can forget as well as learn. One initiative's gains for equitable access may be erased or reversed by some other element of the program. The time that students save thanks to one initiative may be wasted by a poorly designed course they take later. In the end, what counts are the cumulative gains in quality, access, and affordability.

Actually, There Are at Least Two Learning Paradigms, Not Just One

Barr and Tagg (1995) asserted that their learning paradigm treats time as variable and learning as fixed—after each student masters something, they can move on to the next thing. That's an accurate description of SNHU's CfA programs, but it doesn't describe the GSUs. To develop students' capabilities, the GSUs use evidence-based educational strategies such as learning communities (LCs). LCs are almost impossible to implement in a program like CfA's, where students work at their own pace and largely by themselves. Let's nickname the GSUs' shared assumptions the *Integrative Learning Paradigm*, while *Individualized Learning Paradigm* will be shorthand for the assumptions underlying institutions or programs such as CfA. To save even more words, we'll sometimes say *Integrative (or Individualized) institution* when we're talking about an institution that is shifting its educational strategies toward one or the other learning paradigm.

> The *Individualized* and *Integrative Learning Paradigms* (capitalized, in this book) begin with the same assumption, that the mission of colleges and universities is to help students improve selected capabilities and personal attributes. The difference between the two paradigms, as the old saying goes, is "He who travels alone, travels fast, but they who travel together, travel far."
>
> The Individualized Paradigm (travels alone) assumes that students learn best when they each start from what they already know and proceed as quickly, or as slowly, as their learning allows. Because of this assumption, student learning relies on materials much more than on expert instruction and coaching; traditional faculty wouldn't have time to teach one student at a time.
>
> The Integrative Paradigm (travels together) assumes that the most lasting, useful learning stems in large part from a variety of kinds of interpersonal interactions such as expert–novice discussions, debates, teamwork, peer critiques, role playing, and competitions. An old friend once told me that the most powerful learning—changes in how the learner sees and feels about things—can emerge when friends muse together (Ehrmann, 2006).

The Individualized Pursuit of 3fold Gains

The theory of how to use Individualized practices to achieve 3fold gains is as follows.

Quality should be improved in an Individualized program because assessment helps keep the student's next task not too easy, not too advanced, but just challenging enough. Also, the CfA version of Individualized education is organized around project-based learning, a high-impact practice (HIP). Both these features should help improve quality.

Access is improved by that same accommodation of pace to individual differences. Presumably the worst-prepared students can go from success to success at their own pace. The best-prepared students can progress more quickly and are not bored. And the students with the most relevant experience can leapfrog forward. Individualized institutions focus on access for working adults and others who need the time flexibility of self-paced programs and who can discipline themselves to study alone much of the time.

Affordability (price for students, cost to the institution) is improved by a rethinking of the role of experts. Giving every student an expert teacher or coach would make Individualized programs too expensive. So, instead of faculty as the primary means of instruction, materials are used to present information and then to guide students in practicing and developing their skills. Once the institution has invested in materials, those resources can be used by any number of students, at no additional cost to the institution. The more students the institution enrolls, the less the per-student cost for materials. Individualized programs are also likely to be offered completely online, thus reducing costs of (now unnecessary) classroom buildings.

Another gain in affordability comes from the staff. Subject matter experts (SMEs) curate the materials, aggregating some and developing others. The other major role for SMEs at CfA is to critique student projects, offer coaching, and assess whether a project demonstrates the desired competencies. Some roles often assigned to faculty (academic advising) are instead the province of specialists without terminal degrees. The use of expensive experts to explain content in live classrooms is eliminated.

Caution: Only a handful of online, competence-based academic programs currently exist. As we saw, CfA has produced some encouraging initial results. But the field of educational research hasn't told us much yet about how, and how well, these Individualized programs and institutions work. For example, the research on their affordability is mixed (Desrochers & Staisloff, 2016). And we don't yet know how well these models work in developing deep understanding. Might the absence of a convenient expert be an advantage, forcing students to think more for themselves, or a damaging disadvantage? Do students from underserved minorities and poor households fare as well as others, or are they more likely to drop out?

The Integrative Pursuit of 3fold Gains

Georgia State and Governors State are examples of how to pursue gains in quality, equitable access, and affordability. Elements of both institutions' constellations include

- defining essential learning outcomes and the means to assess them, at the student and program levels;
- using HIP educational strategies (chapter 10) to assure that students develop toward those desired outcomes;
- identifying specific barriers to student success and remedying some of them; and
- creating the infrastructure needed to support and sustain these educational strategies. We'll have a lot more to say about infrastructure in later case histories (chapters 7 through 9) and in the chapters on organizational foundations and management of interactions with the wider world (chapters 11 and 12).

Georgia State has the most extensive documentation about how their constellation of strategies has helped create 3fold gains. (This book usually uses *constellation* as a shorthand for an Integrative constellation). Redesigned courses, learning communities, and other Integrative educational strategies helped graduation rates to increase substantially (quality). The same educational strategies also reduced or eliminated performance differences between students from underserved and privileged groups (equitable access). And, by improving retention and lessening time to a degree, both students and the institution saved time and money (affordability).

Turning the Page

For our purposes (developing a widely adaptable framework for 3fold gains), the Instruction approach is off the table because it does nothing to improve learning or equitable access outcomes. The Individualized pursuit is still rare, and there is comparatively little research or evaluation of whether 3fold gains are being achieved, especially gains in graduates' ability to critically and creatively apply what they have learned in new and unpredicted contexts.

So, from here on, we'll focus on the Integrative pursuit of 3fold gains. Far more institutions are beginning to shift in the Integrative rather than the Individualized direction. For that reason, there's more relevant research and more kinds of initiatives have been tested. The first two case histories told the story of how the GSUs' Integrative educational strategies had developed at scale, but we didn't say as much about how they were trying to sustain their work.

So let's turn to Guttman Community College in New York City, which was designed from the start to pursue Integrative strategies for quality and access. It was Guttman that opened my eyes to how institutions could sustain Integrative educational strategies by turning some institutional facts of life on their heads.

PART THREE

SUSTAINING THE INTEGRATIVE PURSUIT OF 3FOLD GAINS

Each of the three case history chapters that follows focuses on a different approach to institutionalizing and sustaining Integrative educational strategies.

Guttman Community College (chapter 7) was designed from the start to help set new standards in quality and access. Some of its unusual features are educational strategies (e.g., the importance of engaging students with their city in many different courses); some are organizational features (e.g., no traditional academic departments); while still others involve novel approaches to interacting with the wider world (e.g., how the college recruits students and prepares them for Guttman's unusual academic program).

The transformation of the University of Central Oklahoma (chapter 8) from an Instruction-aligned institution to an Integrative institution began with a new presidential catchphrase, "transformative learning" (TL), to describe and guide formal and informal learning. Over the years, the commitment to TL influenced the creation of six learning outcomes, proactive networking with like-minded pioneers at other institutions, a new institution-wide system for assessing and documenting student learning, and incremental curricular change.

The University of Central Florida (chapter 9) relied on its blended (the same as Georgia State University's "hybrid") and fully online courses to achieve its 3fold gains. This cumulative development took off, partly due to a very early university commitment to train and support all faculty who were teaching online. The resulting confidence in quality led to aggressive growth and substantial savings, especially reductions in the need for new, expensive classroom buildings.

Part Four describes what the three case histories have in common.

7

GUTTMAN COMMUNITY COLLEGE

Designed for Integrative Education

The important thing about [Guttman] Community College is not any one thing they're doing, but that they're doing all of them together. All the research shows that if you do them alone, for a modest amount of time, they have a modest positive effect, but it doesn't last. This will be a chance to see what happens if you do them together, consistently, over a longer period of time. (Weinbaum et al., 2013a, p. 10)

In 2008, the City University of New York (CUNY) began planning a new community college in Manhattan. At that time, CUNY faced a problem. In the years leading up to the new venture, only 11% of full-time first-time first-year in CUNY associate degree programs graduated within 3 years, and only another quarter of the entering cohort were still enrolled. But some community colleges around the country were graduating more students and doing it faster, with programs based on research into learning.

CUNY comprised six 2-year institutions, 13 senior colleges, and seven graduate and professional institutions. It was (and is) one of the largest public systems of higher education in the United States. Chancellor Matthew Goldstein charged the planning team for the new college with improving graduation rates without lowering standards. A primary goal for the new college was to attain a 30% 3-year graduation rate for the very first cohort of students, increasing to 40% over the following few years. Goldstein recognized that such large changes could be brought about by only fundamental changes in how students were educated. He directed the planners to pay attention to what more-successful community colleges were doing and to related research on learning. From the start, the planning team aligned Guttman's design across three interdependent domains: educational strategies, organizational foundations to support those strategies, and interactions with the wider world aligned with those strategies.

The new college (temporarily named New Community College) began educating its first entering class of 289 students in fall 2012. In 2013, in honor of a $25,000,000 gift to CUNY that included a $15,000,000 endowment to support student learning, the new institution was renamed Stella and Charles Guttman Community College. (We will refer to it as "Guttman.") As of 2019, Guttman has not been able to move to a larger home so its enrollment is capped at around 1,000 students.

Founding Principles Aligned With the Integrative Learning Paradigm

Guttman had the luxury of being new and, therefore, from the outset, guided by an explicit set of founding principles (City University of New York, 2008):

- As an open enrollment institution, the new college should *pursue inclusive excellence* (rather than the exclusive excellence model that filters out "poor students").
- The choice of educational strategies should *increase student chances for real achievement* by admitting students who are willing to commit to full-time study; developing student capabilities with respect to agreed-upon learning outcomes, cumulatively over many courses and life experiences; using evidence-based teaching and learning strategies such as experiential learning in authentic settings and the social construction of learning; connecting students with each other, faculty, and staff; offering a few well-organized pathways to degrees and transfer, rather than drowning students in options; and integrating academic learning with vocational learning, developmental learning, and student services.
- Everyone at Guttman should work together to share responsibility for student success.
- The college should be organized to use evidence to guide continuous improvement.

To implement and sustain these principles, Guttman had to depart from some CUNY and community college norms. For instance, Guttman's *Faculty Handbook* (2018a) asserted, "We hold in common the following teaching and learning principles" (p. 21). (It's the first time I've ever seen that sentence in a faculty handbook.) The principles embrace interdisciplinary curricula and opportunities for students to learn to solve complex problems; a culture of collaborative inquiry about teaching and learning; classroom interactions among students; consistent opportunities for faculty, staff, and peer mentors to learn from each other inside and outside the classroom; scaffolded and differentiated instruction and assignments to address the needs of a diverse group of students; and a culture of academic rigor, specifically one that affirms that disciplines have bodies of knowledge and ways of knowing that are foundational for students in a postsecondary setting.

Educational Strategies to Implement Guttman's Principles

The new community college was committed to achieving inclusive excellence, but it wouldn't be easy. As one study reported,

> It came as a shock to many students that they were expected to do reading in advance of classes and be prepared to discuss it, that reading and writing assignments required considerable work beyond the classroom, and that instructors expected a high level of participation in class. . . . The first semester aimed at moving students from a prior learning situation that for many was rote to one that was analytical, from one that focused on individual short assignments to one that emphasized both individual and collaborative long-term learning projects, and from a classroom that permitted short answers to a teacher's questions to one that encouraged lively discussion. (Weinbaum et al., 2013b, p. 13)

To educate these students, the team developed a constellation of mutually supportive educational strategies. All academic programs are organized around *active engagement with New York City* (NYC) and other major global centers. This experiential learning enables students to immediately apply what they learn. In addition to motivating students, the resulting work demonstrates the value of students' developmental, academic, and vocational work for students themselves, for their instructional teams and instructors, and later for 4-year institutions and employers. Its goals include providing a meaningful motive for students to develop the capabilities they need for real-world activities.

All academic programs, including the first year, are organized around five clusters of Guttman learning outcomes (GLOs). The GLOs were adapted from the Association of American Colleges & Universities's (AAC&U) Essential Learning Outcomes (ELOs) (AAC&U, 2018a) and the subsequent Lumina Foundation's Degree Qualifications Profile (DQP) (Adelman et al., 2011): broad integrative knowledge; applied learning; specialized knowledge; intellectual skills for life-long learning; and civic learning, engagement, and social responsibility. Many of Guttman's educational strategies help students develop these academic capabilities. In contrast, many institutions think of first-year requirements in terms of content coverage.

First-year students are organized into *houses*, each consisting of three *learning communities* (LCs) of 25 students who take first-year courses together. Each house is led by an instructional team consisting of full-time, tenure-track faculty from different disciplines, a staff student success advocate, librarians, a graduate student coordinator, and second-year peer mentors. The team meets weekly to assure that courses reinforce one another and to discuss how each student is doing across courses. Each student has a faculty adviser, drawn from the house team, who also teaches one of their courses. The sense of community is real—Provost Wach recalls a faculty member commenting that, when the houses dissolve at the end of the first year, half the students rejoice while the other half have wet eyes.

First-year courses combine academic work, developmental work, and field work. This combination of course components is intended to prepare students for college work in general, including active academic engagement with the city. Along with the LC design, this combination of components is intended to help students develop college level skills (e.g., reading and math) while also developing their GLOs (capabilities).

Full-time study (30 credits) is required in the first year, and strongly recommended for subsequent years. That was a significant but not impossible step for Guttman; at the time it was being planned, 87% of entering students at CUNY community colleges were already registered for full-time study. (Research suggests that full-time study makes a significant difference to completion rates [Complete College America, 2013].) Full-time study is easily achievable because the academic schedule is organized so that students need come to campus only twice a week, for 5 continuous hours each day.

Guttman makes extensive and varied use of *peer mentors* to provide coaching and other kinds of support for students. The 60+ peer mentors in 2017–2018 took on a variety of roles. Some worked with students in their first-year LCs, facilitating group work and other class activities and leading study sessions. Others specialized in admissions or worked mainly with students preparing for transfer. We'll say a bit more about Guttman's peer mentors in the discussion of educational strategies in chapter 8.

All students use *ePortfolios* to assemble key assignments from throughout their course of study and to reflect on the capabilities their work reveals. For institutions that organize learning around the cumulative development of broad capabilities such as GLOs, ePortfolios are virtually essential tools for deepening that learning, assessing it, and documenting it (Bauer-Maglin et al., 2014).

To understand what a few of these strategies look like in practice, let's examine just one required first-year course, Ethnographies of Work (EOW), as it worked in 2017 when I visited Guttman. From their first week in this two-semester course, students began observing and analyzing nearby workplaces. Students were encouraged to pick workplaces that would help them understand careers they might pursue. Every week, students went through this cycle:

- Students did readings for the coming week and wrote a paper drawing on what they had learned in the previous week.
- The 3-hour, once-weekly class session began with a quiz on the preclass readings. This quiz encouraged students to do the reading and learn from it.
- The class and the professor discussed the readings.
- Guttman is in the middle of the city, so 20 to 30 minutes is all it took for students to leave the classroom, visit a workplace, record observations, and return to EOW. A Facebook group enabled students to communicate with the professor and other students in real time while they were off-campus.
- After students returned from the field, they debriefed during the remainder of the day's session.

Associated with EOW was a weekly session called Learning About Being a Successful Student (LaBSS), led by a student success advocate who was also a member of that house's instructional team. In LaBSS, students learned how to identify resources both on- and off-campus, improve their interpersonal and professional communication, and understand academic and financial aid policies.

Organizational Foundations for Sustaining Integrative Educational Strategies

Let's look at just a few of the *organizational foundations* by which Guttman was designed to scale and sustain its Integrative educational strategies.

> *Organizational foundations* are elements of infrastructure, policies, and culture that can either sustain educational strategies at scale or contribute to difficulties in sustaining and scaling them.

Planners decided early on to *tailor job descriptions and allocate workload* in ways that support Guttman's Integrative educational strategies. For example, faculty earn teaching credit for their own courses and also for the time they spend with their teams planning and guiding their LCs. Some faculty serve as area coordinators, tenure-track teaching positions with 40% time assigned to work with colleagues on issues such as experiential learning, ePortfolios, or globalizing the curriculum. Librarians' jobs include a responsibility to work closely with faculty in designing and teaching LCs.

Guttman rejected the idea of *academic departments* on the grounds that disciplinary silos would interfere with interdisciplinary thinking and teamwork. In the early years, all 30+ faculty reported directly to the provost. By 2017, when faculty numbers had increased to 54 full time and 19 part time, it was no longer practical for the provost to be solely responsible for faculty personnel decisions, so faculty personnel committees were created for three interdisciplinary practice areas of social sciences; science, technology, engineering, and mathematics (STEM); and humanities. Each committee consisted of five full-time faculty elected from and by full-time faculty within the appropriate practice area. The goal was to improve the integrity of faculty personnel decisions while avoiding creating organizational barriers to interdisciplinary collaboration (Guttman Community College, 2018a).

Guttman's *criteria for reappointment, promotion, and tenure* are anchored in the college's mission and principles; they detail how teaching should align with those principles and give examples of relevant evidence about whether that alignment is happening. The guidelines (Guttman Community College, 2013) lead with a description of the distinctiveness of Guttman: "The college seeks to be an innovative laboratory focused on enhancing teaching and learning through active pedagogical strategies, sensitive and relevant to the culturally, academically, linguistically and economically diverse community it serves" (p. 2). In chapter 6, we saw how the Instruction Paradigm prizes individual faculty effort and autonomy; in contrast, the learning paradigms need a balance between autonomy and collaboration. The Guttman guidelines quickly establish that collaboration with other faculty and with staff is fundamental to the job description. The guidelines include a dozen instructional principles such as "integrative learning opportunities that enable students to study and participate/contribute in meaningful ways to NYC and communities they identify as important to them" (p. 3). These principles are illustrated with the following, even longer list of example practices that inform teaching at Guttman: interdisciplinary curricula and learning opportunities for students to solve complex problems; integrative learning opportunities that enable students to study, participate, and contribute in meaningful ways to NYC and their communities; and culturally responsive pedagogy that values and affirms students' diverse backgrounds and lived experiences as a starting point for all learning.

The guidelines include other unusual content. In the discussion of expectations for faculty service, the policy asserts that "at a minimum, all faculty are expected to regularly participate in College Council meetings" (Guttman Community College, 2013, p. 8). This reinforces the principle that education has to be a team sport. Another repeated assertion is that continually becoming a better educator is as important as the quality of current teaching; evidence is requested about how the faculty member has been working to improve. The guidelines even provide a framework for observation of the candidate's teaching. Among the questions the observer should keep in mind is, "Is this course taught in a manner that is consistent with the . . . College Instructional Principles?" (p. 21). Faculty are asked to include in their promotion and tenure materials their reflections about the relationship of their teaching with college principles and on how they use peer observations and student teaching evaluations to guide their own continuing professional development.

Guttman is one of several CUNY institutions that uses a 12-week plus 6-week *academic calendar*. Students can use the full 18 weeks to complete a course. Other students can complete the same course in 12 weeks and can then take an additional 6-week course for the remainder of the semester. Guttman clears the calendar for an unusually large number of days for college-wide activities. The calendar includes 10 assessment days each year for assessing student learning via ePortfolios, meetings around different GLOs, studying recent college data collected through surveys and assessments, assessment design workshops, and other professional development activities. Two community days each semester involve students in projects intended to improve the lives of New Yorkers through political activity, community service, and advocacy. Each project is overseen by instructors and must include students' intentional and guided reflection on what has been achieved and learned.

Guttman organizes *learning spaces* to support its educational strategies. Instead of a library, planners created an information commons (IC). The IC was designed to support student research (e.g., for problems arising from their work in NYC), so librarians are recruited with the explicit responsibility of also serving on instructional teams for LCs. Physically, the IC was originally designed to support the development of the whole student; it has been described as "workspace, student union, and lunchroom" (Herrington, 2013, p. 62). Reality doesn't always imitate intention. Experience showed that cramming those three functions into one comparatively small space didn't work. As of 2019, food is prohibited and nonacademic activities are redirected elsewhere. Affordability was a consideration so the new IC began with only 2,000 volumes and had capacity for only 4,000. However, as CUNY students, Guttman's students have borrowing privileges for the system's millions of books, journals, and research collections. Guttman also has a partnership with the New York Public Library (Herrington, 2013). The IC provides education in information literacy through discovery and active learning; one IC goal is to teach students about the social impacts of information.

At Guttman, *technology* pervades the learning process. In addition to the ePortfolios described earlier, teacher and student presentations and in-class group work are supported in most or all Guttman classrooms by a cart with 30 laptops for student use during class; a class set of iPads, available on request; and a computer display projected onto an interactive whiteboard that faculty or students can control by touching the whiteboard or using a special pen (Bauer-Maglin et al., 2014).

As part of efforts to continuously strengthen a culture of evidence and improvement, President Scott Evenbeck made small *internal innovation grants* available to faculty to enhance and study Guttman's educational strategies. In 2017, a dozen grants were made to 17 faculty; clusters of two or three projects working on a common theme were organized into faculty LCs. For example, one faculty project evaluated several ways to improve academic success in the first-year statistics course. Another project evaluated the effectiveness of faculty development services for part-time faculty and made recommendations to improve it.

Managing Interactions With the Wider World

Guttman has also designed many of its interactions with the wider world in order to better support its Integrative educational strategies.

One of the most important transactions for any college is the *recruiting and admission of new students.* Most colleges say little to prospective undergraduates about their educational strategies. For example, one of the other CUNY community colleges takes the conventional path on its admissions web page: the first two paragraphs describe the college's growth from small beginnings, its size, its beauty, its "cutting-edge academic programs" (without saying what they are), its "outstanding" faculty, its affordable tuition, its flexible class schedules, and its majors. In contrast, Guttman looks for students who might be attracted to its particular academic strengths. In 2019, the first two paragraphs on its admissions web page read, in part:

> Guttman was designed with student success at the heart of its mission. From the time you begin the application process, you will experience our commitment to supporting each student as an individual.

> Our distinct first-year program uses New York City as a learning laboratory where you can connect classroom learning with field experiences. Whether you're studying the sustainability of Times Square in your City Seminar class or observing the workplace in your Ethnographies of Work class, our unique first-year program will provide you with a college experience like none other. (Guttman Community College, 2019b, paras. 1–2)

Guttman is an open admissions institution, but to assure that people who choose Guttman are prepared for what they will encounter, *three preparatory steps are required before admission is granted*: attend an informational session about the college, participate in an individual meeting immediately afterward, and sign a contract agreeing that they understand the expectations of the college. Potential students are invited to bring family or other supporters to participate with them throughout the process. The students who have signed then attend a 2-week summer bridge program, which is free to and compulsory for admitted students. When students begin the bridge program, they join their LC right away. They immediately begin academic work to clarify and develop their goals, strengths, and needs; engage in fieldwork activities in NYC; begin creating their ePortfolios; and learn about other features of college study, including Guttman's nontraditional program design. These same LCs continue into the fall and spring semesters. Of almost 1,800 people in fall 2017–2018 who expressed initial interest in attending the informational meeting, only 460 actually completed all three preparatory steps plus the summer bridge program and entered Guttman. That yield was satisfactory because Guttman cannot grow its student body until additional space is secured by CUNY.

From its beginning, Guttman *sought and developed a corps of faculty and staff* who already believed in its principles and had the skills to implement its practices. For example, Guttman was designed around the assumption that lasting learning is developed cumulatively through a number of courses and cocurricular experiences. Personnel searches sought candidates who wanted to work both individually and in collaboration with other faculty and staff in order to advance student learning. The faculty and staff have available a range of professional development opportunities. To strengthen a culture of faculty inquiry, in 2017–2018 Guttman offered a series of five workshops on practicing the scholarship of teaching and learning (SoTL). The workshops attracted widespread interest because SoTL is recognized as a form of faculty research for tenure and promotion purposes. None of this is to say that Guttman and CUNY have been completely consistent in attracting staff specifically interested in Guttman's way of organizing education. For example, in early 2018, Guttman was looking for an assistant director of human resources (HR) to take charge of onboarding new part-time employees. The position description, posted by CUNY, said nothing about Guttman's special character or how its goals and organization might influence HR functions such as onboarding new staff.

One of Guttman's educational strategies is to assure that all academic programs are organized around active engagement with NYC and other global centers. Faculty can't create and sustain such opportunities alone. So Guttman created an office of partnerships and career engagement (OPCE) to *create and sustain a network of "community partners"* which each offer at least some of the following: fieldwork and case studies; community service projects; part-time employment opportunities; paid or unpaid internships; and career planning and preparation programs for Guttman students, including workplace observations, professional networking events, mentoring relationships, skill-building events, and customized events to meet the needs of the partner.

Managing interactions with CUNY has been an ongoing effort. CUNY's chancellor had called for the new college to be designed to assure better graduation rates and better learning, and a large CUNY task force created the initial design. But being a CUNY campus posed some challenges at the beginning, when many at CUNY believed the new funding should be allocated to existing CUNY campuses, not to the creation of a new one. And there was significant pushback from the CUNY faculty union about some of the proposed new principles, including doing without academic departments and sharing responsibility for the academic program across faculty and staff. Later, the new interdisciplinary first-year experience had to be adapted to articulate with CUNY's disciplinary first-year requirements. With the backing of the chancellor, Guttman was able to surmount such barriers.

Evidence for 3Fold Gains at Guttman

Evidence for quality gains: In the years just before Guttman's founding, about 11% of CUNY community college students graduated in 3 years. Guttman's goals called for 3-year graduation rates of 30%, then 40%. Table 7.1 shows how Guttman exceeded these goals from the start.

Meanwhile, Guttman has been developing infrastructure to assess and improve the capabilities of its graduates. Evidence collected in 2018 suggested that while in many ways graduates did well in 4-year colleges, their math achievement after transfer was not yet meeting Guttman expectations. Improving student math performance for 4-year institutions is now a priority for Guttman.

TABLE 7.1
Retention and Graduation Rates of Guttman's Inaugural and Three Subsequent Classes

Year Entered	*First-Time Students*	*1-Year Retention Rate*	*2-Year Graduation Rate*	*3-Year Graduation Rate*
2012	289	74%	28%	49%
2013	278	69%	30%	44%
2014	410	73%	28%	46%
2015	444	70%	31%	43%

Note. Data from Guttman Community College, 2018b.

Evidence for equitable access gains. Since its inception, Guttman's entering students have been majority Hispanic (61% in fall 2015); then African American (26%) and White (9%). One quarter of incoming students were under the age of 18, another 67% were aged 18 to 20 years, and only 1% were age 25 or older. Pell-eligible entering students were 76% of the total, and at least 47% were first-generation college students. Of entering students, 22% reported a disability and 11% that English was their second language. Guttman's graduation rates are more than twice as high as those of other CUNY 2-year institutions. But those success rates vary by population. Overall, 43% of all students entering Guttman in 2015 graduated within 3 years. That matches the 3-year graduation rate for incoming Hispanic students, but only 32% of African American students graduated within 3 years, while 54% of the White students did. Guttman's (2018b) 2018–2022 strategic plan notes that "data show our men of color are the least successful constituent student group, which reflects the national trend but is unacceptable to us" (p. 5).

Evidence for affordability gains: To my knowledge, none of the Guttman founding documents explicitly mentions the pursuit of affordability, but they do emphasize the importance of timely completion of the program, which reduces demands on student (and institutional) time and money. One affordability advantage is Guttman's low tuition, $4,800/year for NYC residents. For comparison, CfA programs (at a private university) charge $5,000/year for 2-year and 4-year degrees, before factoring in the tuition assistance that some of its employer partners provide. Guttman's Integrative educational strategies and comparatively high graduation rate make it likely that students will save money and time by the time they graduate and probably lower costs for students who are able to pass courses the first time they take them. Another affordability advantage for students is the block course schedule that enables full-time first-year students to come to campus only twice a week for 5 hours.

A different slant on affordability is the institutional cost of educating each student. In 2019, President Evenbeck told me that Guttman's instructional costs were similar to those of Hostos, another small CUNY community college. And the relatively high persistence and graduation rates at Guttman save students time and money while increasing the return on their investment in college. On the other hand, Guttman's administrative costs are much higher than the CUNY average per student, mainly because Guttman was designed to grow to serve thousands of students. That is, to handle the demands of what is now a small student body, Guttman has had to rent expensive office space near its main building in midtown Manhattan. That excess expense is likely to persist for several years because growth plans have been on an extended hold while CUNY tries to provide an appropriate campus.

Turning the Page

Guttman was chosen for this book because it illustrates what can happen when an institution is designed from the start to align with Integrative assumptions and when practices such as its distinctive admissions process (wider world interaction) and its faculty rewards system (organizational foundation) sustain its Integrative educational strategies.

The University of Central Oklahoma, the next case history, is in at least one sense the opposite of Guttman. Founded in 1890, by the late 1990s it was a fairly conventional regional public university. Its first steps toward what became an Integrative vision began in an ordinary way with the desire to make the university more distinctive. The grand vision wasn't imposed. It emerged.

8

UNIVERSITY OF CENTRAL OKLAHOMA

Transformative Learning Sparks Institutional Evolution

The beginning of transformative learning at UCO was somewhat chaotic and unplanned. It was a transformative event in and of itself. (Cunliff, 2011)

In the late 1990s the University of Central Oklahoma (UCO) was not so different from other public regional institutions. But over the next 20 years, a series of challenges and initiatives created an unusual degree of agreement about the why and how of a UCO education, a cultural shift as well as a shift in educational strategies, organizational infrastructure, and the university's relationships with its wider world. How and why did this transformation happen?

UCO was founded in 1890 as a normal school for teacher education, one of three such institutions created at the same time for the Oklahoma Territory. Its original three-story brick building towered over a flat, unpopulated plain near Oklahoma City. From the beginning, I've been told, the founders had a sense of mission to bring education to the territory; that spirit continues.

UCO has since become a regional comprehensive institution, offering a range of 4-year and master's degrees to about 16,000 students, of whom 14,500 are undergraduates. It's located outside Edmond, Oklahoma, a city of 91,000, and is a half hour drive from the state capital, Oklahoma City. Most of its students have been commuters. By 2018, the university had over 400 full-time faculty and 400 adjuncts.

Dating back to its normal school days, UCO has always seen itself as a teaching institution. For example, its colleges are required to count teaching-related work as a minimum of 50% of what faculty need to do for promotion and tenure.

Early Transformative Steps

In 1997, Roger Webb became president of UCO. He brought with him a commitment to developing students' leadership abilities. Webb and his UCO colleagues soon defined *leadership* in terms of three C's: character, civility, and community. Such ideas influenced the development of programs and infrastructure. For example, UCO students in every major were offered the opportunity to minor in leadership. A new academic administrative position, director (later, vice president [VP]) of leadership, was created to develop and coordinate these programs.

In 2002, Webb's provost, Don Betz, helped the American Association of State Colleges and Universities (AASCU) develop its American Democracy Project (ADP). ADP's goal was to help institutions develop students' civic engagement, the community side of Webb's leadership priority. In 2004, the National Survey of Student Engagement (NSSE), in which UCO had begun participating, and the Association of American Colleges & Universities (AAC&U) formulated a list of ten high-impact practices (HIPs, described in chapter 10) (AAC&U, 2013). Research indicated that HIPs could improve what all students learn (quality) while being even more helpful for students from underserved groups (equitable access).

That same year, the National Association of Student Personnel Administrators and the American College Personnel Association issued a national report, *Learning Reconsidered: A Campus-Wide Focus on the Student Experience* (Keeling, 2004). The report began by defining *learning* "as a comprehensive, holistic, transformative activity that integrates academic learning and student development, processes that have often been considered separate, and even independent of each other" (p. 2). *Learning Reconsidered* shared the assumptions that define the NSSE annual survey: that lasting changes in students are the product of a broad array of experiences in college, and are not limited to what students do in courses. For some readers, the report did represent a reconsideration, especially at institutions where academic affairs and student affairs were slightly contemptuous of one another as they competed for budget and for student time and attention. The report recommended that academic affairs, student affairs, and other units work together to make their institutions more educationally effective. Student affairs at UCO experienced *Learning Reconsidered* as a "lightning bolt," recalls faculty member and later VP for Student Affairs Myron Pope. The report provided a clear, detailed explanation of how traditional goals of liberal learning had to be achieved through contributions from inside and outside courses. Within 2 years, HIPs and *Learning Reconsidered* would both influence the evolution of UCO.

In 2005, Betz left UCO for a presidency. As part of institutional strategic planning, Webb's new provost, Bill Radke, charged academic deans and his senior staff to meet until they had agreed on a new mission statement for academic affairs. After the staff had wrangled vigorously for days, Radke and Webb visited them to see what they'd decided. Radke recalls, "They were each holding up a sign that said, 'helping students learn.'" While that sounded like a platitude for some, many saw it as a transformative change from "helping faculty teach."

Around this same time, Radke began talking regularly with Kathryn Gage, VP of student affairs. Gage told the provost about *Learning Reconsidered.* It made immediate sense to Radke that student learning was the responsibility of the entire university, not just academic affairs; the leadership program provided an earlier instance. Radke began inviting Gage and other vice presidents to academic affairs planning retreats so that, together, they could develop comprehensive and coordinated support for helping students learn. That didn't mean that the other vice presidents were expected to serve academic affairs; rather, they would work together to serve student learning, with no one vice president in charge of the others.

Radke played other important roles in building a coalition that could take action. A number of people I spoke with commented about how well and how frequently Radke explained the emerging work to different audiences. Jeff King (2018a) summarized Radke's roles during this period:

> He recognized his leadership role with faculty but eschewed top-down, mandated messaging about how faculty must teach at UCO, knowing that would be counter-productive. Instead, he was careful to urge, to invite, to cajole, to "strongly suggest," and not to communicate with a big stick. At one point, he did require faculty to identify in syllabi how one or more of the Central Six Tenets would be addressed in the class, but this was not until the 2012–2013 academic year. His reasoning was that shared governance meant a "pull approach" had to be employed instead of a "push approach." (p. 12)

And if there were signs that a senior leader might be drifting out of the coalition, Provost Radke would have a closed-door session with that person, usually with good results, I'm told.

Transformative Learning and the Central Six

The pivotal cross-silo conversations were sometimes quite informal. For example, a revolving group of middle and senior leaders began having lunch together, talking about whatever. Every so often, their discussion would turn to how they might focus and improve UCO's efforts to "help students learn." They eventually nicknamed themselves the Burrito Buddies for what many of them were eating for lunch. "Helping students learn," many agreed, was at least partly about how college can transform students, especially recent high school graduates, into new people they hadn't previously dreamed of becoming. The Buddies made up a term, *transformational learning*, to label this process. Later, as they became aware of scholarship in this area, they identified their work with ongoing work on *Transformative Learning* (TL) (e.g., Mezirow, 1990).

UCO came to define *TL* as a developmental process for students

- willing to be transformed;
- having an experience, perhaps a disorienting one, that could prompt them to engage in critical reflection about what could be learned from that experience;
- engage in rational discourse, orally or in writing, about the experience and reflections; and
- gain from those activities an expanded perspective and, sometimes, a dramatic shift in worldview or belief.

There was nothing particularly systematic about the Buddies' lunch discussions. A leading member of the group, Professor Ed Cunliff, recollected later what this deliberation had been like. His 2011 memo is worth quoting at length (italics are mine):

> From where I sit now, the beginning of transformative learning at UCO was somewhat chaotic and unplanned. It was a transformative event in and of itself. Mezirow, who is considered the originator of transformative learning theory, describes the process as being somewhat sequential but not necessarily planned. We were certainly not in a planning mode and little, from my perspective, could be called sequential . . .
>
> Ironically, *one critical element is the respect for "not knowing."* Much of education centers on knowing. . . . There is a need to let go of that sense of having the answers before learning can take place. We had entered a discussion to talk about measuring outcomes, and became distracted from that process by the vague sense that there was something out there that we could feel but didn't know what it was.

> We didn't know, but we were ready to explore. There was also a sense that *whatever was out there was not something that anyone owned.* We had to let go of the sense of boundary—this is my turf and that is your turf and you better stay out of mine. In order to collaborate and to operate with a sense of community we had to give up professional territory . . . letting go of turf and ego is another critical element.
>
> There were those who initially said, "Isn't what we already do transformative learning?" Maybe, but we think we can do better. *We can take a look at ourselves, maybe reinvent ourselves, and maybe through the process of reflection we can come out a little bit better. Sounds like what we hope for our students.* (Cunliff, 2011, p. 1)

This realization—that the university could and should transform itself in ways that resembled how students transform themselves through their college experiences—spurred and widened the conversation at UCO.

In addition to the Burrito Buddies, between 2006 and 2009 a group of senior vice presidents was discussing the university's growing agglomeration of offices and programs to help students learn; every year or two, it seemed, a new one was added. The 12 programs they identified included the leadership program, ADP, undergraduate research, peer health leaders, and TRIO (a federal program that serves individuals from disadvantaged backgrounds). The vice presidents needed some way to make sense of these unrelated and sometimes competing programs. They tried to create a conceptual scheme that they could use to prioritize existing work while revealing missing elements.

Influenced by the emerging goal of TL, the VPs began formulating a set of overarching educational goals (*tenets*) that could contribute to students' development and transformation. Leadership, undergraduate research, and service-learning were obvious starting points. Eventually, the central six tenets were defined: disciplinary knowledge; global and cultural competencies; health and wellness; leadership; research, creative and scholarly activities; and service-learning and civic engagement. The vice presidents soon realized that at least three of the six tenets (research, creative and scholarly activities; service-learning and civic engagement; and global and cultural competencies) aligned with HIPs that already existed at UCO (undergraduate research, service-learning, study abroad). If the central six were implemented well, the HIPs could improve student engagement and learning and perhaps reduce achievement gaps in the process.

At first, it was assumed that faculty would be responsible for only the disciplinary knowledge tenet while other parts of the institution would be responsible for the other five. Within a few years, views had changed.

Specifically, people realized that coursework could help develop all six tenets. Thus academic affairs and student affairs came to share responsibility for global and cultural competencies. Because all six tenets represented serious commitments to improvement, UCO's leadership decided to designate a center for each tenet in order to stimulate, support, and document work done under that banner. Some such centers already existed, while others had to be created. A set of assumptions and goals was beginning to change the way UCO organized its work.

Those two lines of discussion, about TL and the tenets, had converged by 2009. That was also the year that *transformative learning* began appearing publicly as a goal for a UCO education. To accelerate the work, faculty were invited to a regular "share fair" where they could discuss one another's efforts to transform student learning. The fair quickly evolved into a university-wide conference on TL. Faculty and staff debated how to assess student transformation and progress toward the central six, questions they knew their accreditor was bound to ask. UCO made a lasting and public commitment to TL in the form of the new Center for Transformative Learning building, opened in 2010. The facility housed a number of flexible active learning spaces, equipped with technology. No lectern marked the front of the classroom. In order to teach in this building, faculty had to submit proposals for how they would take advantage of such a learning space.

Takeoff and Title III

In 2011, former provost Don Betz returned to UCO as its new president. Action with respect to TL picked up speed. In 2011, UCO had a Faculty Enhancement Center run by a single faculty member. When that faculty member retired, Betz and Radke took the opportunity to reconceive and enlarge the office as the Center for Excellence in Transformative Teaching and Learning (CETTL; it's pronounced "kettle," a fitting metaphor). CETTL's goal was to spread the word and support activities to achieve the potential of TL. Founding Executive Director Jeff King was chosen after a national search and quickly began working with the academic deans. In addition, King joined the existing Transformative Learning Steering Committee as cochair, working alongside the existing chair as the group launched the *Journal of Transformative Learning*. The team also expanded the TL Conference (discussed later) as well as taking on the charge from VPs Bill Radke and Kathryn Gage to become the face of TL at UCO.

Ramping up TL would take more money. King and colleagues from the Office of Research and Sponsored Programs began developing a multimillion dollar proposal for the Federal Title III Strengthening Institutions Program (which helps institutions of higher education expand their capacity to serve low-income students by providing funds to improve and strengthen academic quality, among other things). Their goal was to transform every student's development, especially students who were first-generation, low-income, and/or underrepresented (minority) students. The percentage of students in each category comprise between one-third and one-half of the entire student body.

Cunliff and King (2018) recalled several lessons they learned from the experience of developing the Title III proposal about promoting cross-silo collaboration and pulling people into the effort. They realized how important it was to involve deans, department chairs, office directors, and faculty in the implementation process. To aid the proposed work on assessment, program development, and outreach, each dean recommended a faculty member to serve as a champion for TL and the six tenets in their school. Department chairs convened faculty to figure out how course syllabi could advance the six tenets. In the end, everything was optional, an opportunity for interested faculty, staff, and students. But participants needed to be motivated to work in the interest of students in areas beyond their direct responsibilities and authority. One meaningful kind of encouragement came from changes in the UCO budget, for example, to provide direct support for faculty to encourage undergraduate research. To engage more faculty, work on TL had to be regarded as a way of advancing faculty careers. That's one reason why, in 2012, UCO turned its campus Transformative Learning conference into an annual national conference. Submissions to that conference could be a first step toward publication in UCO's *Journal of Transformative Learning,* an open-access, double-blind peer-reviewed electronic journal published twice a year. Both conference and journal submissions counted as faculty scholarly output for purposes of tenure and promotion.

In 2012, an interaction with the wider world helped prompt the next stage of work: feedback from its regional accreditor that they thought the emphasis on TL was worthwhile but that it would need some way to measure implementation and success in achieving it (King, 2018a).

Student Transformative Learning Record

The team agreed that it would be important to assess and document student progress through the tenets toward TL. Eventually the team decided to call this document the Student Transformative Learning Record (STLR, pronounced "stellar"). STLR would contain evidence of student development in five of the six tenets, as described by using a rubric. The sixth, disciplinary knowledge, is assessed in the traditional way through courses, assignments, and grades.

Other than assignments in formal courses, everything about STLR would be voluntary. Faculty would have the option of aligning assignments with one or more of the tenets. Course assignments could include a STLR activity that faculty or staff would rate using an activity-specific, STLR-aligned rubric. The activity might be a course assignment, a cocurricular activity such as undergraduate research, or an extracurricular activity. Interested faculty and, notably, staff would be taught together how to create and rate STLR-relevant activities. Students' STLR submissions would usually include an artifact (i.e., the results of the activity), the rubric used to assess their progress toward transformation, their written analysis of how their artifact provides evidence for this rating, and the rating itself. Faculty or staff could create activities challenging students to rise to rise to one of three levels for any tenet. (Recently a process was created whereby a student could identify prior learning and document it with an interview with an outside expert paid by the university.) Eventually it was decided that students could earn badges at each of three levels of achievement (exposure, integration, and transformation) in each tenet (Table 8.1).

STLR, in combination with the academic transcript, would comprise the comprehensive student record (CSR). When the student sent the CSR to a potential employer or school, the reader could choose to drill down from the tenet and the badge name in order to see examples of the actual work. Students might easily graduate with a couple of hundred assessed pieces of work, but each time they requested their CSR, they were limited to 10 artifacts for each tenet. (An online article by King [2018b] provides a wealth of information about the history and operations of STLR.)

Earning the Title III Grant

The 2011 application for a Title III grant was denied but UCO was encouraged to try again. President Betz declared that UCO would go forward with implementing STLR, whether or not grant support was found. The tenets were instantly appealing because of their clear relevance to what students would be doing after graduation. One persuasive reason to push ahead was the strong positive reaction from employers, parents, students, and others. That helped in creating the cross-silo coalition that would be necessary if the funded project were to succeed. The executive director of CETTL

TABLE 8.1

Five STLR Tenets, Three Levels of Achievement

	*Global and Cultural Competencies*		
	Transformation	*Integration*	*Exposure*
	Keen sense of cultural self and an identity as a global citizen has emerged	Developing sense of cultural self; and relation to the global community	Beginning awareness of cultural self; openness to learning
	*Health and Wellness*		
	Transformation	*Integration*	*Exposure*
	A holistic view of health and wellness for self and community is articulated and practiced	A developing holistic view; some application to self and community with some ability to evaluate own behavior	Beginning awareness and understanding of health and wellness; initial attempts at personal change
	*Leadership*		
	Transformation	*Integration*	*Exposure*
	Leadership knowledge and skills are applied effectively to community or campus issues	Leadership is developing; knowledge and skills are applied at a basic to intermediate level	Leadership skills are being tried out with increasing understanding

(*Continues*)

TABLE 8.1 *(Continued)*

	Research, Creative, and Scholarly Activities		
	Transformation	*Integration*	*Exposure*
	The "why" and the "how" of research and creation are grasped and show in work	Relevant inquiry about research and creative process and skills are developing	Skills in research and the creative process are developing; ideas are beginning to emerge
	Service II Learning and Civic Engagement		
	Transformation	*Integration*	*Exposure*
	Deep engagement in the community, both through learning and helping	Awareness of community issues and the importance of engagement	First experiences in volunteering and civic interest

Source: UCO Center for Excellence in Transformative Teaching and Learning (2020); reproduced by permission.

led the project team. An assistant VP for information technology served as project manager. Student affairs appointed multiple representatives to the team, as did academic affairs. Faculty were represented along with UCO's Office of Institutional Assessment. In addition, an ex-officio member of the project team was the associate VP for academic affairs.

A key aspect of the project team's structuring was sponsorship by three UCO vice presidents: VP for academic affairs and provost, VP for student affairs, and VP for information technology. This ensured a direct line of communication from the project team (and its constituencies) to the president's cabinet. One of the revisions in the proposal was to include the goal of helping other institutions use STLR. In 2012 the second proposal was approved, resulting in a $7.8 million, 5-year grant to develop and disseminate STLR.

Implementing STLR

One of the sources of STLR success was that a number of faculty had always made STLR-like assignments but, until now, they had had no way for students to document their development nor any way to see for themselves what the impact of their assignments had been on student development. That's why, instead of responding to STLR as an insult, these faculty were early champions of STLR, helping their colleagues understand what it could become: a way to further develop students' beyond-disciplinary skills as well as expanding their perspectives of their relationships with themselves, others, communities, and the environment. The first cohort of first-year students began using STLR in fall 2014.

In the early years, entering first-year and transfer students were initially unaware of TL, the six tenets, or STLR. So, early and often, TL leaders took up the challenge of informing and then persuading students. A required course, Success Central, in which students create an artifact and reflection for one or more of the tenets, was developed for incoming students. Students also learn that, when they graduate, their STLR record will be especially valuable if by then they have earned a transformation rating in one or more of the five nondisciplinary knowledge tenets. To symbolize these achievements at graduation time, each tenet has a signature color. For every tenet for which students have submitted artifacts demonstrating transformation, they receive a cord of that color to wear around their necks as part of their graduation regalia; honors graduates of UCO also have gold cords. These graduation cords raise the profile of STLR achievements among the graduates, their parents, younger siblings, and guests.

STLR Faculty and Staff Development

Creating a STLR assignment in a course encouraged faculty to consider how their course might contribute to TL by their students. The head of the chemistry department, interviewed in a video about STLR, talks of STLR as a prompt for faculty to improve their own capabilities in the five transdisciplinary tenets, a new way to interact with their students, and as a stimulus to see their course as a contribution to student development in some or all of the tenets (University of Central Oklahoma, 2016, at 1:33).

One indicator of faculty engagement in TL, the tenets, and STLR is the popularity of relevant workshops, conferences, and other events offered by CETTL. For example, the fall collegium on college teaching practices, starring an outside speaker, routinely draws about 70% of UCO's full-time faculty. Attendance at the national conference on Transformative Learning is usually capped because its facility can handle only about 350 participants (of which about half are usually from UCO). In 2019, the conference received 120 proposals for sessions, of which peer reviewers selected 90 (plus 50 posters, 35 by students). Half of the proposals came from UCO. For those conference attendees who are interested in TL, the tenets, or STLR, there are plenty of UCO folks to talk to. Meanwhile the UCO folks learn from the outside participants.

All of these activities are organized wholly or in part by the 21st Century Pedagogy Institute of CETTL, which offers about 40 events per year. The institute focuses each event on one or more explicit learning outcomes for faculty that were selected by an advisory board: course design around TL theory; active learning strategies aligned with student learning outcomes; methods to assess learning; improving the environment for inclusion, technology, and the human dimension; academic professionalism. Each outcome can be developed at any of a dozen or so events. From August 2018 through January 2019, 114 different faculty participated in at least one institute event.

Faculty new to UCO must attend at least four teaching workshops during their first year in order to be recognized as teacher-scholars by the president and provost at an annual spring gala. Other teaching-related awards include Distinguished Teacher-Scholar and Lifetime Teacher-Scholar, each of which requires the creation and review of materials fitting one or more of those faculty learning outcomes. In response to a simple survey, 46 faculty respondents suggested that the workshops are having desirable effects. To the question about whether attending even one workshop on TL was worth the faculty member's time, the average answer was 4.3 on a scale from strongly disagree (1) to strongly agree (5). All the questions elicited encouraging responses, including whether a colleague doing a peer observation would be able to see the difference (3.4).

Spreading the Use of STLR

One institutional attribute that was instrumental in the wider use of STLR was UCO's promotion and tenure (P&T) policy. That policy

> was weighted toward quality of teaching as evidence of success supporting promotion to tenure and for posttenure review. This provided one lever to message STLR to faculty because STLR would provide training and support in authentic assessment, prompting student critical reflection, use of rubrics, and other teaching strategies. Participating in STLR training and practice, then, could be evidence of professional development in teaching, a positive factor in one's P&T dossier. (King & Wimmer, in press, pp. 16–17).

Also encouraging faculty were positive student reactions.

The annual Transformative Learning conference is one way to spread the word about STLR. With the help of its Title III grant, UCO has been able to work with other institutions interested in adapting the STLR framework to their own needs (e.g., developing their own tenets or rubrics). Western Carolina University has been working on its own cocurricular adaptation (Degree Plus) for several years, while abroad, at Massey University in New Zealand, students use portfolios of academic work and cocurricular activities to document five main employability characteristics: self-management, information literacy, global citizenship, exercising leadership, and enterprise.

Internally, the university has been building an endowment to widen and deepen STLR use by students and student groups working together on research projects outside of classes with faculty and/or staff. Students create reflective artifacts on these projects, and faculty or staff assess them in the same way as they would judge course artifacts created for STLR assignments. Students can be paid $10/hour for their time spent developing and reflecting on these artifacts.

STLR and Online Courses

Here's an example of how two seemingly unrelated initiatives can be aligned to support one another. UCO has a Center for eLearning and Connected

Environments (CECE) that provides staff professionals to work with faculty on creating courses to be offered in online or hybrid learning spaces. One CECE staff member recalled getting a fresh sense of the importance of STLR when a panel of local employers explained how STLR provided everything they needed to judge the value of a potential employee, including evidence not included in a traditional transcript. Today CECE staff help faculty integrate STLR assignments into new online courses.

Evidence for 3Fold Gains by UCO

Increasing use of STLR: The first kind of useful data deals with process. STLR won't have much influence if it's only used by a small choir of devotees. One way to gauge the institutionalization of STLR is the number of artifacts that faculty and staff assess each year. In 2015–2016, the first operational year of STLR, 2,620 artifacts were assessed, most for integration or transformation. (For initial exposure, students would attend events, swiping their ID cards at the entrance; that evidence of attendance is sufficient to demonstrate exposure.) By 2017–2018, the number of artifacts had swelled to 7,743. By 2017–2018, 351 course sections included at least one STLR-rated assignment, as did 271 cocurricular activities. Drivers of growth included a new cohort of entering students and cumulative growth of STLR-related activities across UCO.

About 20% of students graduating in spring 2018 had at least one transformation rating. By summer 2019, over 70% of current full-time UCO faculty had participated in at least one faculty development workshop in which they created a STLR assignment for a course they would be teaching. The STLR staff aims to get that number to 100% and, perhaps more importantly, to deepen the involvement of trained faculty, encouraging and helping them to incorporate at least one STLR assignment in each of their courses.

Evidence for quality gains: The first class to have STLR opportunities for all 4 years graduated in spring 2019. For this group, using STLR at any level, even just to document exposure experiences, strongly correlated with higher graduation rates. That's consistent with the correlation between increased year-to-year retention and STLR use by students in earlier classes. And compared with their peers, STLR-using students who transferred from UCO were three times as likely to graduate from that other institution within a total of 4 years of college work if they had used STLR while at UCO. These are correlations, of course, but UCO's unpublished predictive analytics show that students who use STLR graduate at higher rates than would be predicted from their ACT scores and high school grades. And students who submit at least one transformation artifact are over twice as likely to graduate from UCO as students who get exposure credit for attending STLR events but don't submit artifacts.

STLR's positive impact on students also shows up in interviews with students. Here's what one student had to say about personal transformation stemming from an outside-of-class STLR project:

> When I think about the art and music that I create [now], I'm less concerned about making something that's a representation of myself, about my own personal emotion. I want to be the kind of artist and consume the kind of media and art that's more important than the individual. I've been thinking more about what I can do as a student, an artist, and musician about these much more important topics than a self-indulgent kind of art. (King & Wimmer, in press, p. 30)

A different undergraduate said of her STLR experience:

> These are the most valuable experiences that I have from my college career. This [STLR] project remained with me because it contributed to a bigger picture. There was a real audience and a real need. I was actually helping others, and I found that's the best way for me to learn. (p. 30)

An indirect, unexpected quality outcome was the impact on faculty of reviewing students' reflections on their work in their courses. In 2019 ongoing formative and summative evaluation began to hint that, for some faculty, their own experience was transformative. These faculty had previously seen their job as content delivery; they didn't believe they could affect students' development. However, when student reflections explained just and how why these transformative effects were occurring, their faculty began to reconsider what it meant to be an educator. A Business School faculty member reported that

> just the transformation in the students. I mean, this is what you live for, you know? And to see that you can actually flag it and demonstrate it, note it, get your hands on it. It was amazing to me. (p. 35)

For some, STLR provided the occasion for a series look at what outcomes faculty wanted from an assignment. A survey of full-time faculty/staff in summer 2018 found that over 58% of faculty reported modifying or planning an entirely new activity to STLR-tag. In addition, over 78% reported that being involved with STLR impacted their teaching or how they interacted with students. By 2020, over 70% of full-time faculty had asked for and received STLR training (King & Wimmer, in press).

This faculty approval also came from the wider world outside UCO. Department chairs have reported that STLR was the reason a new faculty member accepted UCO's offer instead of higher-paying offers from other institutions. In fact, chairs in some departments now regularly bring new faculty candidates to CETTL to learn about STLR as part of campus visits. Some candidates who already know about STLR want to discuss potential STLR projects with CETTL staff during their visits (King & Wimmer, in press).

Other encouraging evidence for quality enhancement came from a board of local employers that has helped to plan and assess STLR. One of its members described interviewing a UCO graduate for a position:

> My expectations initially, based on experiences with near-college-graduates or recent college graduates, is [of] their inability to articulate to me [how their prior work experiences and/or internships translate] into real tangible work product or work-related things. So my expectations were that that would occur again, especially with someone who hadn't graduated. I found quite the contrary in my interview, and even the review of the ePortfolio with this UCO student. In fact, she took experiences from jobs and industry and hourly kind of part-time college jobs that you would expect a college student to have, and transferred skills and knowledge from that into hard-and-fast employer questions that I ask every candidate, and did a better job than folks I've had with years of experience and years of situations to draw upon. That was probably the most profound thing for me. (King, 2018b, section 5)

Since its inception, STLR has earned state and national accolades. For instance, AASCU named UCO a 2018 Excellence and Innovation Award winner in the Student Success and College Completion category, specifically highlighting the STLR program and its role in student success and retention.

Evidence for equitable access gains: UCO is beginning to gather data about student development in the tenets and their assessment through STLR. A group of first-time, first-year students, comprising low-income, first-generation and/or underrepresented students, all of whom used STLR, was tracked. The group began at UCO in fall 2015, with year-to-year retention 13% higher compared with the retention of non-STLR users in the same cohort. Grade point averages within the STLR group were more than half a grade higher. By the time this first group of STLR-using students graduated in spring 2019, STLR engagement had statistically eliminated the 4-year graduation rate gap between at-risk and non-at-risk students (King, personal communication). Such data suggest the possibility that UCO's emphasis on TL (including STLR) might be particularly beneficial for the underserved students who are the primary target of Federal Title III funding. Such a result would be consistent with findings at other institutions that rely on HIPs (for more, see the discussion of HIPs in chapter 10).

Evidence for gains in stakeholder affordability? Improving graduation rates for all students, and for students from underserved minorities and poor households—those constitute gains in quality, equitable access, and affordability. As of early 2020, however, UCO hasn't estimated the amount of time or money saved by the students or by the institution due to increased rates of graduation and speed to graduation.

Turning the Page

Chapter 2 expressed skepticism of institutions that were attempting to improve quality, access, and affordability with scattered, often short-term initiatives, each competing with the others for funding and institutional attention. That's probably how UCO looked before 1997. In retrospect, President Webb's investment in developing students as leaders was a first step toward the UCO of today. Meanwhile, a bottom-up step was taken when senior leaders, the Burrito Buddies, worked out a conceptual scheme of six tenets that could bring order and priorities to UCO's gaggle of apparently disconnected initiatives. Almost 15 years later, TL and the tenets are quite real for UCO, as manifested by the many initiatives and other activities that are strengthening themselves by joining the constellation.

Our final case history analyzes the University of Central Florida through the lens of its uses of blended (hybrid) and online courses. Its strategy opens up an additional Integrative route toward 3fold gains.

9

UNIVERSITY OF CENTRAL FLORIDA

Using Online and Blended Strategies to Pursue 3Fold Gains

In the 1960s, the University of Central Florida (UCF) was founded in Orlando to help provide an educated workforce for the burgeoning space program. By 2019, over 58,000 undergraduate and 10,000 graduate students were enrolled. Since the late 1990s, the role of online and *blended* learning has been widening and deepening at UCF.

> What UCF calls a *blended* course (and once called a *mixed modality* course) is what some others (e.g., Georgia State University, chapter 3) call a *hybrid* course and still others call a *flipped* course. What UCF calls a *fully face-to-face course*, this book often labels as a *campus course*. Each of these is a different type of learning space, not a pedagogy. But each type of space tends to make certain pedagogies a little easier, and other pedagogies a little more awkward. A UCF blended course is supposed to foster a good deal of interpersonal interaction both online and in the classroom. Blended courses allocate fewer hours to time in a physical classroom compared with fully face-to-face learning spaces, in order to free up time for faculty and students to work together online. We'll have more to say about blended courses in this chapter and in chapter 11 on organizational foundations.

The development of online and blended learning at UCF was shaped by many factors, which we explore in this chapter. 3fold gains developed steadily at UCF over the next 20 years, in the forms of good instructional practices embodied in hundreds of courses, access for tens of thousands of additional learners, and a smaller budget for building construction for the university. Today, another institution with little or no online presence might glance at UCF and fail to see any way it could follow in that university's footsteps. What's important to remember, however, is how many years of determined effort underlie UCF's transformation in these ways. Let's start at the beginning, in 1995.

As the Twig is Bent . . .

In 1992, John C. Hitt became president of UCF, a position he held until his retirement in 2018. Soon after taking office, Hitt announced five strategic goals that would guide his administration (Barnes, 2013). When I visited UCF in the early 2000s, one of my contacts repeated these five priorities from memory. For our purposes, the most important is goal 1, "to offer the best undergraduate education available in Florida." It is striking because the undergraduate education goal was first in the list, because the declaration was coming from a regional public campus and not a flagship institution, and because the context was the state of Florida (not just the region around Orlando, which UCF had been created to serve).

In 1995, the first commercial web browser was a year old, there was no Google, and another dozen years would pass before the first iPhone was sold. And 1995, as it turned out, saw the baby steps that led toward UCF's transformation. It's worth paying attention to the details of this genesis because these precedents contributed to the distinctive institution-scale approach embraced by UCF today.

UCF's engagement with online learning began on the university's margins, in continuing education for teachers in school vocational programs. At UCF and statewide, enrollments in such certification programs for those teachers had long been declining. A dozen institutions had competed for a share of the shrinking pie. By 1995, only UCF and one other remained. There was a real chance that, at some point, UCF's program would have too few students to continue. Yet demand, albeit thinly scattered, existed for these programs statewide. Periodically, Professor Steve Sorg was contacted by teachers from around the state asking whether the UCF program could be offered near them.

Sorg proposed to his department head that part of a state grant be used to create UCF's first online course, Special Methods in Teaching Vocational Education, to be offered to high school teachers in summer 1996. As development of the course's website began, a programming policy roadblock stymied Sorg and his colleague Barbara Truman. The pair appealed to UCF's chief information officer (CIO) Joel Hartman. Hartman hadn't known about their project; thus far it had been authorized only by Sorg's department head. Hartman agreed to change the policy and then he told Sorg something unexpected: A presidential task force was hosting meetings to elicit ideas about online learning at UCF. Hartman invited Sorg and Truman to describe their plans to the task force and to college deans. At the meeting, Sorg and Truman described how online learning could become an important university strength and how faculty leadership was crucial. The dean of UCF's largest college, Arts & Humanities, liked what she heard. When Sorg asked what her own college would need to take its next step, the dean responded crisply, "You two, because you're the only ones who can help my faculty understand this opportunity." The deans began to see online courses as an integral part of their colleges, rather than as a cash cow to be milked to subsidize other operations. It also aligned with President Hitt's number one priority: to provide the best education in Florida.

The campus version of the vocational teacher certification course had previously attracted 25 students. Sorg predicted that the first offering of the online course might draw 30 students. Surprisingly, in summer 1996, 72 students registered, suggesting that online learning might open access in a big way. The new revenues for the university would also help pay for intensive training and support for faculty to create the next rounds of online courses. In designing the course and in his orientation of the high school teachers, Sorg emphasized:

- *Applying their new knowledge at work in order to understand it*: These teachers would need to do research, evaluate, synthesize, and integrate this new material with their existing knowledge in order to improve their own programs. And as working teachers, they already expected to apply their new knowledge in their own jobs and, in the process, to more deeply understand what they'd learned.
- *Collaboration*: Each time a student had a question, they should address it to one particular person, instructor or student, and copy it to all the other students. It was a requirement of the course that students read all of these online exchanges. For a group of working teachers, it didn't seem odd to help one another out in applying new ideas and technologies in their home schools.
- *Using the most powerful pedagogies possible*: One example was using asynchronous conferencing to encourage students to work together rather than just waiting for the expert to give them the final word.

The approach of using teacher projects to improve their high schools resolved worries about cheating: Students were graded by projects that they developed and implemented in their schools, not by multiple-choice exams. One of Sorg's colleagues recalled that "Steve's hallmark phrase was 'student-centered.' That was the hallmark of everything we did. Not just a change in modality, *per se,* but a move from teacher-centered to student-centered and all the ripple effects from there."

Soon after, Sorg accepted an offer to form a center that would develop and support faculty users of online learning, reporting to Vice Provost for Academic Programs Frank Juge. The center was later named the Center for Distributed Learning (CDL). During that same period, Truman was appointed director of course development and web services, reporting to CIO Hartman. Crucially, support from the deans enabled UCF to institute a pivotal policy: All interested faculty *must* take extensive training in the pedagogical potential of, limits of, and best practices with the new technology and *must* work with professional instructional designers as they developed their first course. Although Sorg's and Truman's units reported to different people, Sorg (faculty), Truman (staff), Juge (provost), and Hartman (CIO) met weekly for an hour. They jokingly called themselves the Four Musketeers ("all for one, one for all!").

In 1997 the Research Initiative for Teaching Effectiveness (RITE) was created, a formal unit to research the strengths and needs of the university's online program. (Anyone who has been following research into online and blended learning over the years is likely to know the work of Charles [Chuck] Dziuban and Patsy Moskal of RITE. Much of UCF's awareness of the strengths and needs of their online programs is due to RITE research.) By this point the direction of UCF's online program was set, with the following crucial features in place:

- Leadership and support from the deans, the provost's office, and the CIO
- Faculty and staff working together to use what we're calling Integrative principles for course design and teaching
- Significant financial support reinvested from distance learning fees
- A research unit using evidence to describe and analyze what was happening with online and blended courses

Two additional factors influenced the rapidly unfolding action. First, the demand for a UCF education exceeded the supply. It takes years to build a new classroom, and online learning was helping the university deal with a substantial shortage of classrooms, even as some new classroom buildings came online (this at a university whose nickname for itself was "UCF: Under Construction Forever"). Second, UCF's college and department budgets are substantially influenced by the number of credit hours generated in the previous year. By encouraging increased faculty involvement in online learning, deans could grow their enrollments and budgets faster than if they waited years for new buildings. It's also important to note the principle that revenues from online operations were reinvested in online operations, not used to subsidize campus activity.

By 2017 or so, UCF had developed extensive infrastructure to support expanding and enriching education using digital technologies. The lion's share of the support for faculty is provided in-house, not through vendors. As someone explained about UCF, "It's who we are, not just what we do."

IDL6543

After years of offering student- and faculty-centered workshops and resources, CDL created a new faculty development course. Known by its number, IDL6543, this noncredit course requires an 80-hour time commitment from participants, including 11 weeks of work on seven online units, four 3-hour workshops, mandatory technology labs, one-on-one instructional design consultations, and faculty completion of weekly assignments. The blended course features online work and collaboration, along with face-to-face interaction and hands-on education in using the technology. In IDL6543, each faculty member develops their course design and materials with their own instructional designer on call. That particular instructional designer remains assigned to them until one of them leaves UCF. Once those faculty had used best practices in their online teaching, they were likely to use them for campus courses.

The cost for this support is an estimated $20,000 per faculty member. As of 2019, over 1,000 faculty had taken IDL6543. UCF can train at most 120 faculty per year. But in recent years, UCF has been hiring 200 faculty annually. By 2019, there was a faculty waiting list for IDL6543 of 4 years.

To support all this activity, CDL has continued to expand. In 2019 its staff numbered about 90 people, including instructional designers (who have faculty rank and obligations for scholarship and service), videographers, graphic designers, staff who assure copyright compliance, and Techranger students to help faculty with technology issues. The current $18 per credit distance learning fee, introduced in 2007, provides a substantial share of the CDL budget and pays for faculty training. CDL also has explicit governance authority over the university's online instructional technologies and standards such as the learning management system, online program standards and expectations, and Massive Open Online Course (MOOC) approvals.

The Faculty Center for Teaching and Learning

UCF's Faculty Center for Teaching and Learning (FCTL) also has a tradition of working with educational uses of technology. For example, working with CDL, FCTL staff plan and support multimedia classrooms designed specifically for active learning activities. UCF conducted several years of surveys of students who took courses in these classrooms. About one third of respondents reported increased learning in the new rooms due to debates, group presentations, group tests, online discussions, peer evaluations, and team research. Two thirds of respondents reported gains from in-class discussion groups. Survey responses also suggested that students were engaged in higher level learning, not just remembering facts, opinions, and scripted procedures (Marshall, 2006).

FCTL uses a variety of resources, including testimonials from faculty, to encourage faculty to consider developing blended courses. A 2014 video illustrated how going online provided an opportunity for rethinking a course. Associate Professor Dan Murphree wanted to change pedagogy for his history course from lecture to more writing-intensive (a high-impact practice [HIP]), and with more discussion among students and with their instructor. On the video, which is no longer available on the FCTL website, he described what motivated him:

> In my discipline . . . students tend to be very passive. They . . . want to accept the facts and the interpretations from the instructor without taking ownership of their understanding history themselves. . . . A writing-intensive course might be a way for students to . . . actively engage and even be . . . critical of the history they were learning.
>
> One of the things I knew going into flipping . . . was that I was changing the way I'd been teaching for 10 years with . . . a standard lecture format and . . . exams in class. . . . I was abandoning all that and it was an uncomfortable feeling, to be honest. . . . [But] I thought it would be worth it to get to the goals I had set.

The CDL and FCTL websites both make it clear that the creation of an online or blended course creates an occasion to qualitatively improve student learning and expand the teaching repertoire of faculty. Melody Bowdon, then director of FCTL, coedited a book entitled *Best Practices in Flipping the College Classroom* (Waldrop & Bowdon, 2015) that includes case studies of several UCF courses.

Experimenting With Personalized Adaptive Learning

For many years, UCF had been experimenting with various forms of adaptive courseware, in which students' previous responses and preferences influence their individualized path through course material; when initial assessments demonstrate that the student already understands upcoming material, the student can skip ahead to the next topic. As has been true in the adaptive learning field generally, early results at UCF were mixed but encouraging enough to keep exploring the options.

Course Redesign Initiative

UCF trustees heard the evidence from CDL/RITE research and other sources on the successes of blended and online courses and adaptive courseware. Impressed, they allocated $2 million from reserves, matched by another $2 million of operating budget, for a 3-year initiative called Digital Learning Course Redesign (fall 2017–2019); as of this writing, it's still underway. The initiative's goals are to reduce D/F/Withdrawal rates, to improve student success and satisfaction, and, by using alternative scheduling, to make more productive use of the university's limited inventory of classrooms. Each redesigned course takes advantage of fully online course formats, blended formats, active learning, and/or adaptive learning. Foundational; general education; and science, technology, engineering, and mathematics (STEM) courses are given high priority; also favored are courses of strategic importance for degree completion (nominated by faculty) and large enrollment courses.

To implement the program, UCF's Division of Digital Learning (which includes CDL) partnered with FCTL and five of UCF's colleges to get the word out and ensure that the resulting proposals concerned high-priority courses. The initiative's 3 years of funding were enough to support development of 50 fully online or blended courses and another 50 that used adaptive courseware. The initiative included stipends to train up to 120 faculty as well as funding to transform eight classrooms into additional flexible, technology-enhanced active learning spaces. The initiative is intended to benefit up to 50,000 students a year after all the redesigned courses are in place.

The demand for online and blended courses has increased steadily. In 2018–2019, 47.4% of all credits from UCF courses were generated in totally online or blended courses, and only 18% of UCF students took all their courses in traditional campus formats. Most students take several online or blended courses on their way to a degree.

Evidence for 3Fold Gains by UCF's Online and Blended Programs

Evidence for quality gains: On average, online course sections have almost twice as many students as face-to-face courses. However, there's no evidence that net outcomes have suffered. To assess the learning outcomes of its online and blended courses, RITE analyzed grades earned in all UCF courses taught from fall 2014 through fall 2015, focusing on grades, withdrawals, and student course ratings (Dziuban et al., 2018). Courses were sorted into three categories: fully on-campus, fully online, and blended. To remove discipline-specific grading patterns as a factor, final course grades were divided into two categories: any grade enabling a student to make progress toward graduation (A/B/C) versus any grade not enabling progress (D/F/W). The authors concluded that their data analysis methods precluded the calculation of statistical significance. Nevertheless, the findings are intriguing:

- Students in blended courses earned slightly higher grades (2–3% advantage in achieving course success) compared with students in fully on-campus or fully online courses that includes case studies of several UCF courses.
- Students in blended courses withdrew at about a 1% lower rate, compared with on-campus or online courses.
- On the standard UCF student rating form, more students in blended courses consistently rated their course as "excellent" than did students on-campus and online, again by a narrow margin.

These findings are consistent with several other studies of blended courses (e.g., Bernard et al., 2014; Means et al., 2013). The consistency of this finding is of practical significance because so many students are involved that small percentages represent large numbers of students.

With the data available, it doesn't appear that class size makes a difference for course outcomes. That's consistent with evidence from educational research cited in chapter 1. Online courses at UCF have substantially higher student-faculty ratios (around 70:1), followed by blended and then by fully on-campus courses, which have the lowest student-faculty ratio. However, evidence suggests that UCF blended courses are slightly more effective than the other two modes.

Evidence for equitable access gains: UCF's primary access goal has been to offer greater educational opportunities to people who for any reason can't study a particular course on campus during traditional hours. Most UCF students take a mix of campus, blended, and online courses. That mixing makes it tough to sort out whether those three learning spaces have different implications for equity. Making it even tougher is the fact that student learning is evolving on campus, too, not least because faculty who've learned about educational research, multimedia, and course design for their online courses often apply those lessons and materials on campus. However, in an unpublished study, UCF researchers examined the percentage of students earning a passing grade (A/B/C) in courses offered between fall 2013 and fall 2015. They found that courses offered in online and blended learning spaces had slightly smaller grade gaps between Pell- and non-Pell-eligible students. For example, in fall 2013's face-to-face campus courses, 84% of Pell students and 89% of non-Pell students earned a passing grade. Meanwhile, in blended courses that semester, 89% of Pell-eligible students passed compared with 92% of non-Pell students. In other words, there was a 5-point difference between Pell-eligible and not-eligible student grades in the campus courses versus a 3-point difference in the blended courses (and a 4-point difference for the fully online courses). Every semester, Pell-eligible students had small comparative advantages when they took blended courses (Boston Consulting Group and University of Central Florida, 2017).

These apparent differences between modes probably stem, at least in part, from the teaching and learning activities favored by each kind of learning space. For instance, face-to-face (shoulder-to-shoulder) campus courses probably encourage faculty to do most of the talking, lessening the time available for two-way interactions among students and their instructor; blended courses can favor enhanced interaction both online and in classrooms.

Evidence for affordability gains: The program of online and blended courses has affordability implications as well. UCF would need to construct approximately 8,000 square feet of classrooms every year to keep up with increasing enrollment. Each additional classroom seat that does *not* need to be created saves approximately $6,500 in construction costs and $330 per year in operating costs. Creative scheduling of blended courses also helps reduce plant maintenance and operations costs. UCF can schedule two or three courses into the same weekly time slot for the same classroom because each course meets perhaps one third as often as it would in a face-to-face format (Dziuban et al., 2011). In 2015, UCF's Office of Space Planning, Analysis, and Administration estimated that it would have cost $192 million to build the classroom space needed to offer all of UCF's online and blended courses in face-to-face formats, plus an additional $7.2 million per year for operations (Brown & Kurzweil, 2015).

Other affordability gains affect students' money and time directly. For example, when students graduate sooner, they and the institution can save both time and money, as we saw at Georgia State in chapter 3. On the average, 2015–2016 graduates who had taken a greater percentage of their undergraduate courses online also finished their degrees earlier. For example, graduates who began their higher education at UCF, attended full-time, and got none of their credits online took 4.3 years to earn a 4-year degree. However, those who took 61% to 80% of their credits online graduated in only 3.6 years (Figure 9.1). Similar trends were seen for transfer and part-time students.

Figure 9.1. UCF students who take more courses online tend to graduate sooner.

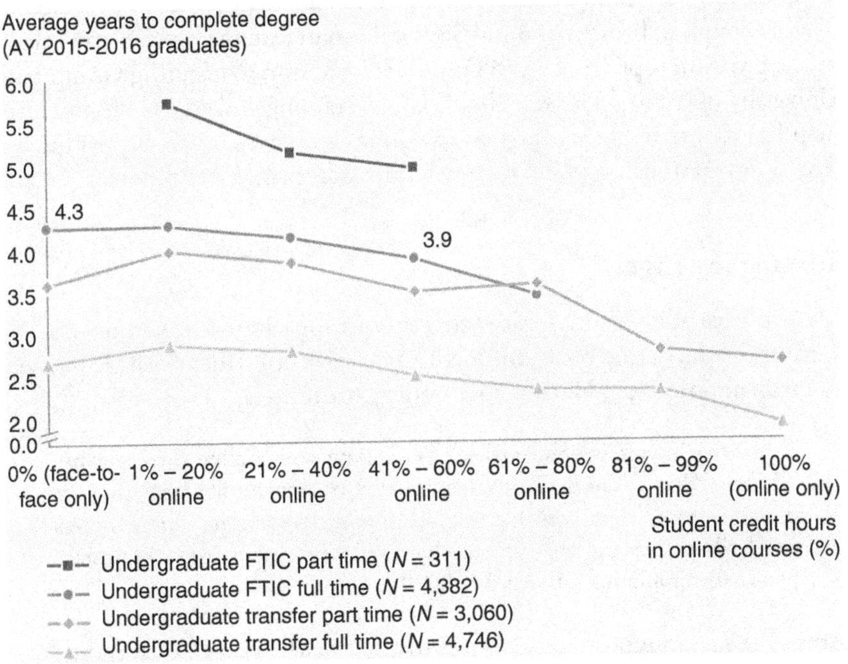

Note. Time-to-degree data is for 2015–2016 graduates who started in summer 2005 or later; online activity is shown. Points are excluded where *N* was less than 30 students. "Student credit hours in online courses (%)" includes student credit hours in fully online and lecture capture courses. AY=academic year; FTIC=first time in college.

Note from author: At UCF, lecture capture courses consist of online video recordings of lectures, recorded live in classrooms, plus readings and assignments. Only a tiny fraction of students come to the room to hear the lecture live, nor would the room be big enough to hold more than a fraction of them. This is a different pedagogy than used in UCF's online or blended courses. Fully online courses almost never have long video lectures although they may include shorter videos; there's more emphasis on interpersonal interaction online in fully online courses. Because of this difference, I wouldn't have grouped the two modes in this figure.

Source: Adapted from Boston Consulting Group & Arizona State University, 2018. Reproduced with permission.

There are at least two reasons why speed to graduation might vary with the percentage of credits taken online. First, required courses are always available to students, even when they're away from campus or when their regional campus doesn't offer a required course when the student is ready for it. Second, we saw that UCF's online and blended courses have slightly higher rates of student success (progress toward a degree) and lower rates of withdrawal; that too speeds students toward graduation.

Fully online students (i.e., students who take all their courses online) can save some cash as well. For in-state undergraduate students who take 14 online credits per semester, tuition is the same as for on-campus learners but the total fees are $926 less, despite the fact that the fully online students pay a distance learning fee. Florida allows its public institutions to charge a fee of up to $30 per online credit; however, UCF has kept its fee at $18/credit. That's enough to bring in around $8.5 million in revenues, which pays most of the program support costs ($8.6 million) (Boston Consulting Group and University of Central Florida, 2017). UCF's training and course support also help faculty teaching their first course online to rely as much as possible on free or low-cost instructional materials, another savings for students.

Turning the Page

Many people at UCF emphasized that subsidizing campus programs was not a driver for the online program. Joel Hartman went further. As he explained to me in an interview, Hartman tells other institutions,

> If making money is your goal for developing your online program, my advice is, "don't!" The decisions that optimize chances for financial gains are different from the choices that optimize academic gains. Academic success can lead to financial success but the reverse is seldom true. (Hartman, personal communication, April 1, 2020)

Among the counterproductive moves that occur when quick cash is the goal, Hartman continued, are,

> administrators getting way out ahead of their faculty; overestimating revenues while underestimating the costs of quality; the false assumption that there would be a large external market for the institution's online programs; the panic that the train is leaving and we need to get on. (Hartman, personal communication, April 1, 2020)

In contrast, in the early days of the online program, UCF was trying to serve students nearby and across the state who couldn't otherwise get an education.

Even then, in Sorg's first course, the goals were also to use the most powerful pedagogies possible and to take advantage of digital technology to make them still more effective. Since 2010, the online and blended programs have taken on added significance as a source of inspiration and support for faculty who want to improve student learning in campus courses, too.

None of this could have happened without extensive and intensive collaboration across organizational boundaries (e.g., the Four Musketeers) along with the gradual and cumulative development of large-scale organizational infrastructure to support faculty work. Former provost Dale Whitaker provides a fitting period for this case history, "When we all lean in the same direction, it results in remarkable impact" (University of Central Florida, 2016, p. 13).

Postscript in a Pandemic

This book was researched and written from 2016 through 2020. In the final weeks before it went to the publisher, the COVID-19 pandemic swept in. As you might guess, UCF was unusually well prepared to respond. That wasn't just because of its faculty's experience with technology per se. Also helpful were UCF's early commitment to educational excellence (the best quality in the state) for its online courses as well as for its blended and campus courses. The creation of CDL, the later creation of the Division for Digital Learning, the decades of faculty development about how to help students learn effectively (online), and consistent leadership by the president and his cabinet—virtually every element of UCF's constellation for 3fold gains contributed to its ability to respond quickly and smoothly to the pandemic.

Unintentionally, the federal government had also aided the university's readiness to respond to disaster. Some years earlier, UCF had been audited to check if there was "regular and substantive interaction" between faculty and students online, as was required for UCF to continue investing federal financial aid to these students. In the wake of the audit, UCF had decided to require that every course in the catalogue have its own course shell in the Canvas learning management system. And every faculty member was asked to do something usefully interactive during the first week of the semester. By the time the pandemic struck, all those routines were in place.

Then, the virus rocked the world, including higher education. Within days the shift had been made to online by one of the larger universities in the country. CIO Joel Hartman recalls that feedback from stakeholders, especially faculty, was surprisingly positive. UCF's approach to pursuing 3fold gains turned out also to be excellent preparation for swift response to disaster while maintaining quality, equitable access, and affordability. In fact, the response represents a 3fold gain, in and of itself, compared to what a less well-prepared UCF might have been able to achieve.

Institutions should not postpone pursuing 3fold gains until the virus and economic crises pass. On the contrary, if an institution works to improve quality, access, and affordability, partly by taking pragmatic advantage of digital technology as UCF has, that preparation can help the university survive current disasters while preparing to respond even more effectively to future disruptions.

PART FOUR

ALIGNING INITIATIVES ACROSS THREE DOMAINS

Many initiatives to improve quality of learning focus mainly on adopting new educational strategies, but such initiatives often clash with institutional facts of life. For example, preparing all students for and involving them in undergraduate research may be constrained by faculty roles and rewards at that institution.

One of the distinguishing features of our six institutions is that none of them has been working *only* on changing educational strategies. In fact, our six institutions caught my eye because they were taking on coordinated, mutually reinforcing initiatives across three domains: educational strategies, organizational foundations, and wider world interactions. To illustrate what I mean by "mutually reinforcing," Table P4.1 summarizes a constellation of five programs across three domains that, in combination, should assist 3fold gains. The right-hand column summarizes some of the ways in which these five elements reinforce each other at this first hypothetical institution. For fostering specific gains within the categories of quality, access, and affordability, the two educational strategies provide the power, aided directly by the program for making technologies affordable and indirectly by the faculty rewards system and the kinds of new faculty being hired.

Remember that the alternative to pursuing 3fold gains is to pursue three gains, each with a different agenda. Such an institution might look more like Table P4.2, which lists elements of educational strategies, organizational foundations, and wider world interactions that could, as a group, be self-defeating. For this second institution, the impact and sustainability of each element are weakened because each element stands alone, and there is less chance for it to be scaled up or sustained in the long run.

To put this comparison between two hypothetical institutions more generally, constellations are composed of institutional assets and initiatives that can be scaled and sustained because those elements support one another across

TABLE P4.1
Mutually Reinforcing Constellation of Elements

Program/Initiative	*Domain*	*Alignment*
Academic programs are organized around capabilities to be developed by graduation	Educational strategy	Capability of clearly thinking and writing about many topics, including the major, is one of those educational goals.
Writing in the discipline courses (high-impact practice [HIP])	Educational strategy	Students learn to reflect in writing about their learning in their field, a skill that is crucial for ePortfolio reflections. Quality impact improves when students engage in multiple HIPs during their academic programs.
Programmatic ePortfolios (HIP)	Educational strategy	Students reflect on and improve their communications skills, including writing. ePortfolios help faculty analyze effectiveness of writing-intensive courses.
Faculty rewards system	Organizational foundation	Faculty dossiers include evidence of student learning (e.g., to write well), which can be drawn in part from students' ePortfolios.
Availability and affordability of technologies for writing	Organizational foundation	Policy helps all students, especially Pell-eligible, afford their own computers, tablets, and needed software. Participation in HIPs is more equitable because all students have the needed tools.
New faculty hiring	Wider world interaction	Recruitment of new faculty in the disciplines prioritizes those with documented history of helping students improve their writing. Qualified faculty support more "writing in the discipline" courses.

three domains. Year by year the Integrative constellation can be expanded to make that mutual support even stronger so that its initiatives become even more effective and sustainable. In contrast, aggregations of initiatives that don't support each other are more difficult to sustain or scale. The impact of such aggregations on institutional quality, access, and affordability will likely be far less and far briefer.

TABLE P4.2
Aggregation of Unrelated Elements

Program/Initiative	*Domain*	*Alignment*
Academic programs are organized around content delivery	Educational strategy	That's a strategy aligned with the Instruction Paradigm, not the Integrative Paradigm. It doesn't, for example, align with writing across the curriculum or writing in the disciplines.
Writing in the discipline (WID) courses	Educational strategy	WIDs are awkward to implement because in an Instruction institution, there is little cumulative development of capabilities, just cumulative content coverage.
Faculty development	Organizational foundation	Teaching center chose to improve faculty's lecture skills because that was most in demand. But that doesn't help the cumulative development of communications capabilities.
Faculty rewards system	Organizational foundation	For teaching segment of dossier, no evidence of student learning is requested.
Availability and affordability of technologies for writing	Organizational foundation	No alignment between space planning, academic planning, and IT. So there's a shortage of computer classrooms and student labs. The poorest students may not be able to afford a computer.
New faculty hiring	Wider world interaction	Recruitment and interviewing new faculty involves no effort to see whether they can or would teach a WID course in their field.

In both tables, the Integrative elements for achieving 3fold gains are sorted into three domains. Each of the next three chapters looks in depth at one domain. Chapter 10 describes a set of mutually supportive educational strategies. Chapter 11 discusses the kinds of organizational foundations that can potentially support those strategies. And chapter 12 talks about ways the institution can manage its interactions with the wider world so that it can support its evolving educational strategies and organizational foundations. These three domains are good for sorting, but many initiatives have elements in two or all three of these categories. For example, the Student Transformative Learning Record (STLR) at UCO (chapter 8) has elements of educational strategy (infusing STLR assignments across the curriculum); organizational foundations (its academic records); and interactions with the wider world (providing employers and graduate schools with detailed insight into what students have achieved, and collecting feedback from employers to help influence and institutionalize STLR within UCO).

Let's begin with a few of the most widely used, high leveraged, and mutually reinforcing Integrative educational strategies.

10

INTEGRATIVE EDUCATIONAL STRATEGIES FOR 3FOLD GAINS

Learning results from what the student does and thinks and only from what the student does and thinks. The teacher can advance learning only by influencing what the student does to learn.
(Herbert Simon, quoted in Ambrose et al., 2010, p. 1)

At the heart of any Integrative constellation are its *institutionalized* educational strategies. In chapter 6 we described the Integrative assumptions about learning that provide a rationale for these strategies. In this chapter we will describe a few common strategies, each used by at least one of our five Integrative institutions.

> When we say that an educational strategy has been *institutionalized*, we mean that it's been going on this way for years, that students, faculty, and staff all consider it normal, and that a number of other educational strategies, organizational foundations, or interactions with the wider world help to support and sustain it.

The examples of institutionalized Integrative educational strategies include

- defining 3fold goals for degree programs and for the institution;
- creating cumulative learning with purposeful pathways;
- using asynchronous exchanges to help students learn to write and think;
- engaging in active and collaborative learning . . .
- . . . with help from learning assistants to facilitate small group work and coaching in large classes; and
- building a program spine of high-impact practices (HIPs).

To differing degrees these educational strategies can all contribute to equitable access and affordability. At the end of this chapter, we'll look at how one institution tried to improve quality of learning and faculty satisfaction with their roles while also cutting unnecessary costs.

Defining 3Fold Goals for Degree Programs and for the Institution

The important outcomes, the ones that matter most and are most readily observable, usually are attained more by institutions and programs than by particular bits, as we've observed before. A single composition course may not by itself lead to noticeable changes in the writing abilities of graduating students. But several courses, each emphasizing and aiding the development of writing (and associated thinking) skills are more likely to do the trick. Something similar is true for programmatic gains in access and affordability. For example, affordability gains from one redesigned course may be noticeable but not big enough to be of practical use; the important point is for enough people to participate in enough small changes so that, by programs end, the gains are big enough to really matter. That may be self-evident but it has a challenging corollary: it's likely that many different people need to be committed to the same goals for 3fold gains. How does such a working consensus emerge?

The University of Central Oklahoma (UCO) case history (chapter 8) illustrated how such agreement can sometimes emerge from years of effort. Year by year, as agreement spread and coalitions grew, UCO was able to take on more ambitious efforts to improve their academic program. The same kind of coalition building is necessary to attain gains in affordability and equitable access.

Creating Cumulative Learning With Purposeful Pathways

At the dawn of online learning, in the mid-1980s, Starr Roxanne Hiltz (1988) did a study comparing a composition course taught online (a course that encouraged plenty of academic interaction among students and the instructor) with a different section taught on campus. The first and last essays of the semester were collected from both courses. Without knowing which course each essay was from or when it was written, several well-prepared reviewers rated each paper on a scale of 1–10. In which section would you guess that students' writing improved most? The online section? Or the campus course?

Actually, each of the four sets of essays (pre/post, online/on-campus) got the *same* average rating (Hiltz, 1988, p. 162). There was no real difference between before and after essays in either course. Nor was there was any difference between the two modes, online or on-campus. And for anyone in composition research, that result was probably no surprise. With a holistic rating of essays (i.e., a simple scale of 1–10), many first-term composition courses don't move the needle. Simply put, one course is often insufficient to create noticeable gains in student writing or anything else of value.

That's one reason why, in an Integrative-aligned institution, it's essential for faculty to plan essential learning outcomes for the institution and its programs (degree programs and university requirements) and then design an academic program that cumulatively helps its students develop those capabilities. The resulting description of the sequential process of how courses (and other experiences) develop student capabilities is sometimes called a *curriculum map*. It is one component of what are often called *purposeful* (or *guided*) *pathways*. Capabilities aren't the only outcome that need to be developed intentionally and cumulatively. I haven't seen such a thing yet, but it may make sense to "map" strategy over a course of study for assuring the students from underserved groups can accelerate. As for cumulative affordability for stakeholders, suppose a focus for this program is cumulative instructional dollars per student; by the time the student completes the program, cumulative spending should be no more than a certain figure. Wouldn't it be helpful to have some way of tracking that spending, even approximately, so that the budget of costs per graduate isn't exhausted by the end of the first year? I'll leave it to the kind of experts I've interviewed to see whether this kind of mapping is worth the effort.

Let's return to the curriculum map of goals and cumulative learning. One way to use such a map is as part of a campaign to inform and remind students about how today's activities relate to their own and the program's ultimate goals. Bailey et al. (2015), Leskes and Miller (2006), and Veney and Sugimoto (2017) all provide insights into this essential educational strategy.

Let's look back at just one example of guided pathways in our case histories. Georgia State University (chapter 3) has been improving its pathways to careers for years. We've already seen how freshman learning communities organized around meta-majors are preparing students for a set of related majors. The development of its College to Career (CTC) initiative was influenced by research showing that low-income and first-generation college students are less likely to have known college-educated professionals. Nor do they know much about their wide range of career options. One consequence of not understanding where pathways can lead is that more students from underserved groups unwittingly choose majors that lead to lower-paying jobs, exacerbating inequality. CTC's primary goal is to ensure that, over 4 years, students become prepared for careers of their choice, ready to succeed from the first day on the job. The process begins with students uploading pieces of their work to their new ePortfolios, along with their written reflections about the evidence their work provides about what they can already do. The ePortfolio offers the ability to tag artifacts related to categories such as leadership, communication skills, and service-learning, thus drawing students' attention to the particulars of their progress. Throughout their course of study, they add more such artifacts, some the products of course assignments specifically designed to create such evidence. A peer mentoring program uses qualified undergraduates and graduate students to help review ePortfolios of senior undergraduates. Students use a variety of online tools to navigate their curricular pathway, such as exploring majors, selecting courses each term, and creating a personal calendar that includes coursework and personal events. As we mentioned in chapter 4, the online scheduling tool immediately alerts students if they schedule a course that does not move them toward their degree requirements.

All of these strategies help students get on track early toward their educational and career goals and stay on track with a minimum of wasted money, time, and effort. Obviously a program like CTC does not prevent students from "going off course" in order to explore a new possibility for their lives; it does remind them of the costs in time and money of that experiment.

Using Asynchronous Exchanges to Help Students Learn to Write and Think Critically

I hope it's clear by now that I don't see any technology as a driver of learning outcomes such as critical thinking. But the use of certain technologies, such as those that enable *asynchronous exchanges*, can help faculty and students accelerate or enrich learning.

> Synchronous exchanges are driven by the clock. As soon as one contribution is made, silence usually forces a response within seconds (e.g., face-to-face conversation or a telephone call). In contrast, the timing of *asynchronous exchanges* is up to each participant (e.g., exchanging love letters, posts and comments on a blog).

To understand the potential importance of asynchronous exchanges, let's go back to perhaps the first important technology: writing and reading. Walter

Ong's classic little book *Orality and Literacy* (1982) explains vividly how writing changed the way people think about their thinking. Spoken words can't be taken back and they vanish as soon as they're spoken. Writing makes critical thinking possible by freezing thought in flight for thoughtful reconsideration and critique later; writing also enables people to discuss the content over a period of minutes, months, or years. The invention of the printing press and the typewriter increased the potential for developing skills of critical writing and thinking by making writing easier to create and disseminate. In the late 20th century, word processing created even more such opportunities.

To be clear, word processing does not automatically improve critical thinking. But during a visit to Reed College in the late 1980s, I first realized that computer writing can be used to develop critical thinking. The day-long visit was part of an informal inquiry into what faculty at different institutions had learned so far about how they could improve learning when all their students had computers. Reed's seniors were the first class to have had their own computers since their first semester. The faculty I talked with that day all had different things to say about how their courses gained some advantage from universal ownership of computers by students. But they all volunteered one similar point, "I'm no longer embarrassed to ask the student to do it over again." Their syllabi now included fewer papers but required more steps in writing each one: submitting outlines, giving and receiving peer critiques, discussing early drafts, getting faculty feedback, and, finally, submission of the completed papers. I wondered whether this added up to anything so I visited the director of Reed's writing program. She told me that, since this initiative had begun, bachelor's theses had become more coherent. Certainly, she told me, the computer makes it easier to rewrite and reorganize. But she suspected that the change revealed that this crop of seniors was better at critical thinking than their counterparts 5 years earlier. They had learned to hone their arguments, draft by draft. That day I asked a senior about what he'd learned about writing and he replied that "the only important draft was the last one." "In what course did you learn that?" I asked. He replied, "I don't think I could have learned that from just one course. But over a lot of courses, it gradually sank in" (Ehrmann, 1995, p. 26).

Traditional academic assignments used to (and many still do) conclude after the following conversational "turns": (a) faculty member presents the assignment to the student, (b) the student sends the completed work to the faculty member; (c) the faculty member sends a grade and comments back to the student, ending the discussion, and usually ending the student's thinking about that assignment even before reading the comments. In contrast, Reed faculty were extending and deepening that academic discussion. A few years later, a professor of philosophy remarked,

> I can't talk philosophy with undergraduates! They just don't know enough. Ah, but email! With email they have time to consider what's been said and to think about what to say next before they respond. If we're using email, I *can* talk philosophy with them. (Ehrmann, 2011, p. 37)

I understood still more about the potential of asynchronous exchange for developing critical thinking when I visited a Spanish class taught at the University of Arizona, where online written asynchronous discussion was substituted for language labs in two sections of Spanish III. Some of the topics posted for online discussion came from faculty, and just as many were initiated by students. One dealt with students planning a party, another with how to help a troubled fellow student. Students had to write Spanish—no English—with one another online. Only some of their discussion was graded at all, and that grade was only for the fluency with which they expressed themselves. Meanwhile, in other sections, students spent that time in a language laboratory; audio recordings led each student through drills in Spanish pronunciation, vocabulary, and grammar. I visited a section that was using online discussion. Its students were excited about using Spanish for their own purposes without having to worry about their accents. Asynchronous exchange also gave them the time they needed to translate what the other students had written, think about it, and decide how to reply.

At the end of the term, students in both sections took oral examinations of their ability to carry on a real-time conversation in Spanish. Despite the fact that the section using online conferencing had spent no time drilling their speaking and listening skills, those students scored better in conversational Spanish than the students from the language lab sections. Online asynchronous discussion helped students become comfortable expressing themselves in Spanish. During the final oral examination, doing so was second nature, so they could focus their attention on their accents (Smith, 1990). (After her tenure at Arizona, Karen Smith went to University of Central Florida [chapter 9]; their Faculty Center for Teaching and Learning was named for her after she died, far too young.)

The significance of Smith's study for fluent thinking transcends language learning. Any discipline, not just Spanish, requires that novices develop new capabilities for thought and expression. And mastery requires many healthy doses of conversation, much of it with peers.

Engaging in Active and Collaborative Learning . . .

The sort of asynchronous discussion that was just described is only one example of *active* and *collaborative* learning.

Active learning is a confusor. By one definition, *active learning* consists of visible student activity such as original writing or working with interactive software; by this definition, students in lecture halls are, by definition, learning passively as they sit silently and copy some of the speakers' words in their notes. This book, however, uses an equally common definition: *active learning* describes a way of thinking. By this definition, students listening to a lecture are learning actively if they mentally interrogate the lecture as it unfolds, for example by questioning how the lecturer's message relates to what they already know.

Collaborative learning, one type of active learning, involves interactions with one or more other students. It can take many forms, of which the most widely known include debates, role plays, competitions, team projects, seminar style discussion, games, and peer critiques. And, as a pattern of thought, it involves a meeting of the minds.

An early higher-education example of the potential of collaborative learning highlighted its importance in learning physics. Eric Mazur's YouTube video, *Confessions of a Converted Lecturer* (2009), recalls his slow realization that even his "A" students at Harvard University were fooling themselves and him; their high scores on final exams (and their high ratings of Mazur as a teacher) concealed the fact that they understood very little of what he tried to teach them about how the physical world works.

> I thought I was a good teacher until I discovered my students were just memorizing information rather than learning to understand the material. Who was to blame? The students? The material? I will explain how I came to the agonizing conclusion that the culprit was neither of these. It was my teaching that caused students to fail! (Mazur, 2009)

So Mazur began to experiment with techniques pioneered by physics education researchers (PERs). Eventually he developed an approach he called *peer instruction* that combined active and collaborative learning. As described in his video, Mazur began to ask students in the lecture hall conceptually challenging, multiple-choice physics questions, questions that could not be answered by simple recall nor by crunching numbers. The answer options were carefully crafted; all but one reflected misconceptions held by many students. To respond to his questions, students used a digital device nicknamed a *clicker* (today students usually use mobile phones instead). After students had all chosen their responses, a bar graph was displayed instantly to the learners; it charted how many students had chosen each response. If it turned out that many students disagreed, Mazur asked them to pair up; students would explain to their partners why they'd each selected their response. The lecture hall would roar as hundreds of students talked one on one. After a minute or two, Mazur repeated the original question; students were free to change their minds if their discussion had convinced them another answer was better. This second round of responses was usually closer to the mark. More important, the thinking and the conversation helped students, bit by bit, to think like physicists. End-of-course tests of conceptual understanding revealed dramatic gains by students, not just for Mazur but also for many other faculty members who tried peer instruction for the first time. An assistant professor once confessed to me that, when he used PER techniques like peer instruction for the first time, and did it badly, his students learned more than through his lectures, even though he was a good and experienced lecturer.

Let's look at just two more examples of applying active and collaborative activities to deepen student understanding in large enrollment classes. It's not a coincidence that all of these examples are drawn from science, technology, engineering, and mathematics (STEM) research; a disproportionate amount of the research on active and collaborative learning has been done in lower-division STEM courses. In those courses, active learning is the greatest departure from the norm. It's also easier in these courses for faculty to assess students' understanding and misunderstanding rather than being fooled by what students remember. I've chosen two specific studies of the impact of active and collaborative educational strategies, each because its way of assessing student understanding was memorable and powerful.

First is a study of a second-semester analytical chemistry course at the University of Wisconsin (Wright et al., 1998), which compared learning in two sections of the course, each section numbering about 100 students. The experimental section's entire semester featured frequent collaborative, research-like activities. The control section course was designed and taught by one of the department's most respected lecturers. Presentations in this section were carefully planned to encourage student questions and participation. The researchers observed earlier offerings of each section to confirm that each faculty member was actually teaching as advertised.

Then the researchers asked faculty in the department what kind of learning assessment could potentially produce findings that could persuade them to change how they taught their own students. The chosen method was one-on-one oral examinations of each undergraduate by a faculty member who was not their instructor. Each of the 25 faculty interviewers began by creating the criteria they would use to rate their eight interviewees' responses (four from each section, so all students were interviewed). Of course, the faculty interviewers were not told from which section of the course each interviewee came.

The investigators identified four different categories of criteria developed and used by the interviewers, and looked at the student ratings by each of the four groups of interviewers. In all four categories, the collaborative learning group did better. The most common category of approach (represented in 11 of the 25 interviewers' criteria) was to rate each student's patterns of thinking (e.g., as they responded to the interviewer, did the student self-correct? use a variety of perspectives? understand the larger context surrounding a particular problem? relate theory and practice?). The 44 students from the collaborative section who were rated on this criterion were far more able to use higher order thinking than the 44 from the lecture section.

Two decades later, a similar comparison, this time of a second-semester physics course, made headlines (Deslauriers et al., 2011), partly because its findings were published in *Science*, a preeminent journal for STEM research (not just STEM education research). Two sections of physics at the University of British Columbia, each with about 270 students, were studied. The sections met three times a week for 50 minutes each time. Both were taught by experienced, highly rated instructors. For 11 weeks both sections used identical teaching strategies; students in each section averaged the same scores on quizzes. Then, for week 12 only, the experimental section was taught differently. Before each of its three 50-minute classes, students were assigned a three- or four-page reading as well as a short true-false quiz about what they'd just learned from the reading. During class sessions, Mazur's peer instruction approach was employed. The class sessions also featured small-group active learning tasks and targeted in-class instructor feedback. In all other respects, the two sections were taught in the same way that they'd been taught for the first 11 weeks. The outcome? When both sections were tested for conceptual mastery at the end of the 12th week, the *lowest* scoring group of students in the experimental group did about as well as the *highest* scoring group in the traditional section. Also, attendance and classroom student engagement were both higher in the experimental section.

These one-course studies are no fluke. In 2020, a meta-analysis of 41 published studies of active learning in STEM fields, many of them from research-intensive universities, concluded that active learning helped everyone, but helped students from underrepresented groups even more. Active learning reduced performance gaps in examination scores by 33% and narrowed gaps in passing rates by 45%. These narrowed performance gaps were found mostly in courses that invested a lot of classroom time in high-intensity active learning. The authors hypothesized that these gaps could be narrowed further when students have plenty of coached, deliberate practice and when faculty use inclusive teaching approaches (e.g., helping students deal with imposter's syndrome—"No one knows it, but I really shouldn't be here") (Theobald et al., 2020).

. . . With Help From Learning Assistants

When section sizes are large, well-prepared *learning assistants* (LAs) can help faculty succeed with active and collaborative learning activities. Let's look into the uses of undergraduate learning assistants as a contribution to 3fold gains.

> A trained *LA* works with faculty to help students with the processes of learning. That's a broad-brush definition; many ways to use such students fall under this umbrella. And the various roles are called different things in different institutions. Some of the more common titles are *peer mentors, lab assistants, teaching assistants*, and *Supplemental Instruction leaders*. LA is a confusor because two institutions may make identical use of these LAs but have different titles for the role; similarly, two institutions may use the same title for their LAs but use them quite differently.

Typically LAs are only a semester or two beyond having taken this same course themselves. Their training and empathy should be good preparation for discovering how students in the course are thinking. They may help facilitate small groups in the course, making collaborative work more feasible for faculty to manage. They have often been trained to observe closely and ask questions in order to figure out what might help students learn for themselves. To put it another way, LAs are not there to give students answers or hints, but to ask questions that may help students see things differently. Because LAs work closely with the instructor, they know what the faculty member is trying to accomplish. As a result, LAs can help faculty understand what's working well and not so well for the class. In addition, LAs provide students with personalized attention at far less cost (thus improving affordability) than either graduate teaching assistants or smaller class sizes. Access benefits for underserved groups are also possible; having a mentor or two in the classroom can help faculty assist students with different misconceptions. Some LA programs are designed to provide targeted help for students in an underserved group (Crisp et al., 2017).

Guttman (chapter 7) has institutionalized the use of LAs; in 2018, the college employed about 60 undergraduate *peer mentors* in a variety of roles. Guttman's strategy for recruitment and self-selection of LAs parallels their practice for recruiting and onboarding new students: as the potential mentors decide whether or not to commit to the program, they're also getting a running start on their education as mentors. Two weeks before Guttman's Summer Academy (the bridge program for entering first-year students), the new cohort of peer mentors begins their own intensive 2-week training program, for which they are paid a competitive wage, just as they are paid for all training over and above their 12 hour per week commitment to mentoring. At some other institutions, LAs enroll in an academic course about, for example, relevant learning science, how to conduct inquiries into student thinking, and tactics for coaching and consulting. They earn credit rather than (or in addition to) wages.

Evidence is mounting that LA programs, by whatever name, can help transform courses and the curriculum, stimulate discipline-based educational research by faculty and LAs, and influence mentors to take up teaching as a career (e.g., Otero et al., 2010). Another example of the value of LAs comes from a study of course redesign at the University System of Maryland (Ehrmann & Bishop, 2015). In 12 redesigned courses that did *not* use LAs, D/F/Withdrawal (DFW) rates fell by 2 percentage points (e.g., from 24% to 22%, or from 12% to 10%). In contrast, in 25 redesigned courses that used LAs, DFW rates fell by an average of 8 percentage points.

Building a Spine of HIPs

As Jillian Kinzie described in the foreword, the National Survey of Student Engagement (NSSE) and the Association of American Colleges & Universities (AAC&U) identified a set of teaching and learning activities that seem to foster academic success, later labeling them HIPs (AAC&U, 2013; Kuh, 2008). The current list includes

- first-year seminars and experiences,
- common intellectual experiences,
- learning communities,
- writing-intensive courses,
- collaborative assignments and projects,
- undergraduate research,
- diversity/global learning,
- ePortfolios,
- service-learning, community-based learning,
- internships, and
- capstone courses and projects.

If you're not familiar with HIPs, Flack et al. (2018) posted an extended description of each HIP that you might find helpful.

Each HIP represents a major investment of student and program time; it can also serve as an observing post for assessing what students have mastered to date. So, in devising a curriculum map for an academic program, it makes some sense to first figure out how to assure that students engage in at least one HIP each year; and then develop the plans for cumulative learning around those HIPs, helping ensure that students are prepared to take advantage of each HIP opportunity.

Finley & McNair's (2013) analysis of the literature indicates that *well-implemented* HIPs not only improve learning for all but also tend to reduce achievement gaps between students from favored and underserved groups. The more HIPs in which students engage, the more likely those students are to earn a bachelor's degree within 6 years and the more they learn compared with their counterparts who have not had such an experience. HIPs benefit first-generation students, transfers, and those from different ethnic backgrounds to a similar degree.

> *Well-implemented* means that the local execution of an innovation is based on a good understanding of both its letter and spirit. Virtually all adoptions are actually adaptations. That is, the institution may have to tweak the innovation to ensure a better fit. The institution may also need to tweak itself for that same reason: to ensure the HIP will be successful at scale. In contrast, poorly implemented innovations only mimic certain features of earlier successes without emulating what helped those earlier programs be effective. For example, a poor implementation of undergraduate research might ask participating students to do only menial work for faculty. The moral here is not to trust literature reviews or meta-analyses that analyze all programs called *undergraduate research*, for example, without regard to what those programs actually do. At best, such analyses understate the innovation's effectiveness.

What's the source of this HIP magic? Kuh et al. (2017) ascribe it to

- performance expectations set at appropriately high levels;
- significant investment of concentrated effort by students over an extended period of time;
- interactions with faculty and peers about substantive matters;
- experiences with diversity, wherein students must contend with people and circumstances that differ from their own experience;
- frequent, timely, and constructive feedback;
- opportunities to discover the relevance of learning through real-world applications;
- public demonstration of competence; and
- periodic structured opportunities to reflect on and integrate learning.

Our six case history institutions rely heavily on many HIPs, including learning communities, undergraduate research, capstone courses, service-learning, internships, and ePortfolios. In addition, ePortfolios and capstones help make cumulative learning visible to students, faculty, and others.

Creating and Maintaining Affordable Educational Strategies

As I've mentioned, my first professional position was at The Evergreen State College. And almost immediately, I learned how an ambitious Integrative institution could nonetheless have about the same instructional costs per student as its peers. As I recall, the planners looked at what traditional regional institutions in Washington were spending per student and designed Evergreen's educational strategies so they would cost about the same. It was conceptually rather simple. In Evergreen's planned program students would take, and faculty would teach, only one program each quarter. To keep to the budget constraint, each program should be planned at a student to faculty ratio of 22 to 1. And that's how it was done. The programs were team taught and interdisciplinary but that didn't change the math. A three-faculty team should be prepared to educate 66 students, for example. If enrollment fell far short, one of the faculty team would be eliminated. I remember a study by the state higher education coordinating board that found that Evergreen had met its goal of having its marginal instructional cost be about the same as at other Washington State institutions.

Turning the Page

Within an Integrative constellation, educational strategies need to rely on and reinforce one another. For example, writing intensive courses can support the use of ePortfolios in that students' earlier practice in writing reflections for their ePortfolio helps prepare them for writing-intensive courses. Both are among the elements that can prepare students for a successful capstone experience.

Institutionalized educational strategies should support one another but, to be sustained and scaled, they also need to rest on appropriate organizational foundations. That's the topic of the next chapter.

11

ORGANIZATIONAL FOUNDATIONS THAT SUSTAIN INTEGRATIVE EDUCATIONAL STRATEGIES

From medieval times onward, institutions of higher education have relied heavily on Instruction-aligned educational strategies such as lecturing. Their *organizational foundations* developed to sustain and scale such strategies.

> *Organizational foundations* are attributes of culture, physical space, administrative structure, and policies that have evolved in part to sustain an institution's long-time educational strategies. For example, the Instruction Paradigm assumes that faculty have little influence over students' development of new capabilities; that's consistent with a faculty evaluation system that does not require that faculty assess student capabilities. In another example, Instruction-aligned courses are defined by their content; both the course catalogue and transcripts align with that educational strategy. Suppose that institution begins changing toward Integrative educational strategies. The old organizational foundations will hamper those efforts, unless the foundations themselves are realigned. As a reminder, within an institution's constellation for pursuing 3fold gains, organizational foundations are one of three domains, along with educational strategies (chapter 10) and interactions with the wider world (chapter 12).

Unfortunately, some organizational foundations that sustain Instructional educational strategies have the opposite effect on efforts to scale up Integrative (or Individualized) educational strategies. Table 11.1 illustrates

TABLE 11.1
Different Paradigms Need Different Organizational Foundations

Type of Foundation	*Supports Instruction Educational Strategies*	*Supports Integrative Educational Strategies*
Academic culture	Based on assumptions such as, "The students who do poorly are the poor students" and "In teaching, faculty should be left alone by colleagues and should leave colleagues alone"	Based on assumptions such as "Faculty can and should improve student learning by any means necessary" and "Sometimes, faculty need to collaborate with peers and staff to improve learning"
Faculty rewards for teaching	Based largely on student opinions and teaching load	Based largely on learning outcomes and their improvement
Learning spaces (physical and online)	Designed for presentation of content	Designed for active and collaborative learning and for presentations
Support for HIPs at scale	Instruction Paradigm assumes many students aren't good enough to benefit from HIPs, so scaling less important; used by only the best, most motivated students	Curricular design helps to ensure that every student engages in at least one HIP each year; organizational infrastructure exists to sustain and improve HIPs at that scale of use
Centers for Teaching & Learning	Marginally important; beneficiaries are usually faculty who are early adopters	Integral contributor to the institution's pursuit of 3fold gains; scaled to serve large numbers of faculty and instructional staff
Organizational unit(s) and budgets to aim, implement, and assess the pursuit of 3fold gains	Unnecessary because, according to Instruction assumptions, outcomes are the students' responsibility, not the institution	Several case histories highlight organizational units with at least some responsibility: for example, at Georgia State University, it's the Office of Student Success; for online learning at UCF, it's the Center for Distributed Learning; at several, it's the Office of the President

this difference in six pairs of organizational foundations that we'll explore in this chapter. One set (column 2) of organizational foundations developed to support Instruction educational strategies; the other set (column 3) can help the institution scale and sustain Integrative educational strategies

Organizational foundations such as those in Table 11.1 can't support different paradigms equally well. That's because they require mutually exclusive choices. A room configured for lectures (tightly packed seats in rows) hampers collaborative learning, while a flexible classroom is an awkward and inefficient space for nonstop lecturing. So faculty and staff whose work aligns with Instruction assumptions (e.g., content delivery) are likely to oppose efforts to shift toward Integrative-friendly foundations. Another source of opposition will be people who don't see the necessity of changing time-honored practices and policies.

We'll focus on just enough of these widely used and influential organizational foundations to understand their roles and explore one or two ways in which each foundation can be transformed to support Integrative educational strategies. At the end of this chapter, we'll mention additional foundations that are common to and influential in institutions shifting toward the Integrative Learning Paradigm.

Academic Culture

The National Survey of Student Engagement (NSSE) team took a closer look at 20 institutions that had been systematically improving student engagement. They identified six conditions that matter to student success (Kinzie & Kuh, 2004). I don't think it's a coincidence that the following conditions relate at least partly to academic culture:

- "Living" mission and "lived" educational philosophy
- Unshakeable focus on student learning
- Improvement-oriented ethos
- Shared responsibility for educational quality and student success

I saw signs of all four in our six institutions. These elements of culture are important because they reinforce Integrative educational strategies.

How is it possible that an Instruction-aligned culture can hamper the spread of Integrative educational practices? A decade or so ago I recall reading an online post about a young engineering faculty member at a regional state university; the post was written by the director of the institution's teaching center. This assistant professor was dissatisfied because too many students in one of his courses received poor grades or failed. So, aided by the teaching center, the faculty member reconsidered the goals of the course, then its assessment methods, and then its design and materials. The new design was more competency-based, designed to help each student master the material. In the first offering of the revamped course, performance on quizzes and final exams improved sharply; almost no one failed. Shortly afterward, the dean of engineering summoned the young professor. The dean complained that any course in which the average grade was so high must be sacrificing rigor, lowering its standards. The young professor tried to persuade his superior that the course was, if anything, more rigorous than before by showing the dean some of the new assignments, tests, and test results. The dean didn't look at them and warned the assistant professor that his tenure chances were at risk. So the junior faculty member simply scrapped the new design and reverted to the old one. Student grades and failure rates reverted. Soon the director of the teaching center left the university.

So, to pursue Integrative educational strategies, such an institution's culture will need to be gradually realigned. Our cases suggest at least two strategies. At Georgia State (chapter 3), early initiatives yielded surprisingly large improvements in the rates at which students passed courses. The improvements became a source of visibility and pride for the institution, and the additional revenues were plowed back into the next wave of improvements. Many faculty became convinced that they and staff could positively influence the development of students, beyond simply conveying content, and that realization was a culture shift.

At University of Central Oklahoma (UCO, chapter 8), evaluation of student work prompted an unanticipated cultural change among faculty. For several years, the faculty development initiatives that support the Student Transformative Learning Record (STLR) had helped faculty design assignments that both fed into the student course grade (using content-relevant criteria) and also into the STLR snapshot of the students' development (using criteria related to one of the other five tenets). The faculty judge the student's work (for the grade) and also the student's reflective essay about its influence on their development (for STLR). Here's the surprise: It appears that judging these essays influenced what faculty believe about teaching. Some students described specific ways in which the assignment and the course were helping change their lives. For faculty accustomed to thinking of teaching as content delivery, this was a revelation. Some faculty wrote (as inputs to the evaluation of the Title III grant) how this experience helped them see that they could have far more influence on students' futures than they had imagined. STLR shows every sign of cumulatively impacting cultural change in at least some departments. In 2020, I'm sure that many faculty already believe in their role in student development. But this realization constituted a changed worldview for at least some faculty.

Another way to change cultures relates to helping faculty develop the concepts and terminology needed to describe their own teaching in ways other than content coverage. In the early 2000s, I sat in on a planning session for a 5-year, $4 million teaching improvement project called the Visible Knowledge Project (VKP), led by Randy Bass and Brett Eynon (Bass & Eynon, 2009). One of many project elements was expecting participating faculty to keep a reflective journal about their teaching over the 5 years of the project so that they and others could see whether and how their approach had changed. A faculty member on the planning team applauded the idea, but hesitated: "I tried to write such a journal entry about my own teaching. But I couldn't do it, because I have no language to describe how I am teaching my courses." It's hard to improve what you can't describe.

This inability to describe features of learning and teaching makes it harder for faculty and academic administrators to get past confusors and develop a shared sense of how their institution has been working or to develop a shared plan to improve the future. In chapter 10, we suggested the importance of collaborative learning to develop students' capabilities for critical thinking. The point holds for faculty as well. Traditionally, faculty teach in isolation from one another; traditionally, faculty have little or no formal education about teaching and learning in higher education. As the VKP anecdote suggested, artisans of teaching may lack robust, grounded concepts to compare what they have been doing to what they might be doing. (*Grounded concepts* are derived from specific instances in order to identify a class of such instances.)

The multi-institution Global Skills for College Completion project was created to promote such faculty–faculty discussions that could develop grounded concepts. Led by President Gail Mellow of LaGuardia Community College and funded by the Bill & Melinda Gates Foundation (Mellow et al., 2015), the project is worth attention, both for its conclusions and its methods, methods that could be adapted by any institution. Rosemary Arca, an English professor at Foothill College, described her experience:

> For example, if we noticed an activity that seemed to create a supportive learning environment for students, we tagged it Comfort. When we noted an activity that scaffolded study habits expected in college, we tagged that College Transition. If we saw a lesson that required analysis, evaluation, or synthesis of text, we tagged it Higher Order Thinking Skills. The tags, or specific descriptors of classroom practice, were grouped into categories or themes that we discussed and refined over the lifespan of the project. Themes included student support, learning environment, instructional

> design, challenges in instruction, and instructional evaluation. Tags within those themes included, for example, accessibility, community building, contextualization, metacognition, and baseline of student knowledge. Over time we created a shared archive of lessons and activities that matched the tags. (Mellow et al., 2015, Foreword, para. 7)

The experience was transformative for Arca:

> For me, the process was heady and humbling. The weekly online posts about what we did in one lesson in one class and the reflection about that class were powerful meditations on what I was doing in the classroom. I had to be an honest reporter of my own practice by using the categories of reflection required by the project. I gained a deeper understanding of pedagogy and what worked (or didn't) in the lesson I'd taught and recorded. (para. 4)

Faculty Roles and Rewards

In the earlier chapter on three paradigms (chapter 6) we described some of the differences in faculty roles between Instruction-aligned and Integrative-aligned institutions. For example, the Instruction Paradigm assumes that a student's ability to learn can't be affected by faculty, whose job it is to convey content. Quality, it's assumed, relates to inputs (e.g., faculty expertise including their research, SAT scores of entering students). Good teaching takes effort but it's well understood; no substantial formal preparation is required. Also, the Instruction Paradigm defines courses in terms of content and assumes that each faculty member is in charge (only) of their own courses.

In contrast, the Integrative Paradigm assumes that faculty and the institution can enhance (or diminish) how well students can learn. Their job includes developing students' abilities to apply the content they've learned. The results of teaching, and of its improvement, influence the quality of learning and the equity of access. Teaching and learning are academically challenging and deserve significant preparation of and on the part of faculty. Also, the Integrative Paradigm assumes that faculty need to spend some of their teaching time in collaboration with colleagues and staff.

Instruction assumptions about the faculty role align with some elements of the faculty rewards system, such as its lack of attention to learning outcomes of the courses and academic programs for which faculty are responsible. One result is overemphasis in the faculty rewards system on student evaluations of faculty performance.

What promotion and tenure (P&T) criteria should an Integrative institution consider?

- *Improving learning and its outcomes*: Perhaps most importantly, Integrative institutions recognize that it's unlikely that they're already doing the best job possible of educating their students. That's why, at institutions like Guttman (chapter 7), P&T cases can be strengthened by the faculty member's history of inquiry and experimentation to improve student learning, especially where the work has been critically reviewed and published in some fashion. (The formal name for this activity is the *scholarship of teaching and learning*, an area of faculty endeavor that is supported by professional societies, including in many disciplines, and by dedicated journals.)
- *Team contributions*: Guttman also assumes that an integral part of a teaching load is the time faculty invest as part of a leadership team (e.g., for a learning community and its house of first-year students). It's also important to credit faculty contributions to teams that work to improve degree program outcomes (quality, access, and affordability).
- *Preparation for interdisciplinary work on real-world problems*: For faculty to teach in an interdisciplinary program, they'll need significant preparation in relevant findings and methods from other disciplines. Consider a program on climate change, for example: Economics should be not be a mystery to an ecologist in such a program, and vice versa. Interdisciplinary programs may also benefit from faculty experience working outside the academy on climate change-related issues. If an institution wants to develop the capacity to offer a highly effective program on climate change-related work and careers, its reward system should encourage faculty to invest time preparing themselves.

Also needed in an Integrative faculty roles and rewards system is the creation of trusted channels for importing and exporting important innovations and experience for pursuing 3fold gains. Not Invented Here (NIH) is a curse at many institutions that assume only home-grown solutions have a chance of success. That's a time-saving assumption, certainly. I remember the first grant proposal I wrote; it included this sentence: "So far as I know, no one has done anything like this." I've been "plagiarized" ever since, as I discovered during almost 20 years reviewing other people's grant proposals! As a grant-maker, I rapidly became convinced of the converse: "Whatever I need has already been conceived and tried elsewhere." So the challenge is to search for just enough of those ideas and experiences. This is a familiar task for faculty doing research in their own disciplines. It seems likely that the most productive faculty researchers are also those with the best networks that actively help them identify and filter the most important research elsewhere. The same is likely to be true in the pursuit of 3fold gains: The institutions that accelerate most quickly and achieve the most are also likely to be the ones whose people have the best networks with likeminded pioneers elsewhere.

How can such networks be developed? And what role could the faculty reward system play in encouraging them? The answer, I think, is something we've already discussed as the most important element to add to the faculty rewards system: encouraging the scholarship of teaching and learning. Especially important is encouraging faculty to build on the work of colleagues elsewhere and to selectively disseminate their findings, methods, and experience. The kind of communication that P&T systems should encourage occurs when someone says to someone at a different institution, "I know enough about your efforts to improve learning to think you might find this new development interesting." Attempts to share such findings and resources help create issue-focused networks (e.g., around using LAs in history courses). Later, those network members have some shared history to help them decide who needs to know about this and how much priority to give incoming suggestions from this individual. I learned about these networks from a study we did of teaching innovations by MIT faculty that were later used (or not) at other institutions (Ehrmann et al., 2006).

Learning Spaces

Any particular *learning space* makes it easier for faculty or students to engage in certain activities. A well-lit classroom with close-packed theater-style seating can help faculty see and hear comparatively large numbers of students while helping students see and hear the instructor. These favored activities are called *affordances* of that particular kind of learning space.

Learning space is a confusor. In this book, learning spaces are the facilities, both physical and online, that are used for teaching and learning activities. To be clear, a learning space is not a pedagogy. I've heard many people ask, "Do students learn worse (or better) online?" The question makes no sense. As we've noted already, students learn because of what students do. Learning places are where students can do things. The more empowering the space is for students, the more choices they have about what to do; the same is true for faculty.

Affordances suggest but don't dictate what actually happens in such a real or virtual room. For example, as I learned as a freshman, a professor can lecture nonstop to six students seated around a table in his office. Conversely, in chapter 10, we saw how physics professor Eric Mazur fosters a roar of productive student–student dialogue in a large lecture hall with tightly packed seats.

Integrative educational strategies need spaces, physical or online, that easily support at least some of the following activities. I'm guessing you know at least as much as I do about the kinds of physical learning spaces with such affordances so, for the most part, I'll focus on describing them online in hybrid or fully online programs.

- *A place for the meeting of many minds*: Some learning spaces are designed for interaction between a learner and some kind of academic resources, for example, a reading room in a quiet space. In this book, however, we're going to focus on affordances that help small and large groups of people understand one another and do things together. Integrative courses, especially those with large enrollments, will probably need to alternate between periods of one-to-many (plenary) interaction (faculty explaining, a few students asking questions or responding) and breakout sessions small enough so that everyone can be expected to play a part. Some of these interactions might be between pairs or trios of students, while others might involve groups of, say, nine students.
- *Enabling more (kinds of) people to participate*: Think back to the days before colleges were invented; comparatively few people could spend time with a peripatetic scholar, and not much time at that. One motive for creating colleges and campuses was to allow more people to spend more time interacting with each other. Scholars and students who couldn't live on or near campus were out of luck. Today's online and hybrid offerings make it far easier to include students who can't participate in daytime, on-campus sessions. And some faculty have realized how easy it can be to include outside experts when the course is online. One format (which also works well in professional development of faculty, administrators, and other staff) is to have students read something and then be able to ask questions or respond to the author. Remember, however, that no learning space is completely inclusive. The affordances of the space ought to align with priorities for inclusion as well as for quality and affordability.

- *Audibility*: The Integrative challenge is to choose learning spaces in which students in small groups find it easy to participate fully. In a large physical space, the toughest challenge is being able to hear one another when a large fraction of students are talking simultaneously. In an asynchronous online session, students can write to one another. In a synchronous online session (e.g., with Zoom), the class can be split into small groups in which students in the group can hear one another and only one another.
- *"Moving the chairs"*: In large classes aligned with Integrative assumptions, students benefit from periodic small-group breakout sessions. Many campuses have at least a few classrooms specifically designed so that a class can easily and repeatedly shift from faculty communicating with all students to students working together in small groups while the faculty (and perhaps learning assistants) circulate, listen, and look over students' shoulders. Such rooms are expensive to build and furnish. With appropriate online systems and policies, small group work is far less expensive when it is done online, either synchronously or asynchronously.
- *"Rewind"*: The instructor's and outside experts' messages need to be available for learners to repeat for a second chance at understanding. In a large campus classroom, cameras and processing are required to make past sessions available to stream online. But it's a useful service. An undocumented survey of students in over a dozen lecture capture courses that we did at George Washington University (GW) asked students how important recorded lectures were for their grades. About half replied that, if deprived of the recordings, their grades wouldn't suffer. A quarter said that the recordings were useful but probably didn't affect their grades. And the final quarter said that their course grades would probably have been lower. We speculated that this last group of students may have included students whose native language wasn't English, students with learning disabilities, and, equally important, students who couldn't think as fast as the instructor talked. Some students could benefit from recordings of their breakout sessions in a large class. Face-to-face (F2F) they could use their phones, if the session weren't too big and the room not too noisy. Zoom, for example, enables online participants in breakout sessions to record those sessions, both the audio and what unfolds on their screens.
- *Pointing and explaining*: In small groups, students sometimes need to display an image or video; they then discuss it while pointing to a relevant element (e.g., "this spot on the X-ray"; "this moment in the film"). Other students may join the discussion, pointing to the

original material or to another image or video that they add to the first. Equipping a classroom to support small group discussions in this way can be expensive. In the right kind of online learning space, synchronous or asynchronous, there's usually no extra cost to support this style of small group work. These learning spaces can also support coaching of novices by experts, near-peers, and peers.

- *Pacing discussion and exchange*: In chapter 10 we talked about some uses of online communications in support of development of critical thinking skills, specifically with respect to allowing time for reflection. Table 11.2 sorts out different kinds of learning spaces that each can support discussion and exchange.

As Table 11.2 suggests, within the broad categories of face-to-face and online learning spaces, there are many specific options, each with its own affordances. Some options are selected as part of course and program design, and faculty and students choose some individual options (e.g., students doing assignments in their living spaces, workspaces, library, or on a campus lawn).

The cost of adding more learning spaces when enrollments increase is certainly less for online courses (adding more servers) than for F2F (building more classrooms). That same cost-saving advantage holds when enrollments

TABLE 11.2
Examples of Learning Spaces for Discussion and Exchange

Type of Space/ Pace of Interaction	*Face-to-Face*	*Online*
Synchronous	The campus, including living spaces and a variety of campus classrooms, laboratories, performance spaces, corridors, and open spaces; off-campus sites for service-learning, internships, study abroad, and traveling to a site for a face-to-face meeting	Telephone, audio conferencing, texting, Zoom, screen sharing with sharing of cursors and annotation tools
Asynchronous	The campus, homes, library, workplaces and other sites where faculty create and grade assignments, and where students work on them	Threaded discussion in a learning management system; texting; annotation and markup tools for discussing course content; video and sound editing tools

shrink substantially: With physical classrooms, some costs persist even if the room is unused for many hours (or months) at a stretch. Online, there's almost no cost to reducing the number of learning spaces. Chapter 10 on educational strategies summarized some persuasive evidence that well-implemented active and collaborative learning activities could substantially improve learning outcomes. So can high-impact practices (HIPs), almost all of which involve intensive interpersonal interaction from time to time. So how are learning spaces like campuses, asynchronous communication, and synchronous communication likely to affect the use of these high-powered learning activities?

As we saw at the University of Central Florida (UCF, chapter 9), evidence suggests strongly that students in its blended programs (combining online and F2F interaction) on the average perform a little better, are a little more likely to persist, and give slightly higher student ratings than students in fully online and fully campus-bound courses (Dziuban et al., 2018). One reason for that persistent advantage, over the years and across institutions, is that faculty teaching blended (hybrid) courses can usually choose from more kinds of learning spaces and affordances than can faculty teaching fully on-campus or fully online courses. What faculty and students do in each of those three spaces determines how big or small an outcome advantage blended spaces have.

Foundations for Scaling and Sustaining HIPs

To make 3fold gains using an Integrative approach, the institution needs to offer HIPs on a large enough scale so that every student is likely to engage in, say, one HIP each year. Our institutions have adapted their foundations to make this scaling more feasible, such as an office that develops and sustains research opportunities in the local area and beyond.

Instead of focusing on a single foundation, let's focus on a single HIP, undergraduate research (UR), and the variety of adjustments to foundations needed to support it at scale. (The Council on Undergraduate Research [www.cur.org] is a good starting point if you want to examine this question in depth.) When I was appointed vice provost at GW, the institution had several supports for undergraduate research. The provost was determined to make UR more ubiquitous and more visible. Here's a quick list of some of the ways we changed the organizational foundations for our UR over the next 3 years.

- The provost and the College of Arts and Sciences expanded their UR budgets to help pay students to do faculty-mentored research over the summer, and to subsidize faculty who wanted to use undergraduate research assistants.

- We institutionalized an annual research day for student posters to be displayed and judged, and as interest increased, doubled it to a 2-day event.
- A council of associate deans worked to engage the large numbers of faculty and students needed for research days to succeed. This UR council began advising the provost's office on other elements of strategy for boosting UR.
- We appointed three faculty fellows, each a long-time, well-known champion of UR, to work with our UR office. Their most important responsibility was to visit GW individual departments to learn about how that degree program was currently supporting UR (e.g., courses that prepare students to do research). The fellows also talked with departmental faculty about how other departments were increasing engagement in UR.
- We worked with the registrar and departments to assure that each department had approved course numbers for summer research. Having UR appear on student transcripts was one way to document their work and signify its importance. These "courses" were zero-credit, so students were not charged tuition for doing this extra work in the summer.
- The university's job-hunting web service was adapted so that students seeking research opportunities could be matched with faculty seeking undergraduate research assistants.
- The development office solicited alumni donations to support students' UR work.
- To help fund-raising, we created several memorable narratives about students' research for fund-raising literature and presentations. A website was created to display descriptions of students' UR. Those narratives also contributed to our second goal: making UR a more visible feature of GW for its stakeholders.
- Several questions were added to the comprehensive graduating senior survey about the nature and value of their UR, enabling us to assess and publish information about the extent and nature of UR from year to year.

The point here is that, to scale and sustain an Integrative educational strategy like UR, quite a lot of changes may be needed, including a number of different organizational foundations, some easy to tweak and others more difficult (e.g., arranging for every department to offer a zero-credit undergraduate course for summer research). The UR effort as a whole was also an effort to adjust the culture so that faculty at this research-intensive institution would embrace a HIP that aligned with research.

Centers for Teaching and Learning (CTLs)

The existence of formal offices on college campuses specifically to support teaching began in the mid-20th century. Subject to ebbs and flows based on funding availability and campus politics, their numbers have been increasing since. Some institutions delegate the support of teaching to a single faculty member with a part-time appointment, others have a large dedicated professional staff. (If your institution does not already have a CTL, it should; the Professional and Organizational Development Network in Higher Education [www.podnetwork.org] is a good starting point.) Such offices typically offer workshops on teaching strategies for faculty and other teaching staff, personal consultations on teaching issues, mentoring programs for new faculty, and a resource library on teaching. Let's talk briefly about what happens to CTLs as an institution shifts from Instruction to Integrative approaches in pursuit of 3fold gains and what roles CTLs might play in that development.

It's safe to say that, for institutions aligned with Instruction assumptions, CTLs are of only marginal significance, usually both small and transient. In part that's because the Instruction Paradigm assumes that teaching is a well-understood activity that smart people can master on the fly if necessary. So there's no reason to equip such a CTL for much outreach; compare CTLs' budget and staffing for outreach to faculty with the admissions, alumni, and development offices' budgets for stimulating external interest and engagement. Another aspect of this marginality is that CTLs in Instruction institutions are often free to set their own agendas, with faculty advice, because few other offices and academic units have reason to care deeply about what the CTL does. All this helps explain why's it's not uncommon for institutions to create a CTL, kill it some years later, and start a new one a decade after that.

For an institution shifting toward the Integrative pursuit of 3fold gains, the nature and role of the CTL needs to be redefined. Such a CTL ought to be a vital partner in a large cross-silo coalition to improve specific facets of the quality of learning, equitable access, and stakeholder affordability of the academic program. We've seen that happen at UCO (chapter 8). A small, marginal teaching center was transformed into a larger, much more strategically important Center for Excellence in Transformative Teaching and Learning (CETTL). CETTL's creation of STLR exemplifies this shift in CTL roles. The STLR project has an institutional scope (e.g., deepening learning in extracurricular, cocurricular, and curricular spheres; assessment; faculty development and course improvement; and academic records). UCO's CTL manages it all, in close collaboration with institutional leadership and other relevant elements of the university. CTLs won't always be the leader—that's not how coalitions work—but for many initiatives they will be a player in setting agenda and implementing plans.

At some institutions, supporting instructional applications of technology is a responsibility of the CTL. We didn't mention this in chapter 3, but Georgia State's Center for Excellence in Teaching and Learning (CETL) in 2019 had this additional responsibility and about 140 staff to serve the main and branch campuses. CETL instructional designers worked with several departments to create new online masters programs. Putting a course or degree program online is a splendid opportunity for faculty, supported by staff and services, to reconsider its goals, assessment tools, materials, and student activities. At UCF (chapter 9), the Center for Distributed Learning (CDL) has about 90 staff members; they often work closely on course redesign with UCF's Faculty Center for Teaching and Learning (FCTL), which has an additional 10 staff.

Finally, in institutions that are becoming more Integrative, spreading infectious teaching ideas is an important role of CTLs. These institutions will, sooner or later, focus more on 3fold gains by their degree, general education, and other academic programs. Changing a degree program requires a group of engaged, prepared faculty and is a more extensive challenge than helping individual interested faculty improve a single course. To help lay the foundation for such educational strategies, CTLs will need an outreach strategy to engage large numbers of faculty in making small, low-risk, easy-to-appreciate changes in their courses. For example, to prepare the ground for better online courses, the CTL might assist faculty who have an itch to improve the quality of student discussions in campus courses. That's far more easily said than done. It's unlikely that such a strategy would work, especially at a large institution, purely by staff reaching out to faculty. At a large institution, the CTL may need to develop an easy-to-use system for faculty to glimpse what a new teaching pedagogy can accomplish, find research on why the goal is important, or access peer assistance in getting past some typical problems for novices. Harvard's *Instructional Moves* (2020), the University of Maryland's *Improve My Teaching* (2020), and Carnegie Mellon's *Solve a Teaching Problem* (2020) web pages are just a few of the scalable approaches helping faculty from their own institutions (and others) explore teaching problems and opportunities. At least two companies, the Association of College and University Educators and the Faculty Guild, also offer scalable support.

I'd add that, for a menu-driven, step-by-step search for material, faculty are more likely to be engaged when they know from the start that some of the use cases will be relevant to their discipline. For example, in spreading the notion of peer instruction, humanists might be more likely to take a serious look if they already know that at least some examples of trigger questions to ask students come from a humanities discipline. One of the challenges for CTL staff is to find, curate, and disseminate disciplinary examples of the teaching strategies they promote.

Organizational Infrastructure to Target, Implement, and Assess Pursuit of 3Fold Gains

To illustrate the variety of ways in which institutions can set a direction, launch initiatives, and assess their collective impact, here are highlights from three of our case histories.

Georgia State University (chapter 3) began its infrastructure development with the appointment of Associate Provost Tim Renick, who identified as a priority work to consolidate data and coordinate administrative supports relating to student success. From the start, the infrastructure aligned with the assumption that all students could be more successful if the institution gave them a fair chance. Over the years, thanks in part to the obvious success of its first initiatives, Georgia State increased the influence of this infrastructure by including more organizational elements. The cycle of its work uses evidence to identify unnecessary barriers to student success, design an initiative to lower that barrier, and evaluate the success of the initiative.

UCO (chapter 8) began by expanding a coalition of academic administrators who wanted to organize a scattering of student success initiatives so that they aligned with common goals. The coalition guided the institution's growing commitment to transformative learning and to the six tenets (essential learning goals for the academic program). The coalition also took steps so that each tenet was supported by an organizational center. Next came the creation of CETTL. The biggest step forward in infrastructure came with the Title III grant that CETTL helped to win. The grant supported the creation of the STLR and its associated infrastructure, consisting of people associated with certain extracurricular and cocurricular activities who were trained to assess student submissions to their STLR record, and a grant-making and faculty development capacity to help interested faculty create STLR assignments in their courses and to assess student STLR submissions.

At UCF (chapter 9), in retrospect an important first step was offering an online course in vocational education that embodied many important evidence-based approaches to teaching and applying them online. The success of the course, including its surprising enrollment, helped convince deans that UCF's new online courses should embody President Hitt's goal of offering the best education in the state. As faculty needs to develop online courses grew, so too did the supportive infrastructure such as CDL. It was perhaps a lucky coincidence that UCF also had a professor, Charles Dziuban, who wanted to study UCF's online and hybrid programs. Incorporating the research of his small group into CDL helped assure that UCF would gain increasing insight into its own educational activities as the online program continued to grow.

Turning the Page

This chapter describes a few common and powerful organizational foundations for supporting Integrative educational strategies. We skipped a number of other foundations that are also common and powerful: academic technology infrastructure and services (e.g., UCF); data analytics and proactive online services for advising (e.g., Georgia State); changes in academic departments (e.g., Guttman Community College); and changed roles for adjunct faculty (e.g., Governors State). This network of organizational foundations in effect points inward; they're the institution's ways of supporting its own Integrative educational strategies. Obviously it's not possible to strengthen even one foundation overnight; as we've said, constellations (including their elements of organizational foundations) are generally grown and refined over many years.

The next chapter, "Leveraging Interactions with the Wider World," delves into the third domain of an institution's constellation for pursuing 3fold gains: how it manages its interactions with its wider world.

12

LEVERAGING INTERACTIONS WITH THE WIDER WORLD

This part of the book began with the observation that institutions shifting toward the Integrative pursuit of 3fold gains need to develop a constellation of appropriate elements, both institutional attributes and recent initiatives. Constellations consist of initiatives in three overlapping domains: Integrative educational strategies (chapter 10), supporting organizational foundations (chapter 11), and aligned interactions with the wider world. Specifically, this chapter considers five examples of how institutions have managed their wider world interactions in order to support their Integrative shifts and their pursuit of 3fold gains. We'll take a look at how institutions

- leverage forces from the field,
- nurture communities of transformation across institutions,
- seize opportunities created by accreditation,
- take Integrative advantage of open educational resources (OERs), and
- recruit and prepare new students for Integrative teaching and learning.

Leverage Forces From the Field

An influential external publication can sometimes spark internal action. For example, the national report *Learning Reconsidered* struck the University of Central Oklahoma (UCO, chapter 8) "like a lightning bolt" (p. 90, this volume). As a result, student affairs and academic affairs began working together even more closely to improve student learning. That happened at UCO (but not at many other institutions) because UCO's constellation, including senior leaders who had already been thinking along the same lines, had laid the groundwork for this report to stimulate another step forward.

Wider world concerns beyond education can provide occasions for an Integrative institution to take another step. Climate change is a perfect example because it's compellingly motivating, and because it's neither well-understood nor the unique province of a single discipline: economics, biology, and chemistry are just a few of the fields that might help educate students to understand and respond to climate change. It's an Integrative opportunity because of the virtual necessity of interdisciplinary learning and because, from the Integrative point of view, high-impact practices (HIPs) such as learning communities, undergraduate research, ePortfolios, internships and service-learning can all be employed.

While some changes in the wider world (e.g., declining job markets in certain fields) almost force an institutional response, in most cases internal champions need to explain the urgency and opportunity created by these shifts. Their role includes suggesting a meaningful, feasible institutional response (in the UCO example, what specifically academic affairs and student affairs could do better together than separately).

Nurture Communities of Transformation

All six institutions in this book, five Integrative and one Individualized, collaborate in many ways and at many levels with other institutions doing similar work. Several of our institutions (e.g., University of Central Florida [UCF, chapter 9], UCO) have created or helped to create annual conferences and peer-reviewed journals. Some participate in multi-institution projects to help their member campuses advance their agendas for student success. Many of their individual faculty, staff, and administrators keep in close enough touch with colleagues at other institutions, sharing information back and forth; sometimes those connections result in publications or in proposals for panel presentations at association meetings. Such scholarly activity around teaching and learning can influence the priorities of funders, especially when champions at institutions go to the trouble of sustaining long-term conversations with leaders of foundations and government discretionary grant programs. Adrianna Kezar and Sean Gehrke coined the term *communities of transformation* (CoTs) to describe collaborations among people across many institutions that support similar improvements across those institutions (Gehrke & Kezar, 2016; Kezar & Gehrke, 2015). To choose just one example, UCO helped create and lead the American Association of State Colleges and Universities (AASCU)'s American Democracy Project (ADP). ADP in turn was a valuable step forward for UCO toward its central six tenets, work on transformative learning (TL), and the Student Transformative Learning Record (STLR). All of these interactions helped create robust networks of people across institutions with some grasp of one another's interests and achievements. When something novel tickles the antennae of one member, they may well reach out to some of their colleagues at other institutions who would appreciate learning the news.

At the institutional level, such long-term, broad investment in progress and networking creates conditions for institutions on the move to make further progress. *"Not Invented Here"* (NIH) is the belief that only home-grown ideas have a chance of success at home. Our six institutions have demonstrated that they believe the opposite; call it "Everything Was Invented Elsewhere" (EWIE). In pursuing 3fold gains, they all use existing lateral relationships to import ideas, export local achievements, and work collaboratively toward shared goals (e.g., improving academic success for a particular ethnic group, or scaling up service-learning). Doing so enables institutions to avoid unnecessary duplication of effort and learn from the mistakes of others.

Such interpersonal relationships do not snap into existence overnight. Usually they're the fruit of years of casual connections. Mutual understanding grows slowly about what the other is working on, what they might have to offer, and what they might need. I learned this partly from a study about how certain MIT faculty teaching innovations were able to take root (or not) in other institutions (Ehrmann et al., 2006). Institutional policies that could nurture such CoTs include periodically inviting participants in coalitions to share what they know from outside that could be useful inside; supporting and rewarding the scholarship of teaching and learning (SoTL) by faculty and staff; putting on small conferences with nearby institutions with similar concerns; and providing travel support for faculty and staff for conferences and visits to other institutions.

Guided pathways were described as an educational strategy in chapter 10; when they span two or more educational institutions they can help ensure that the later institution gets new students who are prepared for an Integrative academic program. Effective pathways between institutions require some transformational collaboration among faculty and administrators, as the Governors State University (chapter 4) experience illustrates. President Maimon and each community college president first had to spend quite a lot of time getting to understand and trust one another as a first step to building CoTs that included administrators and faculty in both institutions.

Not all CoTs are ad hoc. Institutional or professional organizations also stimulate the growth of networks for selective information sharing and mutual support. It's my impression that, among our five Integrative institutions, Association of American Colleges & Universities (AAC&U) and AASCU were most often mentioned as sources of ideas, collaborators, and appreciation, that is, places where their own work can be judged in the context of what other institutions have been doing. For example, UCO's work with AASCU on ADP (civic engagement) created an early foundation on which subsequent work on TL and the six tenets could build. Interviewees at most institutions mentioned the influence of AAC&U, especially its Liberal Education and America's Promise (LEAP) program (AAC&U, 2017) and its Valid Assessment of Learning in Undergraduate Education (VALUE) rubrics (AAC&U, 2018b).

Some grant-funded CoTs are stand-alone entities rather than projects sited in formal associations. These free-standing projects often sustain themselves with institutional dues and, in some cases, additional grants. A few communities came up in my institutional interviews:

- Achieving the Dream is a consortium of over 250 community colleges dedicated to attacking inequity and increasing social mobility. It began with a Lumina Foundation grant in 2005. It's had real impact on student success efforts, including developing a sense that community colleges need to engage as institutions, not just as a collection of faculty and courses.
- Complete College America was created in 2009 to increase college completion rates at 2-year and 4-year institutions, improve job-related credentials, and narrow the gap in college attainment for traditionally underserved populations. It has statewide projects across the country.
- The University Innovation Alliance (UIA) has helped coordinate and synthesize work at 11 major research universities, including Georgia State and UCF. Michael Crow of Arizona State has chaired the group since its foundation; Mark Becker, president of Georgia State, is cochair. From its founding in 2014 through 2019, UIA institutions have increased their output low-income bachelor's graduates by about 30% per year, and graduates overall by 16%. That's nearly 13,000 additional graduates.
- The UNIZIN Consortium emphasizes equitable access and stakeholder affordability ("Affordability, Access, Retention, Graduation") and advances those goals with digital technologies such as online proactive advising, data analytics, OERs, and setting standards for sharing data within and across institutions. In 2019 UNIZIN had 25 member institutions, mainly research-intensive public universities.

Imagine a group of individuals who think their institution has done absolutely nothing yet to pursue 3fold gains. They want help to get started. I'd suggest they alter their assumptions. They and their institution almost certainly have some useful attributes and at least a few recent initiatives that align with Integrative values. What has been learned, including from failures?

What questions does the current work suggest? In what formal or informal CoTs do we already participate? That kind of critical discussion can lay the groundwork for considering the kind of CoTs that could be most valuable for next steps. We'll talk more about getting started in "Implementation: Beginning the Intentional Pursuit of 3Fold Gains" (chapter 14).

Seize Opportunities Created by Accreditation

Since the 1980s, accreditors of colleges and universities have slowly increased their attention to institutional goals and the improvement of institutional outcomes. Requiring institutions to frame learning goals for academic programs was an early step in this direction. More recently, some regional accreditors began offering institutions the option, or perhaps the requirement, of including in their self-study a major institutional improvement project; the project and its outcomes would be reported in the institution's next self-study. One of the regional accreditors, the Southern Association of Colleges and Schools Commission on Colleges (SACSCOC), calls these projects Quality Enhancement Plans (QEPs). Since 2004, SACSCOC institutions have been required to propose, conduct, and assess QEPs as part of the regular cycle of accreditation and reaccreditation.

Georgia State and UCF both took advantage of the QEP to advance their constellations for pursuing 3fold gains. UCF's 2016 QEP, What's Next, focused on enhancing Integrative learning for professional and civic preparation. UCF's definition of Integrative learning, adapted from AAC&U's, is the ability to develop skills across multiple experiences and to adapt those skills to new problem-solving contexts. To show how well-aligned this is with the larger themes of this book, here's a brief quote from UCF's QEP website.

> *What's Next* seeks to help students *plan* for their futures post-graduation: to not only set goals but to identify the knowledge and skills necessary to reach those goals. The initiative encourages students to *connect* their classroom knowledge and skills to real-world contexts and, thereby, to develop the ability to transfer knowledge and skills from one context to another. Finally, this initiative promotes opportunities for students to *reflect* on their experiences, to communicate their knowledge and experiences, and to develop the ability to successfully advocate for themselves in their lives beyond the university. (University of Central Florida, 2020, para. 5)

UCF's Division for Digital Learning (DDL) is represented on its QEP advisory council by two of its senior staff. Connections like these help assure that DDL operates as an integral contributor to UCF's pursuit of 3fold gains. Georgia State has had two QEPs that contribute to the development of its constellation. Its case history describes the 2019 plan, College to Career. Its 2009 QEP focused on enhancing critical thinking through writing, which also aligns with Integrative educational strategies (chapter 11).

The takeaway is that an accreditation requirement like the QEP creates a compelling opportunity to invest in, implement, and evaluate a significant improvement. If the institution is considering a more intentional Integrative pursuit of 3fold gains, it's extremely important to design a QEP that will last beyond the accreditation requirement and perhaps evolve over a decade or more so that the constellation expands rather than churns. The initiative ought to reinforce, and be reinforced by, other elements of that institution's constellation. The SACSCOC's QEPs almost always focus on improving at least one essential learning outcome (e.g., foundations and skills for college success and lifelong learning, critical thinking and analysis, or communications skills) by using practices such as learning communities and other HIPs, and assessment of the project's outcomes are an important element (Smith, 2017). That's more evidence that a requirement like a QEP can be exploited to contribute to an institution's constellation and ultimately to its 3fold gains.

Use Open Educational Resources

Open educational resources (OERs) have garnered the most attention as a way to make major reductions in textbook costs while making those materials available to the student when, or before, the semester begins; both are both hugely important. Our interest, however, is in how to support, scale, and sustain Integrative educational strategies. *OERs*, especially of a particular kind, can make a significant contribution to an Integrative shift.

OER is a confusor. This book uses David Wiley's definition (2018):

> The terms *open content* and *OER* describe any copyrightable work (traditionally excluding software, which is described by other terms like *open source*) that is either (a) in the public domain or (b) licensed in a manner that provides everyone with free and perpetual permission to engage in the 5R activities:
>
> 1. Retain—make, own, and control a copy of the resource (e.g., download and keep your own copy)
> 2. Revise—edit, adapt, and modify your copy of the resource (e.g., translate into another language)

3. Remix—combine your original or revised copy of the resource with other existing material to create something new (e.g., make a mashup)
4. Reuse—use your original, revised, or remixed copy of the resource publicly (e.g., on a website, in a presentation, in a class)
5. Redistribute—share copies of your original, revised, or remixed copy of the resource with others (e.g., post a copy online or give one to a friend)

Instead of the restrictive conditions of a traditional copyright, authors and publishers of all sorts of OERs can substitute a license for users describing how their materials can and can't be used. They should consider including some or all of these five rights in the license. An organization called Creative Commons (CC) (Creative Commons, 2018) supports the OER movement in part by providing templates for such licenses.

In contrast, *OER's* other widely used definitions don't necessarily include any of those five rights. For example, *OER* sometimes include any instructional materials that are available to students at no cost (the institution may well need to pay the vendor a license fee). Some people assume (incorrectly) that all OERs are textbooks, or that OERs are inevitably of lower quality than published materials.

OERs can be very helpful for Integrative educational strategies (e.g., active learning, collaborative learning, HIPs). The 5R activities make it easier for students to use tools and resources to create their own work using resources from many (OER) sources and enable people outside the academy to use the students' OERs and the students' work to create new OERs. If your gut reaction is, "This guarantees plagiarism!" please reconsider. Authors of OERs allow, and sometimes require, that they receive credit when someone else incorporates their contribution into a new OER.

This book has often referred to the crucial importance of cumulative learning. Here are a few examples of how OERs can be valuable for Integrative educational strategies. Depending on the terms set by the author in a CC license, students could:

- Write their own textbook by splitting the work and researching their assigned topics (O'Shea et al., 2011). Alternatively, students in an advanced course can deepen their understanding of the basics by creating instructional materials for a less advanced course. If some of the sources found are OERs, students have the option of adapting them for the specific needs of the course without waiting for permission from the original authors or publishers. Their new OER textbook

can later be made available around the world; faculty elsewhere could, for example, assign their own students the task of upgrading specific elements of the OER textbook. Foreign language students might be assigned to translate an OER textbook into a new language.
- Compose or design creative work that incorporates music, images, videos, or text from other OER works.
- In a service-learning course, create OER materials for use in neighboring communities. The materials might be health care guides, indices of local community service resources, or instructions for how to do something. If their work is available online, service-learning activities elsewhere might adapt them by incorporating local information.

OERs create options for materials that are continually improved by their users. In all these cases, the students need to conform to the license requirements set by the original author (e.g., giving them credit or not selling the new work). Faculty, too, can create or adapt instructional resources for needs for markets that are too small to interest a conventional publisher. The inclusion of a CC license permits other scholars to further adapt or expand the original work.

Recruit and Prepare Students

One thing I learned from Guttman Community College (chapter 7) is that recruiting and admissions necessarily have at least two outcomes: assembling a group of students to enter the program who may or may not realize what this college experience will be like, and preparing them (or not) to hit the ground running as students.

Integrative institutions ought to use their efforts to gain a competitive advantage in recruiting. A good start is to depict students as agents of learning rather than as objects of teaching. All six case history institutions at least allude to their reforms in their online recruiting materials, and some do much more. Governors State's website emphasizes the student as agent in a web page entitled *An Ordinary Freshman Year Won't Do* (Governors State University, 2020a):

> Your freshman year at Governors State University is no ordinary first year of college. It is designed to give you a foundation on which to build during your college career and for life after GSU. As part of a challenging academic community, you'll learn strategies and skills to become a critical thinker. You'll become confident in your abilities as a student and as a member of a diverse community. You'll explore majors and programs through your sophomore year, [providing] you with a solid foundation of values-based learning . . . preparing you for a world that changes almost daily.

The Guttman case study describes how recruitment, admissions, and a 2-week summer bridge program assemble an incoming class that is prepared to engage in Guttman's Integrative education from the beginning of the semester. For example, students join their learning communities and begin doing things together in the bridge program, and then remain in those communities for their first year of college. Guttman's website details these educational strategies. Here is the text that dominated the *About Guttman* page in 2019:

> Created to deliver a community college education with a focus on student achievement and timely completion, Guttman's unique and innovative model features:
>
> - A multistep comprehensive admissions process with prospective students;
> - A mandatory Summer Bridge Program for incoming students before the start of the fall semester;
> - All first-year students are required to attend on a full-time basis and are grouped in learning communities to foster collaboration, teamwork, and peer accountability;
> - Structured core curriculum; no choice of courses in first year;
> - No remedial courses; developmental support is built into the curriculum;
> - Longer academic calendar; 18-week semesters keep students in school September through July to remain on track to complete their studies;
> - Limited number of majors with well-defined pathways to degree, transfer and/or careers: Business Administration (AA); Human Services (AA); Information Technology (AAS); Liberal Arts & Sciences (AA)—Social Science & Humanities Track and Science & Math Track; and Urban Studies (AA);
> - Peer Mentors, Student Success Advocates, Career Strategists, and Graduate Coordinators support students academically, professionally, and personally;
> - Guttman Global, Guttman-Chase Part-Time Teller Pathway Program, and other transformative experiential opportunities (Guttman, 2019a, para. 1).

Most of the programs and practices listed included live links to additional explanatory material.

Deciding what to feature and how to describe it is itself an interaction with the wider world when marketers test out different messages with focus groups of potential students. For example, Southern New Hampshire University (SNHU)'s College for America (CfA) (chapter 5) learned to substitute terms like *project-based* and *course* for *competency-based* to help its nontraditional practices feel familiar to potential students. CfA also took a radically different approach to recruitment, one well suited to its intended student body of working adults. As its case history describes, CfA does not use direct mail, advertising, or any other means to recruit students one by one. Instead, they create agreements with businesses and community service organizations to provide a CfA education as a benefit. Depending on tuition assistance arrangements, the education is likely to be either free or discounted. It has taken a little longer than expected for these partnerships to mature, but CfA enrollments have been steadily growing.

Turning the Page

We've looked at just five of the many ways in which an institution can support its Integrative educational strategies by managing relationships with its wider world: by leveraging forces from the field, nurturing CoTs, exploiting accreditation as an opportunity, engaging with the wider community of producers and users of OERs, and managing how it recruits and prepares students for entry. These are just examples. We didn't talk at all about the important topic of recruiting and preparing new faculty, administrators, and staff and many other strategies; we'll get into other examples of wider world relationships in "For 3Fold Gains on a National Scale, Change the Wider World, Too" (chapter 15).

Now it's time to put the pieces together in a unified Integrative framework for making 3fold gains. Part Five, "Doing It," discusses why the reasons for making Integrative 3fold gains are so universally compelling; the use of paradigms to understand where an Integrative institution is coming from and where it's headed; an Integrative constellation that includes educational strategies, organizational foundations, and wider world interactions; guidance for institutions in assembling and using such a constellation to make 3fold gains; and feasible steps to change the wider world so that it, too, encourages institutions to make 3fold gains.

PART FIVE

DOING IT

So far, we have argued (chapter 1) that improvements in quality, equitable access, and stakeholder affordability are urgently needed, on a national and institutional scale. That's the first piece of our framework: widely understood, compelling reasons to change the status quo. The second piece is using the Instruction Paradigm to describe many elements of how the work of higher education is currently organized, a rationale that also helps explain why the Instruction Paradigm is increasingly seen as ineffective and inefficient as a means for making 3fold gains. In contrast, the assumptions of the Integrative Learning Paradigm help explain where the institution needs to change. (Chapter 6 describes these paradigms and their roles.)

In Part Five, chapter 13, "A Framework for Pursuing, Scaling, and Sustaining 3fold Gains," summarizes a vision of an evolving, improving higher education. It's not pie in the sky. In fact, all its elements are already in use by our case history institutions and many others. As this chapter explains, to scale and sustain the pursuit of 3fold gains, a constellation needs to be a growing collection of mutually supportive institutional strengths and initiatives across three domains: Integrative educational strategies, organizational foundations to support those strategies, and adjustments to wider world interactions that also help sustain and scale those strategies.

Suppose a cadre of people in an institution suspect this new framework might be important for their institution's future. What should they do first? Actually "first" is misleading. It's likely that every institution can take a fresh look at itself, especially its recent history, and find at least a few existing elements and embryos that align with the Integrative framework. So to rephrase, what should the institution do *next*? "Implementation: Beginning the International Pursuit of 3Fold Gains" (chapter 14) suggests possible next steps.

In "For 3Fold Gains on a National Scale, Change the Wider World, Too" (chapter 15), this book, for the first time, looks at individual institutions from the outside, not the inside. It outlines several feasible changes in the wider world that together could encourage larger numbers of institutions to blaze their own trails toward 3fold gains.

This framework is suggestive, not comprehensive. Institutions don't need to adopt all elements of a constellation described in chapter 13. Nor is the framework final: it's inevitable that additional elements will be added to the menu for Integrative constellations, that additional compelling rationales for the Integrative shift will be uncovered, and that additional steps to implement the pursuit of 3fold gains will be put to the test. The framework described in this book is a jumping-off point.

13

A FRAMEWORK FOR PURSUING, SCALING, AND SUSTAINING 3FOLD GAINS

Chapter 1 documented the importance and urgency of improving quality of learning, equitable access, and stakeholder affordability on a national scale, which, in the United States, implies large numbers of institutions each making their own improvements. Doing so in a fragmented, bottom-up fashion can be self-defeating: Initiatives inevitably compete for scarce time and money and they may conflict substantively as well. In contrast, the institutions studied here have each assembled their own constellations of mutually supportive institutional features and initiatives. Each addition should increase the constellation's leverage for improving quality, access, and affordability on an institutional scale (chapter 2). For these constellations to be sustainable, it's important to align elements of educational strategies, organizational foundations that support those strategies, and interactions with the wider world that sustain those strategies and foundations (chapters 10–12).

This chapter draws on material from earlier chapters to summarize a framework that institutions can use to achieve Integrative 3fold gains; chapter 14 discusses how to implement a constellation over the years.

Wherever Possible, Aim for 3Fold Gains

As a reminder, when a mutually supportive set of institutional features and recent initiatives are intended, together, to produce improvements within quality, access, and affordability, we call that set of outcomes *3fold gains*. Because these elements are intended to work in concert, the constellation can attract a coalition working over many years to achieve the goals. In contrast, when quality is pursued separately from access or affordability, iron triangle assumptions come into play (e.g., that widening access will weaken quality and vice versa).

Constellations Should Align With Integrative Assumptions About Learning

The second element of the framework is the notion that a paradigm—a consistent set of assumptions about learning and how best to support it—can be used to align elements of a constellation so they will support each other. Chapter 6 began by describing the Instruction Paradigm's assumptions, for example, that students' attributes (e.g., aptitudes, attitudes toward studying) are set by the time students enter college and that faculty and institutions are powerless to influence those attributes. The Instruction Paradigm assumes that the beating heart of college learning consists of an expert explaining things while students take notes. It also assumes that teaching, learning, and university governance are so intellectually simple that faculty can learn enough about them informally and on the job. Many elements of an institution may currently align with this paradigm.

Almost the opposite of the Instruction Paradigm are our two learning paradigms, Integrative and Individualized. The learning paradigms assume that colleges can and must help students develop their attributes, aptitudes, and capabilities. Also, such learning almost always requires more than a single formal course; meaningful and lasting student development develops across a number of courses plus experiences outside courses. The Integrative Learning Paradigm also assumes that, to foster student development, many dimensions of interpersonal interaction—student–faculty, student–student, and between students and important people outside the classroom—can be invaluable.

In most institutions, many constellation elements align with Instruction assumptions. For example, most classrooms assume that the faculty member is more or less fixed in front of the classroom and furniture is designed for students taking notes. Faculty recruiting may prioritize evidence of subject expertise and skill in explaining the subject. Our case history institutions have taken steps to realign some of their practices with Integrative assumptions.

It Takes an Appropriate Constellation to Make, Scale, and Sustain 3fold Gains

Broadly speaking, an institution's constellation is a set of consistent educational strategies, and of organizational foundations and ways in which the institution manages its interactions with the wider world in order to sustain those strategies. It takes time to change a constellation, more years than it takes to change any one element of that constellation. (A partial exception to this rule is institutions like Guttman [chapter 7], which was designed from the start to institutionalize Integrative educational strategies.) Even institutions that have been moving in the Integrative direction for 15 years or more are still expanding and refining their constellations.

There's no one ideal model of an Integrative college or university. But from the case histories of our five Integrative institutions have emerged some areas of overlap among their constellation elements. Let's start with some of the more common Integrative educational strategies.

Setting Compelling 3Fold Goals for the Institution and Its Programs

By *compelling* I mean that, with enough time and money, the goals for quality, access, and affordability are attainable and, partly because of that, can elicit the lasting commitment of enough faculty, middle managers, donors, and other relevant stakeholders. (If the initial goals don't attract the right mix of stakeholders to invest time or money to advance them, consider changing the goals.) Few if any of these goals for quality, access, and affordability can be delegated to a single course, or to only one cocurricular or extracurricular activity. Instead, institutional and programmatic progress can be made toward goals if enough elements promote cumulative gains.

Creating an Integrative Constellation: Educational Strategies

Some Integrative educational strategies may not have spread far (yet). The Student Transformative Learning Record (STLR) program at the University of Central Oklahoma (UCO, chapter 8) and its influence on course design comes to mind. But some strategies are in wide use already and have been the subject of extensive research.

To achieve 3fold goals, evidence cited in chapter 10 suggests the surprising gains that can be achieved with a critical mass of well-implemented *active and collaborative activities.*

Some *high-impact practices* (HIPs) are among the most powerful forms of active and collaborative learning (e.g., writing intensive courses, undergraduate research, and service-learning). Capstone courses and ePortfolios are HIPs with double benefits: They deepen student learning while also giving students, faculty, and the institution more insight into how students have progressed toward essential learning outcomes.

An additional way to help students learn to think about their thinking is through the moderate pace of asynchronous online discussion and exchange (e.g., debates, peer review of work, role playing simulations, dialogue about difficult questions). Classrooms tend to encourage a pace of interaction that's too fast for most students to engage in critical discussions. Ideally, asynchronous exchange should complement real-time (synchronous) interactions (e.g., F2F discussion, phone calls, video conferencing). An additional benefit of a faculty, staff, and student body adept in online exchange is that it increases the speed and grace with which an institution can respond to catastrophe (e.g., University of Central Florida [chapter 9]).

Organizational Foundations in Constellations

The right organizational foundations can help institutions scale and sustain Integrative educational strategies, as detailed in chapter 11. Here are a few foundations that several of our institutions have been realigning.

Academic culture should affirm the possibility and importance of developing student capabilities and attributes that help them use the content they have learned and will learn after graduation. It should recognize the importance and difficulty of making access to excellence available fairly. And it should recognize the feasibility and importance of making education more affordable to students and other stakeholders. The culture needs to value formal and informal preparation of faculty as experts in teaching as well as content, and it needs to value evidence as a primary guide to action. Cultures can be influenced from several directions. One such influencer is early initiatives that demonstrate that significant, lasting improvements are possible.

Faculty roles and rewards ought to focus more on faculty contributions to quality, access, and affordability. Both roles and rewards ought to recognize that faculty working in a team can sometimes make contributions to 3fold gains that isolated individuals cannot, and that some of the most important outcomes are meaningful only when they're cumulative. The rewards system, in my opinion, ought to drop the Instruction assumptions that the most important faculty contribution to learning is talking in a classroom while students listen. In contrast, the Integrative Paradigm makes the evidence-based assumption that students learn by what they themselves do. So Integrative faculty roles include creating environments in which students of all kinds can develop the critical, creative, and collaborative capabilities needed to work on unscripted problems in unfamiliar contexts. Many of those problems ought to challenge students to draw on what they've learned both formally and informally in their lives. Because of the Integrative assumption that these activities are crucial contributors to 3fold gains by students and by the institution, the faculty rewards system ought to be aligned to encourage these kinds of teaching activities. (Chapter 7 described how Guttman Community College does this.)

Learning spaces, physical and online, need to support many kinds of interpersonal interaction and active learning. SCALE-UP classrooms that facilitate active and collaborative learning for 100 or more students in a studio-like setting are just one example of how pedagogical planning needs to articulate with space planning (National Research Council, 2015, p. 150). Learning spaces resembling the MILE classrooms at Georgia State (chapter 3) reflect a different Integrative educational strategy, one in which student learning is guided by computer tutorials and by advice and feedback from peers and experts in the room. UCF has been a leader in harnessing blended and fully online instruction to contribute to 3fold gains. In any circumstances, blended courses have a special ability to improve student performance and affordability; meanwhile, both faculty and students become more adept and comfortable with online activities. HIPs, too, often need infrastructure to be sustained at scale. For example, Guttman's (chapter 7) office of community partnerships supports internships, service-learning, and other HIPs by matching students with partners in New York City.

Centers for Teaching and Learning (CTLs) need to play a strategic role. CTLs aligned with the Instruction Paradigm are usually small, likely to set their own agendas, and sometimes short-lived. In Integrative institutions, in contrast, many such units play roles in fostering institutional and programmatic 3fold gains. Sometimes the CTL leads; often it is a major partner. Integrative CTLs need to be bigger and more influential than in Instruction institutions, and coordinated with the agendas of other members of coalitions. At UCF, for example, the Center for Distributed Learning has taken on some of this responsibility.

Organizational infrastructure is needed to support the pursuit of 3fold gains. In a way, the entire university comprises this infrastructure. But it's essential to have an organizational unit, perhaps in the office of the president or provost, that supports and guides work toward 3fold gains. The leadership of this office and of the institution should insure that various kinds of stakeholders each provide some leadership in this work. This office should coordinate and support the most promising initiatives for strengthening the emerging constellation. Georgia State's Office of Student Success was the first such unit that I learned about; its annual reports to Complete

College Georgia (Georgia State University, 2018) provide one model for building a constellation and making the initiatives and their outcomes visible to stakeholders.

Wider World Interactions in Constellations

As described in chapter 12, there are many interactions with the wider world that can help scale and sustain the pursuit of 3fold gains. Here are a few.

The needed approach to *recruiting new students, faculty, and staff* is suggested by the expression "you are what you eat." To the extent that new students want what the institution is beginning to offer, they're more likely to be successful. For example, web-based recruiting messages from two of our case history institutions are geared toward students who want to be agents of their own learning, not just beneficiaries of instruction (chapter 12). Active forms of learning and engagement with the world outside the college can be emphasized too. One way to strengthen an institution's constellation in pursuit of 3fold gains is to demonstrate that the changes thus far are drawing more students, especially those who already value Integrative learning. To the extent that new faculty and staff have track records of special relevance to the pursuit of 3fold gains, it becomes easier to scale and sustain that pursuit. Along with recruiting the newcomers must come preparing them. Guttman is one important model of how recruiting and onboarding should be combined.

Communities of transformation are networks of individuals and, often, of institutions that share a commitment to making some kind of academic progress (e.g., service-learning, laboratory research for online students). Countless such networks appear, flourish, and sometimes dissolve. More are needed, especially by those institutions that are not yet close to the leading edge of development. To invent an example, there may not yet be a network of academics and institutions in the midwestern United States that are trying to start and scale programs of agriculture-oriented service-learning. But once institutions or individuals have gotten some kind of start on the issue, institutions can stimulate the genesis and support of networks by, for example, sponsoring cross-institution visits to share insights, recognizing faculty and staff contributions to two-way sharing of experience and developing multi-institution proposals for funding. Based on my own experiences as a program officer, funding programs know they don't have the resources to help every relevant institution do its own thing. So discretionary funding programs are more likely to pay attention to grant proposals from multiple institutions for activities that could benefit them all.

Exploit accreditation. Accreditors sometimes offer opportunities for institutions to focus on new initiatives that can strengthen their constellations. Chapter 12 highlighted how two of our case history institutions had used regional accreditor Southern Association of Colleges and School Commission on Colleges (SACSCOC)'s requirement for a Quality Enhancement Plan to add sustainable initiatives to their constellations. For Integrative institutions, the pursuit of 3fold gains ought to influence such proposals.

As described in chapter 12, *open educational resources* (OERs) are universally available materials whose licenses for use allow incorporation or alteration of the source material. Creators can choose OER licenses that impose a few or no restrictions on how the resulting work is altered, distributed, and cited. OERs can contribute significantly to Integrative constellations encouraging students learning by doing; for example, learning how music works by adapting and analyzing OER music. When OERs are used, the student is free to distribute their own work as an OER. My guess is that the more prevalent are an institution's interdisciplinary student projects, the more student work could be enhanced by adapting and combining materials from many sources.

The Need for Digital Technologies

Across the three domains of an Integrative constellation, we've seen examples of how appropriate use of digital technology can strengthen initiatives: asynchronous exchange supporting the development of critical thinking; offering students more challenging problems and more powerful tools and resources for addressing them; the special roles of OERs; tools enabling advisers and faculty to quickly identify students who may need a little guidance; online learning spaces; communities of transformation that provide resources and support wholly or partly online. These uses of technology are enabling, not driving. And they are virtually always a small but vital element of effective initiatives. UCF provides just one example of how valuable digital technologies can be when treated as one ingredient among many. The further ahead an institution is in making 3fold gains by relying partly on online courses, activities, and services, the more prepared that institution is to provide quality learning and equitable access in affordable ways when disasters strike.

Turning the Page

We can oversimplify this whole framework in just three sentences. Paradigms provide a rationale for constellations. The constellation's elements should reinforce one another's impact across three domains (educational strategies, organizational foundations, wider world interactions). It usually takes many years to build a constellation big enough and well-aligned enough to make visible, valuable 3fold gains.

Chapter 14 suggests how individuals can begin shifting their own institutions toward the intentional pursuit of 3fold gains.

14

IMPLEMENTATION

Beginning the Intentional Pursuit of 3Fold Gains

Implementation is the process by which a typical institution begins to intentionally apply something resembling our framework to achieve 3fold gains. Institutions created from birth to be Integrative have a head start in building their constellations. In this chapter, however, let's think about how an institution begins its shift toward the pursuit. Because a journey of 1,000 miles starts with a single step, what might that step be for an institution? How can it be taken successfully? In this chapter we focus on the following implementation steps with special relevance for institutions using the Integrative Paradigm:

- Describe current assets for making Integrative 3fold gains
- Identify three kinds of goals
- Create committed coalitions ("We can't not do this!")
- Consolidate and validate the evidence that's already being collected
- Encourage senior leaders to work as a team
- Periodically add a few new initiatives to the constellation
- Don't forget the time
- Be alert for confusors and hidden assumptions
- Overcommunicate with stakeholders
- Evaluate the constellation's outcomes and elements

There's no single correct order for these initial steps; they're all potential beginnings. Georgia State University (chapter 3) started by creating a data warehouse. University of Central Oklahoma (UCO, chapter 8) started with a new president who wanted to develop future leaders. University of Central Florida (UCF, chapter 9) began with a single online continuing education course for public school vocational education teachers. Start with any of these activities or with something different if that makes more sense. All the steps are interconnected. In fact, you'll probably need to return to each of them at least once.

Describe Current Assets for Making Integrative 3Fold Gains

Comparatively few institutions have begun intentionally creating a constellation for achieving 3fold gains. But once such a constellation is considered, a possible first step is to realize that Integrative elements in the form of institutional attributes and recent initiatives are probably already in place. Some Integrative educational strategies, such as capstone courses, internships, and ePortfolios, may already be in place in boutique or scaled-up form. In some degree programs, faculty may periodically pool what they know about a student and discuss how to help that learner succeed. Some academic programs may already be using their goals for quality, access, or affordability to adjust their program's design. Some programs and courses may be getting good at teaching students how to write reflections about their work. Some organizational foundations may also exist. How many classrooms already have movable chairs and tables? Has the academic technology unit made headway in helping faculty use digital technologies to improve learning outcomes? Perhaps some wider world interactions already align with the institution's Integrative efforts. Do at least some departments or schools expect all new faculty hires to have some track record of working to improve student learning? Does recruiting of new students tout project-based learning and undergraduate research as signatures of the institution? Begin by inventorying what's already in place to lay the groundwork for the Integrative pursuit of 3fold gains.

Identify Three Kinds of Goals

The goals of *quality of learning, equitable access*, and *stakeholder affordability* are too broad and vague to put an entire institution into motion, but galvanizing goals can be created within those categories. Part of what got Georgia State moving was recognizing that the high attrition rates of African American and Hispanic students could be improved by institutional action. Adding fuel to the fire was the obvious fact that the university was only a mile from Martin Luther King Jr.'s birthplace. Graduation rates and speed to graduation (within 6 years) became measures of quality and equity as well as a way of increasing affordability for both the students and the institution. At Governors State University (chapter 4), an important educational strategy was adaptation of the essential learning outcomes (ELOs) formulated by the Association of American Colleges & Universities (AAC&U, 2018a). Governor State's access crusade had two overlapping drivers: *first generation (!) students* (i.e., potential students who have no one in their immediate or extended family or even in their neighborhoods who have ever graduated from college) and community college graduates who wanted a 4-year degree. The guided pathway from community college through the 4-year program also had the benefit of speeding students toward a degree, increasing affordability.

One goal was notable for its absence across the case histories. Over the years, I've seen institutions treat certain programs as cash cows, creating surpluses that could be reallocated to subsidize other programs and activities that spent more than they earned. I never heard that motive across our six institutions, even at those institutions that were actually were creating such surpluses. Chief Information Officer (CIO) Joel Hartman has already been quoted in the UCF case history: "The decisions that optimize chances for financial gains are different from the choices that optimize academic gains. Academic success can lead to financial success, but the reverse is seldom true" (personal communication, 2020).

Think of your own institution (or an institution with which you're familiar). Within the broad areas of quality, access, and affordability, what potential outcomes could mobilize faculty, administrators, benefactors, and other stakeholders? Can these potential gains also motivate students? To achieve meaningful gains can easily take 5–10 years, so the goals you're defining shouldn't be just an issue du jour. Here's a tip: Motives that will remain compelling for years may well have already been compelling for years, but there may have been little progress because people didn't yet see how to achieve the change.

Create Committed Coalitions ("We Can't Not Do This!")

Goals may begin with shame, pride, or some other motivation, but they don't galvanize cross-silo collaboration until there's also some confidence that a planned response could work. Sometimes all that's needed is for one institution to see a competitor succeed with a strategy they hadn't previously imagined. For decades in the mid- to late-20th century, some universities offered degrees in labor studies; courses, of course, were taught on campus. Then one university in New York created a labor studies program with classes that met in a union's halls. A few years after that, I bumped into someone from labor studies at a different New York university. With quiet pride, he reported that their labor studies courses met in union halls. I asked if this had anything to do with that first university's success. After assuring me that this university was doing things differently, he went on to say, "Once we heard someone else was doing this, we couldn't *not* do it. People who normally ignored or opposed one another's ideas united around this idea." To teach an entire degree program at an off-campus site, imagine the kind of committed cooperation would be needed among faculty, with administrators and staff, and with the union.

From our case histories, perhaps the most obvious example of a galvanizing idea was the impact of *Learning Reconsidered*, the national report that hit UCO "like a lightning bolt." The report defined, "*learning* as a comprehensive, holistic, transformative activity that integrates *academic learning* and *student development*, processes that have often been considered separate, and even independent of each other" (Keeling, 2004, p. 2). The report went on to link this unified concept to the goals of liberal and transformative learning. Working backward from student outcomes clarified how important student experiences outside courses were to achieving traditional academic goals (p. 26). That vision provided a firm foundation for the six tenets and, later, STLR.

Another example: At UCF, the surprising success of their first online learning course and its pedagogy helped unite several deans behind the idea of getting into online learning, while requiring that faculty creating their first online courses be given extensive preparation and support. The agreement that online learning exemplify the best ways to help students learn influenced the whole trajectory of UCF's development and evaluation of online and blended learning.

In all these examples, the problem or opportunity was compelling for many elements and individuals—not for everyone, but enough for a big enough coalition to get things moving. Although it has been outside the scope of this book to look into what other institutions were doing at about that same time, each of the six case history institutions was stimulated by and built upon the achievements and aspirations of other pioneering institutions. Some of those outside initiatives provided evidence that our institutions' plans were feasible. It's easier to create and sustain a coalition when its strategies are at least somewhat proven and when its immediate goals therefore seem within reach.

Consolidate and Validate the Evidence

Georgia State's systematic pursuit of 3fold gains has been guided almost since the start by collecting data from many sources, validating it, cleaning it, and consolidating it so that administrators could easily get answers to questions relating to student progress. Early steps of data cleaning and consolidation are important for establishing base lines. Five, 10, and 15 years into the future, institutions will want to document whether quality, access, and affordability have changed and if so, how. A complementary approach highlights the work at UCF; their scholarly team has been studying blended and online learning locally for many years, developing and testing new ideas and relating their work to research being done elsewhere around the world. This is another example of using evidence to decide next steps. In both of these institutions and in others, evidence has played a role in attracting new resources to the work; both Georgia State and UCF have used evidence to make the case for greater internal funding as well as for foundation and government grants.

Encourage Senior Leaders to Work as a Team

Institutional shifts toward more Integrative constellations are unlikely to get very far without periodic prompting and support from senior leaders. In some of our institutions, action was initiated by a president (e.g., Governors State) or an even higher power (CUNY, which created Guttman as an Integrative college). In interviewing people at UCF, I often heard how President John Hitt repeatedly declared, orally and in writing, the importance of improving quality, access, and affordability. Integrative gains can only be made when there's extensive collaboration between the provost and other senior leaders. That kind of collaborative commitment is more likely when presidents reward it with their attention and support.

Several of our institutions had an informal cross-silo steering group of senior leaders. At UCO, they named themselves the Burrito Brothers. At UCF, they referred to themselves as the Four Musketeers. Those labels reveal that no single member of these groups was the boss of the others, and suggest the shared purpose, mutual trust, and good humor that characterized these self-created groups. Most of the best leaders have a habit of working through coalitions of people who don't report to them; that's perhaps the biggest difference between the best leaders and average ones (Boyatsis, 1982).

Periodically Add a Few New Initiatives to the Constellation

It's rare that an institution has the attention, staff time, and money to implement more than one or two major initiatives at the same time. Yet the institution is invariably a roiling stew of ideas, problems, resources, and occasions. From time to time, some of them stick together and a plan of action begins to emerge.

Early on, the leadership group ought to inventory major initiatives to alter the academic program, its foundations, or relevant interactions with the wider world. Some initiatives will have been conceived with no reference to any notions about 3fold gains. The institution likely can't afford to do them all, or even to refine them all as plans. Earlier we suggested considering what elements of a potential Integrative constellation are already present, at least in embryonic form. Closely allied with that inquiry is asking what proto-initiatives are being considered, initiatives that could be reframed as part of the constellation. All major proposals for initiatives compete to some degree for attention, people's time, and money. Sometimes they're also competing for permission to apply to a certain source of funds.

Only occasionally does an institution have the opportunity to dispassionately choose among all major initiatives seeking support. But it makes sense to compare initiatives as though they were in such a competition. Here are a few perspectives that might help sift the most important initiatives from the almost as important:

- How would the proposed initiative make a visible, valuable contribution to the constellation for achieving 3fold gains for the institution (or the relevant academic program)? At Georgia State, they might ask the question this way, "If this proposed initiative succeeds at scale, will its contribution to improved retention, graduation, and affordability likely to be large enough to notice? To matter?"
- Integrative initiatives usually require cross-silo backing and implementation. Does the proposed initiative rank high enough on the priority list for each of those silos?
- Are we sufficiently confident that this can be scaled, assuming its pilot test succeeds? For example, assuming that the pilot demonstrates what a scaled implementation could mean for the institution and its students, will the institution be able to marshal the resources needed to scale and sustain it?
- Have we allowed time for the learning curve—time for enough participants to develop necessary skills and to become confident and resilient in their engagement with the initiative?
- Are there compelling reasons to believe the initiative is feasible?
- After taking a look at other implementations of this kind of initiative, can potential problems be foreseen? If so, can the institution cope with them? For example, if the new initiative involves an application of technology, have there been earlier efforts, at this institution and others, to make similar gains using earlier technologies? (In my experience, the reasons for earlier failures rarely lie solely in their technology;

by studying the past, institutions can sometimes anticipate and cope with the barriers that doomed earlier attempts.)

- What kinds of evidence could be used to guide the initiative, including evidence that might reveal that the initiative is unlikely to succeed?

Things Take Time

Piet Hein's short poem "TTT" suggests that, "When you feel how depressingly slowly you climb, it's well to remember that *Things Take Time*" (1966, p. 5). That's true in at least two important ways for implementing this framework.

First, as we've seen in every case history, it often takes several years to implement even one initiative. Early successes can help build and sustain support until, after more steps and more years, meaningful 3fold gains emerge. Obviously, it often takes time for a human being to get comfortable with a new way of doing things (e.g., a faculty member gaining confidence in teaching online; administrators becoming acclimated to a new way to manage advising workloads). In this context, let's remember how Governors State took the long view when hit by repeated state budget cuts. To quote again from a conversation I had with President Maimon:

> As people retired or departed, the university did not automatically replace the position. Instead, we developed job descriptions that fit the university's new directions. All departments were alerted that any new hire had to be interested in undergraduate education, even if the larger portion of responsibility might be in graduate programs. In the context of strategic plans that emphasize quality, we tightened up the implementation of criteria for faculty retention, promotion, and tenure. We hired outstanding deans for the four colleges. All of this has led to, on the whole, a more productive, creative, and mission-driven faculty than we had in 2007. (Maimon, personal communication, August 16, 2019)

One of many reasons for a long institutional learning curve is that individuals and units may be asked to reallocate how they spend time. Will they do it? With what effect? That's also an affordability question. Are there activities where time input can be reduced? My eyes were opened about time and money by a study from the University of Pennsylvania. Penn's school of engineering wanted to improve their undergraduate laboratories but also had to cut the cost of running them. A major portion of the operating cost was the time of faculty and staff. Some of their time directly influenced student learning (e.g., coaching students as they did research in the lab) while other activities were burdensome and not linked directly to the laboratories' goals (e.g., training students to use equipment; completing paperwork). A traditional activities-based cost model would have estimated the total time faculty and staff were spending, and then tried changes that would reduce that total, saving money. Penn did it differently. Their interviews broke out time spent in fulfilling activities (e.g., coaching students as they did research) from administrative and other burdensome activities. The goal was to reduce the time (money) spent on the latter and free up more time for the former (Pope & Anderson, 2000; Powell et al., 2002). That's a good lesson to remember during any pursuit of 3fold gains. To improve affordability, the goal cannot be to reduce faculty and student time to zero, yielding instant degrees, because no education is produced. Instead aim for enabling people's time to make productive, fulfilling uses of their time, while guarding them against burnout.

There's a second reason not to forget time. The first time someone tries a new way of doing things, it almost always takes longer than doing that thing the old way. The fifth time someone does things in the new way probably takes less time than their first attempt. That's one of the reasons for granting temporary release of faculty or staff from some other activities when they're creating an innovation. Even in times of tight budgets, it's important to budget for the extra money and time that participants may need temporarily in order to implement an initiative. Such release time and funds could become a significant budget item for initiatives being implemented over a period of years.

Be Alert for Confusors and Hidden Assumptions

We've been pointing out potential confusors throughout the book. Although it can sound pedantic, it's worth reminding people in a conversation, especially a high-stakes conversation, how you define the most problematic terms you're using. It's useful for groups to agree on which definition will be used, but people sometimes refuse to use an unfamiliar definition for a familiar term. The people used to regarding *active learning* as a description of behavior (e.g., writing a paper) may not be able to switch to defining it as a descriptor of what's going on in people's minds. (One option for making headway in that situation: agree that, for the purposes of the work, different terms will be used to refer to the dual faces of active learning.)

Some hidden assumptions can distort or kill discussions of Integrative improvement if they're left unspoken and untested. Many of these assumptions are components of the Instruction Paradigm; over the years I've seen all of the following unspoken assumptions influence discussions:

- "Your proposal for improving something is also an attack on the performance of everyone else."
- "We can't get any better because our students aren't good enough. Period."
- "Faculty do the productive work at this institution; other expenditures are merely overhead and should be cut first."
- "If you mention money or time in describing a proposal, it must threaten people's jobs or autonomy."
- "Let me respond to your proposal by attacking it. That should help you by revealing weaknesses you must not have seen for yourself."

You may wish to discuss these or similar assumptions with your colleagues. Almost every such hidden assumption has some reasonable basis. The assumptions in this list ought to be conversation starters, not conversation stoppers.

Overcommunicate With Stakeholders

As of a few years ago, UCF's College of Business (COB) relied extensively on lecture capture technology to record live lectures (typically two 75-minute lectures per week) and make them available for students to stream on demand. Enrollments in each section rose to 1,200 or more (that's not a typo), but only dozens rather than hundreds of students came to class regularly. By mid-semester attendance was usually below 50 at these optional lectures. About half the students viewed fewer than half the lectures. Faculty were not satisfied by course learning outcomes either.

COB decided to improve the quality of learning by creating a blended program. Working closely with both the Faculty Center for Teaching & Learning and the Center for Distributed Learning (CDL), COB leaders discussed how to expand and enrich active and collaborative learning activities. Their goal was to prepare students to use new knowledge critically and creatively, for example to create businesses and to guide their own development at UCF and after graduation.

COB called its approach relevant engaged active learning (REAL). Students were now required to attend only five sessions per semester, meeting in groups of 200. These face-to-face sessions were organized mainly around active and collaborative learning, such as a continuing role-playing simulation in which small teams of students worked throughout the semester to design a product and plan a marketing strategy. COB's goals were to increase the amount of student interaction with peers, graduate teaching assistants, and their professor during these sessions, while also making the course more educationally effective than the lecture capture model.

There was some student pushback. Two objections appeared repeatedly:

1. Others objected because the addition of required face-to-face, active learning workshops conflicted with their schedules.
2. Some students objected because they were losing the right to attend live lectures every week.

The two kinds of protest were vigorous enough to produce petitions and then national press coverage. In a 2018 podcast (no longer available), Tom Cavanagh, the vice provost for digital learning, and CDL Director Kelvin Thompson discussed REAL, including the student protests; their podcast web page included links to the news stories. A remark by Kelvin Thompson suggested the title for this segment, "You can't overcommunicate. When you think that you've communicated everything thoroughly, do it a bit more." The University of Central Oklahoma (UCO) case history reported that Provost Bill Radke would interject into almost any meeting an explanation of Transformative Learning, why it was important, and what UCO was doing to implement it. And at Governors State, Director of Institutional Research and Effectiveness Marco Krcatovich reported that spending lots of time with stakeholders early to describe the problem and figure out how to respond was more than justified by the quality of the plan and the reduction in time needed to implement it.

Evaluate the Constellation's Outcomes and Elements

Throughout this book, we've argued that sizeable 3fold gains are far more likely to result from a coherent constellation of mutually reinforcing initiatives than from any one of those initiatives alone. *Evaluation* is the term we'll use for documenting and weighing what's happened. Well-designed evaluations ought to be able to start from any possible set of findings to produce recommendations for action; to say this differently, *any* potential recommendation for action should be accepted or rejected based on findings from the evaluative research. For that to happen, the evaluation needs to look at outcomes, the activities expected to produce the outcomes, and the context that influences how those activities unfold. For example, imagine that an initiative is intended to foster deeper learning in part through collaborative learning. One research consideration is whether or not learning is deeper. A second is whether or not the students engage in collaborative learning in both letter and spirit. And the third is, if they didn't, why did that activity fail?

To study the influence of a constellation, it can help to check for relationships between changes in the constellation and changes in quality, access, and affordability. As we first saw in the Georgia State case, improved graduation rates relate to improvements in quality, access, and affordability. When Georgia State mapped its initiatives and graduation rates over the years, it suggests just how helpful those initiatives have been (Figure 3.1).

Affordability is even harder to study than quality or access. Institutions probably know the least about the most important use of time: students studying away from faculty. Nonetheless, even a little evidence about how and why students invest their time (e.g., in commuting, standing in line, child care) might create ideas about how students could receive a greater educational return on their investment of time.

Attempts to increase affordability probably need to be both top-down and bottom-up. By top-down I'm not talking about power relationships but instead about looking at gross expenditures of money and time. Let's stick with money for a moment. Imagine you're examining the annual budgets that contribute directly to instruction at the institution. The institution graduates about 1,000 students a year. Divide the budget total by 1,000 and you've got a crude estimate of how much we're investing to graduate one student. Very crude, but not totally devoid of meaning. It can be difficult to estimate the full costs of a new or existing initiative. One reason is that the time and money may be drawn from several budgetary units. A research and planning approach called *activity-based costing* provides one way to estimate the full cost of current activities and to compare full costs of other options (e.g., Ellis-Newman & Robinson, 1998). That kind of information might help a team and their institution set a target for instructional expenses per graduate in 3, 5, and 10 years. But that has to be complemented by bottom-up studies. The Penn engineering lab research mentioned earlier is a case in point. It was the engineering faculty and staff who figured out how make their time more productive.

Closing Thoughts About the Opening Epigrams

The epigrams opening this book all relate to implementation:

- "That's a great idea but we don't have the money and no one has the time." Chapter 1 describes why, even at well-endowed institutions, most people feel they have little discretionary money and even less discretionary time. Nevertheless, if the goals are widely valued, if the plan works, and if the change unfolds slowly enough those people and that institution can change in major way. Major reallocations are more likely to happen and to stick if they develop at a thoughtful pace. When I first became involved in educational uses of technology, it's likely that almost any institution in the country would have declared it impossible to allocate as much money to technology as those same institutions spend today. The increased spending demands emerged slowly enough to be managed. To pursue Integrative gains, the tortoise often beats the hare.

- "We've already tried that here, and it doesn't work." I've heard many people say this over the years and it might sound sensible. But they've said it about initiatives that worked quite well at several other institutions. Nor did the speakers consider whether someone could learn from those prior experiences, at their own institution and at others, before trying again. Don't let "we tried it before" be a conversation stopper.
- "It takes a village . . ." That's good shorthand for one essential for shifting practice to align with Integrative assumptions: cross-silo collaboration.
- "Know what to leave out" was originally advice for writers. But it's equally apt for implementers. Prune your plans and temper your expectations. For example, as Georgia State began its pursuit of 3fold gains, it focused on just two things initially: data consolidation and discovering spots where the institution was accidentally derailing its own students. At first these efforts didn't involve many administrators or faculty. Early successes then helped them widen their coalition and plan more ambitious steps.

Turning the Page

Let's pause for a minute and for one final thought about implementation. In his classic *Development Projects Observed,* Albert Hirschman (1967) described his law of the hiding hand: Many great projects have succeeded even though their builders failed to anticipate some intimidating obstacles they would encounter. In fact, Hirschman said, if their champions had foreseen all the obstacles, these initiatives might never have begun. But there was something else these pioneers couldn't initially see: the creative responses they and their collaborators would devise once the obstacles did appear. *Development Projects Observed* is a little book, composed of case histories of international development projects in the mid-20th century. For example, a development project might be a hydroelectric dam, and it has a dual purpose: to succeed on its own terms (the dam is built, it generates and sells electricity) while also helping develop the entity that created it (a regional economy gets a boost). The initiatives in a 3fold gains constellation are development projects. You might find the lessons Hirschman draws to be useful going forward.

From chapter 2 until this point, we've been looking at 3fold gains from an institutional perspective. Undeniably, however, some of the serious barriers discouraging an Integrative shift exist outside the institution. We've already investigated how a single institution might make the most of its wider world. In the concluding chapter, let's consider whether it's possible to change the wider world to encourage and help institutions to pursue 3fold gains.

15

FOR 3FOLD GAINS ON A NATIONAL SCALE, CHANGE THE WIDER WORLD, TOO

Chapter 1 summarized urgent needs to improve quality of learning, equitable access, and stakeholder affordability on a national scale. Chapters 2 through 14 described how individual institutions can make institution-scale 3fold gains by leveraging a constellation of mutually supportive institutional strengths and new initiatives. Of the 4,000+ U.S. colleges and universities that meet Federal Title IV financial aid requirements, I'd guess that, in 2020, only a tiny fraction are intentionally assembling Integrative constellations in order to make 3fold gains. Obviously, that's not enough institutions to make a dent in issues such as the capabilities of U.S. college graduates. Somehow, hundreds and then thousands of institutions need to follow suit. For that to be a realistic possibility, the wider world in which they all operate must change, too. In this final chapter we'll talk about some ways to tweak the wider world so that it encourages the Integrative pursuit of 3fold gains on a national scale:

- Educate the public about the advantages of Integrative institutions
- Rethink doctoral programs to prepare future faculty for Integrative roles
- Prepare the next generation of transformative academic leaders
- Develop and sustain more communities of transformation
- Increase competitive grants to help institutions and programs make progress toward Integrative 3fold gains
- Explore accreditation's potential for encouraging 3fold gains

As with earlier chapters, these particular suggestions are illustrative, not comprehensive. What would you add to this list?

Educate the Public About the Advantages of Integrative Institutions

Can colleges change how potential students and the public think about higher learning and its value? One way to change their expectations is through widespread changes in how large numbers of institutions recruit. We're going to talk about students here, but some of the same ideas might be adapted to searches for new faculty and staff.

Chapter 12 on managing interactions with the wider world has already reported how Governors State University (chapter 4) and Guttman Community College (chapter 7) tout their Integrative features to attract and inform potential students. Here's another example of Integrative recruiting, from the home page of the University of Central Florida (UCF, chapter 9) College of Business (University of Central Florida, n.d.):

> For students, we strive to be the place where they can achieve their academic objectives to be the ONE who gets the job, starts a business, makes the sale, makes a contribution and mentors others. Students who graduate from the college will be great communicators and collaborators, risk takers, data-driven decision makers and problem solvers. Our team—faculty, staff, friends, and alumni—is working hard to provide the right resources and environment to ensure we deliver on those promises. . . . A true culture of engagement sets the College apart from other business schools. With hundreds of events, activities, programs, organizations and resources available, students can identify their passion, practice their pitch, network with industry leaders, jumpstart a career or even launch a business before graduating. We push our students to get out of their comfort zones to try new things, communicate and collaborate with people who are different from them and take risks.

Let's assume for the moment that market research and experience show that this kind of messaging provides the institution with a competitive edge. What features of education at the institution might also be powerful selling points in marketing for new students? Here are a few possible Integrative messages ("you" refers to potential students; "we" denotes the institution):

- *You will learn through what you do.* Governors State asserts that "you'll learn strategies and skills to become a critical thinker" (Governors State University, 2020b). UCF can help students become "great communicators and collaborators, risk takers, data-driven decision makers and problem solvers" (University of Central Florida, n.d.). Framed this way, the message reinforces the relationship between what students do while in the program and what they'll be prepared to do after graduation.

- *You will be prepared to deal with unpredictable changes in the world, good or bad.* In this book, this kind of learning is called *liberal learning*; the root of *liberal* has to do with making one's own choices. Change in the world is continual and inevitable. In our program you practice applying what you've learned in new contexts.
- *Our effectiveness helps you afford college.* Our students achieve more and graduate sooner, saving both time and money; you can get a bachelor's level job sooner, too. (The Governors State and Guttman recruiting messages in chapter 12 both allude to this advantage.)
- *What makes you different is also part of your strength.* Learning is, in part, a "team sport." Each student can learn better when they talk and work with students who have different preparation, points of view, strengths, and needs. And, by the way, our institution has a good track record of helping all kinds of students exceed their own expectations.
- *We walk the talk.* On a website, link each spotlighted program feature to web pages that illustrate the feature in use. A claim about undergraduate research (UR) might be linked to examples of student work and how it was used as well as to information about the fraction of all students doing UR. That kind of backup should help potential students and their advisers sift the real Integrative programs from those relying mostly on buzz words.

The more institutions use similar themes for recruiting, the more likely potential students and their benefactors will begin to expect a new normal of colleges: Integrative messages, with evidence to support them. And that could put a little pressure on more institutions to shift toward Integrative strategies.

Rethink Doctoral Programs to Prepare Future Faculty for Integrative Roles

Many students in doctoral programs, even now, may have had high school and undergraduate education more aligned with Instruction than Integrative assumptions. More importantly, these candidates get little or no formal education about student learning and how institutions work because, it's assumed, they can pick up informally what they need to know.

Since the late 1990s, as Integrative assumptions have spread, some doctoral programs have offered candidates formal preparation in the art and science of teaching. Some such programs help candidates learn about relevant educational research, especially in their own disciplines, and how to apply such findings to developing and teaching a course. Preparing Future Faculty (PFF) is a project to foster the development of such programs; hundreds of programs have participated and the PFF website (www.preparing-faculty.org) includes a wealth of relevant material. Are such programs doing enough to equip faculty? Terrel Rhodes, vice president of quality, curriculum, and assessment at the Association of American Colleges & Universities (AAC&U), has doubts about that. At many institutions, elements of PFF have been inserted into a course that doctoral students must, or may, take. Yet, Rhodes's experience indicates that a single course is insufficient for the many graduate students who secure faculty jobs, especially teaching-intensive positions (Flaherty, 2020).

Educating faculty for their institutional responsibilities, including assessing and improving program outcomes, receives even less attention than good teaching practices. An analogy would be if there were no formal education in the United States to give future voters lasting insight into how our Constitution and Bill of Rights are supposed to work and why they were designed that way. For new faculty to make constructive contributions to discussions about degree program or university goals, for example, it would help if they had some understanding about the history of universities and the assessment of programmatic goals for quality, access, and affordability. Future faculty members of committees would benefit from experiential learning about how they can influence the work of such groups so that, for example, stakeholders emerge with a sense of ownership of the group's conclusions.

Imagine that you have the opportunity to design a new doctoral program in your field to prepare doctoral students for faculty positions in institutions shifting toward the Integrative pursuit of 3fold gains (e.g., educational strategies, organizational foundations, wider world interactions). What would they need to master in order to be prepared to be a contributor? How could the doctoral students' readiness to participate in such discussions be assessed? Should this planned doctoral program have equity and affordability goals?

Prepare the Next Generation of Transformative Academic Leaders

Our six institutions have all been lucky to have effective transformational leaders in at least some senior positions. Leaders include not only provosts and presidents but also deans, chief information officers (CIOs), and other vice presidents. Our six institutions were lucky to get them because comparatively few candidates for senior positions have much informal or formal preparation for the transformational aspect of their roles. It's not every day that someone as well-prepared as Elaine Maimon responds to your executive search.

One way to get better candidates is to recruit people who are already prepared for the distinctive roles of transformative leaders. This passage, for example, comes from a posted position description for a new provost at Marshall University:

> Marshall University invites nominations and applications for the position of provost. President Jerome Gilbert has set forth a bold agenda to increase enrollment and improve retention; emphasize service-learning; increase faculty and student research and creative activities; add relevant PhD programs; develop a major program to fight addiction; and expand community outreach and economic development initiatives. Marshall University seeks an accomplished, innovative leader who will serve as the chief academic officer of the university while partnering with the president to implement a progressive and evolving strategy for excellence and growth. The provost must possess the experience, skills and drive required to lead the future of academics at Marshall, while exemplifying the character and qualities expected in a highly visible and trusted university and community leader. (Marshall University, 2018)

From this description, we can see that Marshall is adopting Integrative educational strategies, the president and provost must work in double harness (mentioned twice), and a track record of innovation is desirable. Here are a few suggestions for recruiting such leaders for an institution's pursuit of 3fold gains:

- A track record of *contributions to constellations* capable of improving quality, equitable access, and/or stakeholder affordability (e.g., experience with implementing high-impact practices [HIPs])
- Demonstrated ability to build the kind of *cross-silo collaborations* necessary for the Integrative pursuit of 3fold gains
- Demonstrated experience in advancing strategic goals for a program, unit, or institution by *dealing with the reallocation of revenues, budgets, or time*
- A track record of contributing to initiatives that *use digital technology* to help institutions or their organizational units transform their strategies and achievements

Faculty and staff who want to prepare themselves for future job searches could benefit from substantial programs of professional education. If the number of institutions attempting 3fold gains markedly increases, more and larger transformative leadership programs will be needed. What features might such programs of professional development have?

- *Punctuated intensity*: The term *intensity* is inspired by how UCF prepares faculty to develop and teach an online course with a program that requires 80 hours of faculty work. The term *punctuated* suggests that these programs include some periods of intense work, separated by months or years while the "students" apply and reflect on what they've learned and what they still need to learn. It takes time to develop such leaders.
- *Hybrid programs*: The same arguments made for hybrid learning spaces for undergraduates (chapter 11, "Organizational Foundations") apply to professional development programs for faculty. Some elements of professional development require real-time interaction, ideally F2F. Other elements benefit from the slower pace of asynchronous discussion and file sharing. A good professional development program also needs to ensure that a wide range of faculty can match their schedules with the program's demands on their time.
- *Options*: Anyone who signs up for this kind of professional development will bring with them some strengths and some needs for further development. So three people preparing for provost office positions might need three different mixes of modules. One, for example, might need preparation in budgeting and cost modeling, while another needs stronger qualifications in using digital technologies to strengthen initiatives. If the program is preparing people for different kinds of transformative leadership (e.g., student affairs, CIO), then more options will be needed.
- *Walk the talk*: In other words, do yourself what you're suggesting that others do. Programs of professional development need to pursue 3fold gains for the same reasons that undergraduate programs do: concerns about what's learned, who is able to learn, and what it costs the program and the student for that learning to happen. If the leaders of the professional development program are doing a conscientious job, the program itself will offer many concrete examples of what the program is preparing future leaders to do.

Develop and Sustain More Integrative Communities of Transformation

Chapter 12 ("Leveraging Interactions With the Wider World") defined *communities of transformation* (CoTs) as collaborations among institutions, or among people from different institutions, developed around shared goals for improvement. A number of CoTs were discussed in that chapter. All six of our case history institutions benefited from CoTs such as associations, consortia of like-minded innovation institutions, and free-standing grant-supported projects. All of that CoT activity is a hopeful sign. But to assist hundreds or ultimately thousands of campuses to start the Integrative shift, many more formal and informal CoTs will be needed.

Some new CoTs could provide mutual assistance among institutions (e.g., of a particular type or in a particular region) exploring the potential of pursuing 3fold gains. Others could help local innovators support each other in implementing a single family of educational strategies or organizational foundations or interactions with the wider world.

Many CoTs, such as clusters of faculty who know each other through professional association meetings and help one another as needed, don't have or need external funding to function. But others may need to develop and sustain a body of resources for current and future members, wish to hold their own conferences, or have other tasks that require at least a fraction of a staff member. Here's an example of what kind of funded support can be invaluable. Around 1980 when I was a program officer in the federal Fund for the Improvement of Postsecondary Education (FIPSE), one of our grants went to a coalition of institutions that all offered a Masters in Liberal Studies. Our grant helped them mount a conference to inform other institutions that were motivated to learn more about whether and how to offer such degree programs themselves. The conference was mainly a series of panels, each addressing a different general question about whether and how to design such programs. Let's say that one of those panels was about how to position such a program within the institution. Each panelist's institution did it differently. As I sat in the audience, I heard people mutter that they were pleased to hear options but they also needed advice about how to choose one of those options, a question that the panel (and all the other panels) didn't address. The grant would need to have been larger to sponsor the kinds of reflections and well-edited writing needed to answer such questions, to study the question and develop the resources and networks needed for effective outreach to novice institutions and individuals. To develop more expertise on how to adapt their core concern in different settings and develop resources of lasting value to institutions, it would help to buy some time from a few people. This lesson applies directly to most CoTs that might be developed.

There is no one-size-fits-all model for grants to CoTs. Quality Matters (QM) began with a FIPSE grant to a network of Maryland community colleges that wanted to help each other assure the quality of their online courses.

Since then the program has grown to include more institutions, kinds of institutions, and products and services; that growth has been funded mostly by fees and membership dues. In contrast, Complete College America has received grants from philanthropies such as the Lumina Foundation, the Bill & Melinda Gates Foundation, and the Carnegie Corporation of New York.

Increase Competitive Grants to Facilitate Steps Toward 3Fold Gains

Grants, small and large, play an important role in the development of private and public institutions because "Work expands to fill the time and budget available and is invested this year in ways largely dictated by last year's budgets and activities." To pursue 3fold gains, a process of continuing improvement, institutions need to find ways to avoid that trap. Like Governors State and others, they need to allocate resources for new ventures each year, even when budgets are being cut.

University of Central Oklahoma (UCO) provides a good illustration of the constructive role that competitive grants can play. In retrospect, several lines of work at UCO from 1997 to 2010 had been converging toward Transformative Learning (TL), the six tenets, and organizational changes to coordinate progress in the five transdisciplinary tenets. But the process had been slow. In 2011, the new Center for Excellence in Transformative Teaching (CETTL) spurred new president Don Betz and others to begin work on a Title III grant proposal to step up the pace. Their first proposal was rejected but resubmission the following year was encouraged. Perhaps the most important change in the second proposal: Title III reviewers had urged the proposal to include a major component on spreading the adaptation of STLR to other colleges and universities. The revised proposal was accepted. Paying more attention to far-reaching impact had at least two benefits. The first, from the Department of Education's perspective, was a multiplier of the project's benefits; students from underserved groups at other institutions could also benefit. Second, building networks of influence among institutions often strengthens the work at the grantee institution: traffic in ideas is almost always two-way. And the strong response to UCO's conferences and training programs helped further legitimate UCO's work in the eyes of its own administrators, faculty, and staff. The grant competition had one other major benefit. The extensive planning and coalition building needed to write a good proposal mobilized more of UCO to work on these issues. I don't think it was a coincidence that, after the initial proposal had been written and rejected, President Betz said that UCO would go forward with its STLR plans even if the second version was rejected. That fits with something I learned in the 1970s while working for FIPSE. During that period, FIPSE attracted about 35 preliminary proposals for every grant that was ultimately awarded. The selectivity and the extensive review process made the grants prestigious. As I recall, a 1980 external evaluation of FIPSE's impact discovered that a large majority of all *rejected* applicants implemented at least part of their proposal anyway. And there were 30 some rejected proposals for every grant awarded.

The following are a few thoughts about new funding programs to lubricate the pursuit of 3fold gains:

- The grants should be kept small; applicants should make a strong case that, if the project succeeds, they can move from supporting part of the work during the grant to supporting full operation after the grant.
- Institutions ought to have considerable freedom in defining just where and why an injection of money would help get things unstuck.
- Many projects should not be limited to single institutions; they ought to stimulate and support communities of transformation (discussed earlier in this chapter and in chapter 12).

Explore Accreditation's Potential for Encouraging 3Fold Gains

Accreditation has changed significantly over the last 50 years. Comparatively speaking, its attention has shifted some toward learning goals and outcomes (a learning paradigm assumption about quality) compared with its attention to an institution's or a program's resources (an Instruction Paradigm assumption about quality).

Today, accreditors should start to consider how to encourage their programs and institutions to set goals for equitable access and stakeholder affordability as well as for quality of learning outcomes and practices. Also, accreditors might help their visiting teams understand the concept of 3fold gains toward those goals and how constellations can facilitate or hinder implementation of the team's recommendations for the institution.

Some of Those Tweaks of the Wider World Have Already Begun

It seems to me that the wider world has already become somewhat more supportive of Integrative constellations and gains in many of the areas we've just reported. However, the changes that are the focus of this chapter have been slow enough that not everyone may have noticed them:

- Educate the public on the advantages of Integrative institutions. Here I'll cite MIT, an institution that, 50 years ago, was noticeably aligned with the Instruction Paradigm. As I mentioned in the preface to this book, as an undergraduate I did a quick and dirty content analysis of MIT catalogues in the mid-1960s. The most noticeable term in those texts was *analysis*. In comparison, the MIT Education (MIT, 2020) web page now begins:

  > At MIT, we revel in a culture of learning by doing . . . our students combine analytical rigor with curiosity, playful imagination, and an appetite for solving the hardest problems in service to society. . . . Our campus is a workshop for inventing the future and we are all apprentices, learning from each other as we go. . . . [It] adds up to a prime spot to make the most of your potential (paras. 1–2).

  I suspect a national longitudinal study of institutions' marketing messages might find hundreds of institutions moving toward Integrative language.

- Rethink doctoral programs to prepare future faculty for Integrative roles. It's possible that there are a few hundred doctoral programs preparing faculty to teach, but we don't know much about how extensive or effective that education is. I'm not yet aware of doctoral programs that also prepare future faculty for the changes in the faculty role that accompany the Integrative shift, however. Another recent sign of the times is the development of companies that help an institution's faculty expand their teaching repertoires, for example the Association for College and University Educators (ACUE) and the Faculty Guild.
- Prepare the next generation of transformative academic leaders. This shift, too, has begun. The first example I've found is the Academy for Innovative Higher Education Leadership offered by Arizona State University in collaboration with Georgetown University.

Turning the Page

In short, it looks like conditions are becoming more favorable for institutions to shift toward Integrative educational strategies in order to pursue 3fold gains. But such a shift is not inevitable. One thing I've learned from these case histories is that in no case was their development inevitable. Any changes for good or ill over the next decade depend to a great extent on individuals such as those reading this book, their experiences, commitments, and actions. Here are a few of the propositions explored throughout this book. Might any of them spark good conversations with your colleagues this week?

- It's possible for institutions to make noticeable, continuing gains in quality, access, and affordability.
- It's important and urgent that institutions do so.
- At this institution, our most often used method is to let ideas bubble up and support as many as possible. Some deal with quality, others with access, and still others with affordability. However, looking back a decade or two, should we be happy with that approach? If not, we need to try something different if we want to get different results.
- What if we were to take a broader view, assembling a constellation of *significant, mutually supportive, sustained* changes in our educational strategies over the next 5 to 10 years? HIPs, for example, can help improve learning for all students while being especially helpful for Pell students and students from underserved groups. By improving retention and speeding graduation, HIPs can also help save time and money both for students and for their institutions.
- Maybe we've been too cautious in trying to change the ways our students learn. And maybe we've had good reasons. The facts of life at an institution can make shifting toward more active and collaborative forms of learning difficult. So it's important that some of those initiatives lower barriers to change such elements as Instruction-aligned faculty rewards systems, rigid classroom designs, and the lack of transparent data about where student success may be unnecessarily hampered by how the institution works.
- If we can plan at least the first step or two to improve specific outcomes within quality, access, and affordability, and if the plan seems feasible, we can probably get more people to invest time and money in creating these initiatives at scale.
- Digital technologies can help us get where we need to go. But don't assume they will drive or define our agenda. Instead, after we decide what to change and how, we'll probably find some effective, inexpensive, and safe ways to improve our plan with selective uses of the Internet, digital communications, and other computer technologies.

And that's about it. I'm turning these ideas over to you. If you've read even a good chunk of this book, you have earned some battle scars and a sense of achievement from your own prior struggles to do a better job for our students, our institutions, and our world. Maybe chapter 1 has confirmed or increased your sense of how important it is for thousands of institutions, including your own, to do better. I hope these stories have enlarged your sense of what's possible in other institutions and in your own.

REFERENCES

Adelman, C., Ewell, P., Gaston, P., & Schneider, C. G. (2011). *The degree qualifications profile*. Lumina Foundation for Education.

Ambrose, S., Bridges, M. W., DiPietro, M., Lovett, M. C., & Norman, M. K. (2010). *How learning works: Seven research-based principles for smart teaching*. John Wiley & Sons.

Arum, R., & Roksa, J. (2011a). *Academically adrift: Limited learning on college campuses*. University of Chicago Press.

Arum, R., & Roksa, J. (2011b, May 4). Your so-called education. *New York Times*. https://nyti.ms/2zFxH5K

Association of American Colleges & Universities. (2013). *High-impact educational practices*. https://www.aacu.org/sites/default/files/files/LEAP/HIP_tables.pdf

Association of American Colleges & Universities. (2017). *Liberal education and America's promise*. https://www.aacu.org/leap

Association of American Colleges & Universities. (2018a). *Essential learning outcomes*. https://www.aacu.org/leap/essential-learning-outcomes

Association of American Colleges & Universities. (2018b). *VALUE rubrics*. https://www.aacu.org/value-rubrics

Bailey, T. R., Jaggars, S. S., & Jenkins, D. (2015). *Redesigning America's community colleges: A clearer path to student success*. Harvard University Press.

Barnes, B. (2013, Spring). Group effort. How UCF presidents have each transformed the university. *Pegasus: The Magazine of the University of Central Florida*. https://www.ucf.edu/pegasus/group-effort/

Barr, R. B., & Tagg, J. (1995). From teaching to learning: A new paradigm for undergraduate education. *Change: The Magazine of Higher Learning, 27*(6), 12–25. https://www.esf.edu/openacademy/tlc/documents/FromTeachingToLearningANewParadigmforUndergraduateEducation.pdf

Bass, R., & Eynon, B. (2009). *Themes and findings*. Visible Knowledge Project. https://blogs.commons.georgetown.edu/vkp/themes-findings/

Bauer-Maglin, N., Rodríguez, C. & Weinbaum, A. (2014). *Putting students at the center at Guttman community college: Accomplishments and challenges in the inaugural years*. https://guttman.cuny.edu/wp-content/uploads/2014/08/PuttingStudentsattheCenterReport8-21.pdf

Bensimon, E. M., Dowd, A. C., & Witham, K. (2016). Five principles for enacting equity by design. *Diversity & Democracy, 19*(1), 1–8. https://www.aacu.org/diversitydemocracy/2016/winter/bensimon

Bernard, R., Borokhovski, E., Schmid, R., Tamim, R., & Abrami, P. (2014). A meta-analysis of blended learning and technology use in higher education: From the general to the applied. *Journal of Computing in Higher Education: Research & Integration of Instructional Technology, 26*(1), 87–122. https://doi.org/10.1007/s12528-013-9077-3

Boston Consulting Group & Arizona State University. (2018). *Making digital learning work: Success strategies from six leading universities and community colleges.* https://edplus.asu.edu/sites/default/files/BCG-Making-Digital-Learning-Work-Apr-2018%20.pdf

Boston Consulting Group & University of Central Florida. (2017). *Financial decision support for digital learning: UCF online and mixed modality course scenarios* [PowerPoint slides]. Unpublished.

Bowen, H. (1980). *The costs of higher education: How much do colleges and universities spend per student and how much should they spend?* Jossey-Bass.

Boyatsis, R. (1982). *The competent manager: A model for effective performance.* John Wiley & Sons.

Brown, J., & Kurzweil, M. (2015). *Breaking the iron triangle at the University of Central Florida.* http://www.sr.ithaka.org/publications/breaking-the-iron-triangle-at-the-university-of-central-florida/

Cahalan, M., Perna, L. W., Yamashita, M., Wright-Kim, J. & Jiang, N. (2019). *Indicators of higher education equity in the United States: 2018 historical trend report.* Pell Institute for the Study of Opportunity in Higher Education, Alliance for Higher Education and Democracy of the University of Pennsylvania (PennAHEAD). http://pellinstitute.org/indicators/reports_2019.shtml

Canning, E. A., Muenks, K., Green, D. J., & Murphy, M. C. (2019). STEM faculty who believe ability is fixed have larger racial achievement gaps and inspire less student motivation in their classes. *Science Advances, 5*(2), eaau4734. https://doi.org/10.1126/sciadv.aau4734

Carnegie Mellon University. (2020). *Solve a teaching problem.* https://www.cmu.edu/teaching/solveproblem/index.html

Chickering, A., & Ehrmann, S. C. (1996). Implementing the seven principles: Technology as lever. *American Association for Higher Education Bulletin, 49*(October), 3–6. https://www.researchgate.net/publication/246430027_Implementing_the_Seven_Principles_Technology_as_Lever

Chickering, A., & Gamson, Z. (1987). Seven principles for good practice in undergraduate education. *AAHE Bulletin, 40*(March), 3–7. https://files.eric.ed.gov/fulltext/ED282491.pdf

City University of New York. (2008). *A new community college concept paper.* http://guttman.cuny.edu/wp-content/uploads/2014/08/ANewCommunityCollegeConceptPaperFinalAug152008withoutdraft.pdf

College Board. (2019). *2019–20 Tuition and fees at public four-year institutions by state and five-year percentage change in in-state tuition and fees.* https://research.collegeboard.org/trends/college-pricing/figures-tables/published-state-tuition-and-fees-public-four-year-institutions-state

Commission on the Future of Undergraduate Education. (2017). *The future of undergraduate education, the future of America.* American Academy of Arts & Sciences. https://www.amacad.org/publication/future-undergraduate-education

Competency-Based Education Network. (2017). *What is competency-based education?* http://www.cbenetwork.org/competency-based-education/

Complete College America. (n.d.). *15 to finish.* https://completecollege.org/strategy/15-to-finish/

Complete College America. (2013). *How full-time are "full-time" students?* https://completecollege.org/wp-content/uploads/2017/11/2013-10-14-how-full-time.pdf

Creative Commons. (2018). *Share your work.* https://creativecommons.org/share-your-work

Crisp, G., Baker, V. L., Griffin, K. A., Lunsford, L. G., & Pifer, M. J. (2017). Mentoring undergraduate students. *ASHE Higher Education Report, 43*(1), 7–103. https://doi.org/10.1002/aehe.20117

Cunliff, E. (2011). *In the beginning, there was transformation?* Unpublished memo.

Cunliff, E., & King, J. (2018). Institutionalizing transformative learning: The trees, then the forest, then the realization. *Metropolitan Universities, 29*(3), 8–24. https://doi.org/10.18060/22407

Desjardins, R., & Colleagues. (2013). *OECD skills outlook 2013: First results of the survey of adult skills.* Organization for Economic Cooperation and Development. https://www.researchgate.net/publication/293074894_OECD_Skills_Outlook_First_Results_of_the_Survey_of_Adult_Skills

Deslauriers, L., Schelew, E., & Wieman, C. (2011). Improved learning in a large-enrollment physics class. *Science, 332*(6031), 862–864. https://doi.org/10.1126/science.1201783

Desrochers, D., & Staisloff, R. (2016). *Competency-based education: A study of four new models and their implications for bending the higher education cost curve.* rpk Group. http://rpkgroup.com/wp-content/uploads/2016/10/rpkgroup_cbe_business_model_report_20161018.pdf

Doyle, W. (2006). Community college transfers and college graduation: Whose choices matter most? *Change: The Magazine of Higher Learning, 38*(3), 56–58. https://doi.org/10.3200/CHNG.38.3.56-58

Dziuban, C. D., Graham, C. R., Moskal, P. D., Norberg, A., & Sicilia, N. (2018). Blended learning: The new normal and emerging technologies. *International Journal of Educational Technology in Higher Education, 15*, Article 3. https://doi.org/10.1186/s41239-017-0087-5

Dziuban, C. D., Hartman, J. L., Cavanagh, T. B., & Moskal, P. D. (2011). Blended courses as drivers of institutional transformation. In A. Kitchenham (Ed.), *Blended learning across disciplines: Models for implementation* (pp. 17–37). IGI Global.

Ehrmann, S. C. (1978). *Academic adaptation: Historical study of a civil engineering department in a research-oriented university* [Unpublished doctoral dissertation]. Massachusetts Institute of Technology. https://dspace.mit.edu/handle/1721.1/16288

Ehrmann, S. C. (1995). Asking the right questions: What does research tell us about technology and higher learning? *Change: The Magazine of Higher Learning, 27*(2), 20–27. https://www.researchgate.net/publication/245504962_Asking_the_Right_

Questions_What_Does_Research_Tell_Us_About_Technology_and_Higher_Learning

Ehrmann, S. C. (1999). Access and/or quality: Redefining choices in the third revolution. *Educom Review, 34*(5), 24–27. https://www.educause.edu/ir/library/html/erm/erm99/erm9956.html

Ehrmann, S. C. (2000). Technology and educational revolution: Ending the cycle of failure. *Liberal Education, 86*(4), 40–49. https://www.learntechlib.org/p/92221/

Ehrmann, S. C. (2006). To love the beauty of an equation, what do you need to learn? (Some observations about a liberal education, and three roles for technology). *Grazing.* http://sehrmann.blogspot.com/2015/02/to-love-beauty-of-equation-what-do-you.html

Ehrmann, S. C. (2011). Taking the long view: Ten recommendations about time, money, technology, and learning. *Planning for Higher Education, 39*(2), 34–40. https://doi.org/ 10.1080/00091383.2010.503175

Ehrmann, S. C., & Bishop, M. J. (2015). *Pushing the barriers to teaching improvement: A state system's experience with faculty-led, technology-supported course redesign.* http://www.usmd.edu/cai/sites/default/files/USMCourseRedesignReport-Sept2015.pdf

Ehrmann, S. C., Gilbert, S. W. & McMartin, F. (2006). *Factors affecting the adoption of faculty-developed academic software: A study of five iCampus projects.* http://icampus.mit.edu/files/docs/exec_sum_icampus_assessment.pdf

Ellis-Newman, J., & Robinson, P. (1998). The cost of library services: Activity-based costing in an Australian academic library. *Journal of Academic Librarianship, 24*(5), 373–379. https://doi.org/10.1016/S0099-1333(98)90074-X

Erickson, L. (2020). Congress must address dismal dropout rates. *Education Next, 20*(1), 69–75. https://www.educationnext.org/congress-must-address-dismal-dropout-rates-forum-should-congress-link-higher-ed-funding-graduation-rates/

Ewell, P. (2008). No correlation: Musings on some myths about quality. *Change: The Magazine of Higher Learning, 40*(6), 8–13. https://doi.org/10.3200/CHNG.40.6.8-13

Finley, A. P. (2012). *Making progress? What we know about the achievement of liberal education outcomes.* Association of American Colleges & Universities.

Finley, A. P. (2017). *On solid ground: VALUE report 2017.* Association of American Colleges & Universities. https://www.luminafoundation.org/files/resources/on-solid-ground.pdf

Finley, A. P., & McNair, T. (2013). *Assessing underserved students' engagement in high-impact practices.* Association of American Colleges & Universities.

Flack, B., Dunn, D. & Korth, D. (2018). *HIPS: High impact practices.* https://tips.uark.edu/hips-high-impact-practices/

Flaherty, C. (2020, December 13). Required pedagogy. *Inside Higher Ed.* https://www.insidehighered.com/news/2019/12/13/online-conversation-shines-spotlight-graduate-programs-teach-students-how-teach

Gehrke, S., & Kezar, A. J. (2016). STEM reform outcomes through communities of transformation. *Change: The Magazine of Higher Learning, 48*(1), 30–38. https://doi.org/10.1080/00091383.2016.1121084

Geith, C., & Cometa, M. (2003). Case Study 3: Rochester Institute of Technology cost analysis results: Comparing distance learning and on-campus courses, fall 1997–fall 1998. In S. C. Ehrmann, & J. H. Milam (Eds.), *Flashlight™ cost analysis handbook: Modeling resource use in teaching and learning with technology.* (2nd ed., pp. 61–73). The Teaching, Learning, and Technology Group.

Georgia State University. (2017). 2016 status report. *Complete College Georgia.* https://success.gsu.edu/files/2017/01/Georgia-State-University-2016-Complete-College-Report-with-Appendix-10-26-16.pdf

Georgia State University. (2018). *Freshman learning communities.* http://success.students.gsu.edu/freshman-learning-communities/

Georgia State University. (2019). 2018 report. *Complete College Georgia.* https://success.gsu.edu/download/2018-status-report-georgia-state-university-complete-college-georgia/?wpdmdl=6472128&refresh=5eae0e711d3f71588465265

Gilbert, S. W. (2016). *Introduction to TLTRs: Teaching, learning, and technology roundtables (TLTRs).* http://www.tltgroup.org/anthology/collabcom/tltr

Goldrick-Raab, S. (2016). *Paying the price: College costs, financial aid, and the betrayal of the American dream.* University of Chicago Press.

Governors State University. (2020a). *An ordinary freshman year won't do.* https://www.govst.edu/freshman/

Governors State University. (2020b). *General education advising.* https://www.govst.edu/GeneralEducationAdvising/

Governors State University. (2020c). *Mission and strategic plan.* https://www.govst.edu/About/Mission_and_Strategic_Plan/

Guttman Community College. (2013). *The new community college at CUNY: Reappointment, promotion, and tenure guidelines.* http://guttman.cuny.edu/wp-content/uploads/2014/08/ReappointmentPromotionandTenureGuidelines.pdf

Guttman Community College. (2018a). *Faculty handbook, 2018–2020.* https://guttman.cuny.edu/wp-content/uploads/page-assets/academics/faculty-resources/FacultyHandbook_REV08232018_digital.pdf

Guttman Community College. (2018b). *Strategic plan 2018–2022.* https://guttman.cuny.edu/wp-content/uploads/page-assets/about/strategic-planning-and-accreditation/strategic-plan-2018-2022/Strategic-Plan-2018-2022.pdf

Guttman Community College. (2019a). *About Guttman.* guttman.cuny.edu/about

Guttman Community College. (2019b). *Admissions.* https://guttman.cuny.edu/admissions/

Hansen, S. (2016). *Developing a disruptive innovation in U.S. higher education: A case study of competency-based education at College for America* [Unpublished doctoral dissertation]. University of Pittsburgh.

Hart Research Associates. (2015). *Falling short? College learning and career success. Selected findings from online surveys of employers and college students conducted on behalf of the. Association of American Colleges & Universities.* Association of American Colleges & Universities. https://www.aacu.org/leap/public-opinion-research/2015-survey-results

Hart Research Associates. (2018). *Fulfilling the American dream: Liberal education and the future of work. Selected findings from online surveys of business executives and hiring managers.* Association of American Colleges & Universities. https://www.aacu.org/sites/default/files/files/LEAP/2018EmployerResearchReport.pdf

Harvard University. (2020). *Instructional moves.* https://instructionalmoves.gse.harvard.edu/home

Hein, P. (1966). *Grooks.* MIT Press.

Herrington, V. J. (2013). *The academic library: Cowpath or path to the future?* https://academicworks.cuny.edu/cgi/viewcontent.cgi?article=1018&context=nc_pubs

Hiltz, S. R. (1988). *Learning in a virtual classroom. Executive summary and two volumes.* (No. 25, 26). Computerized Conferencing and Communications Center, New Jersey Institute of Technology.

Hirschman, A. O. (1967). *Development projects observed.* Brookings Institution Press.

Hutcheson, P. (2007). The Truman Commission's vision of the future. *Thought and Action, (Fall)*, 107–115. http://www.nea.org/assets/img/PubThoughtAndAction/TAA_07_11.pdf

Immerwahr, J., Johnson, J., & Gasbarra, P. (2008). *The iron triangle: College presidents talk about costs, access, and quality.* (No. 08-2). National Center for Public Policy and Higher Education. https://eric.ed.gov/?id=ED503203

Kazin, K. (2014). *Kate Kazin on writing, rigor, and the CfA associate's degree.* https://collegeforamerica.org/kate-kazin-on-writing-rigor-and-the-cfa-associates-degree/

Keeling, R. P. (Ed.). (2004). *Learning reconsidered: A campus-wide focus on the student experience.* National Association of Student Personnel Administrators.

Kezar, A. J., & Gehrke, S. (2015). *Communities of transformation and their work scaling STEM reform.* University of Southern California. https://pullias.usc.edu/wp-content/uploads/2016/01/communities-of-trans.pdf

King, J. (2018a). *Operationalizing transformative learning.* [Unpublished manuscript].

King, J. (2018b). Transformative learning in online college courses: Process and evidence. *International Journal for Innovation in Online Education, 2*(2). https://doi.org/10.1615/IntJInnovOnlineEdu.2018028557

King, J., & Wimmer, B. (In press). Operationalizing transformative learning: A case study demonstrating replicability and scaling. In K. Morgan, & K. Bhagat (Eds.), *Learning, design, and technology: An international compendium of theory, research, practice and policy.* Springer.

King, P., & Kitchener, K. (1993). The development of reflective thinking in the college years: The mixed results. In C. G. Schneider, & W. S. Green (Eds.), *Strengthening the college major* (pp. 25–42). Jossey-Bass. https://doi.org/10.1002/he.36919938404

King, P. M., & Kitchener, K. S. (2004). Reflective judgment: Theory and research on the development of epistemic assumptions through adulthood. *Educational Psychologist, 39*(1), 5–18. https://doi.org/ 10.1207/s15326985ep3901_2

Kinzie, J., & Kuh, G. D. (2017) Reframing student success in college: Advancing know-what and know-how. *Change: The Magazine of Higher Learning, 49*(3), 19–27. https://doi.org/10.1080/00091383.2017.1321429

Kinzie, J., & Kuh, G. (2004). Going DEEP: Learning from campuses that share responsibility for student success. *About Campus, 9*(5), 2–8. https://doi.org/10.1002/abc.105

Kuh, G. (2008). *High-impact educational practices: What they are, who has access to them, and why they matter*. Association of American Colleges & Universities.

Kuh, G. D., Kinzie, J., Schuh, J. H., Whitt, E. J., & Associates (2010). *Student success in college: Creating conditions that matter*. Jossey-Bass.

Kuh, G. D., O'Donnell, K., & Reed, S. (2013). *Ensuring quality and taking high-impact practices to scale*. Association of American Colleges & Universities.

Kuh, G., O'Donnell, K., & Schneider, C. G. (2017). HIPs at ten. *Change: The Magazine of Higher Learning, 49*(5), 8–16. https://doi.org/10.1080/00091383.2017.1366805

Kurzweil, M., & Wu, D. D. (2015). *Building a path to student success at Georgia State University*. Ithaka S+R. https://doi.org/10.18665/sr.221053

LeadershipIQ. (2019). *Why new hires fail (Emotional intelligence vs. skills)*. https://www.leadershipiq.com/blogs/leadershipiq/35354241-why-new-hires-fail-emotional-intelligence-vs-skills

LeBlanc, P. (2018). *Some reflections on completing 15 years at SNHU*. http://blogging.snhu.edu/leblanc/2018/07/some-reflections-on-completing-15-years-at-snhu/

Leskes, A., & Miller, R. E. (2006). *Purposeful pathways: Helping students achieve key learning outcomes*. Association of American Colleges & Universities. https://doi.org/10.1111/j.1467-9647.2008.00496.x

Levine, A. (1980). *Why innovation fails: The institutionalization and termination of innovations in higher education*. SUNY Press.

Maimon, E. (2018). *Leading academic change: Vision, strategy, transformation*. Stylus.

Marshall, R. (2006). The University of Central Florida: Collaboration and multimedia classrooms. In D. Oblinger (Ed.), *Learning spaces* (pp. 39.1–39.8). EDUCAUSE.

Marshall University. (2018, February 13). Provost [Job description]. *Inside Higher Education*. https://careers.insidehighered.com/job/1506508/provost/?TrackID=13&utm_source=Inside+Higher+Ed&utm_campaign=4e1a705308-DNU20180111&utm_medium=email&utm_term=0_1fcbc04421-4e1a705308-197398593&mc_cid=4e1a705308&mc_eid=8ee9f96e99

Mazur, E. (2009). *Confessions of a converted lecturer* [Video]. https://www.youtube.com/watch?v=WwslBPj8GgI&t=534s

McNair, T. B., Albertine, S., Cooper, M. Asha, McDonald, N. L, & Major, T. (2016). *Becoming a student-ready college: A new culture of leadership for student success*. Jossey-Bass.

Means, B., Toyama, Y., Murphy, R., & Bakia, M. (2013). The effectiveness of online and blended learning: A meta-analysis of the empirical literature. *Teachers College Record, 115*(3), 1–47.

Mellow, G. O., Woolis, D. D., Klages-Bombich, M., & Restler, S. G. (2015). *Taking college teaching seriously: Pedagogy matters*. Stylus.

Mezirow, J. (1990). How critical reflection triggers transformative learning. In J. Mezirow & Associates (Eds.), *Fostering critical reflection in adulthood: A guide to transformative and emancipatory learning* (pp. 1–20). Jossey-Bass.

MIT. (2020). *Education*. http://web.mit.edu/education/

National Research Council. (2015). *Reaching students: What research says about effective instruction in undergraduate science and engineering.* National Academies Press.

O'Shea, P. M., Kidd, J. K., Baker, P. B., Kaufman, J. A., & Allen, D. W. (2011). Student-authored textbooks: Why they're necessary and how they can be done. In S. D'Agustino (Ed.), *Adaptation, resistance and access to instructional technologies* (pp. 76–86). IGI Global.

Ong, W. J. (1982). *Orality and literacy.* Methuen.

Otero, V., Pollock, S., & Finkelstein, N. (2010). A physics department's role in preparing physics teachers: The Colorado learning assistant model. *American Journal of Physics, 78,* 1218–1224. https://doi.org/10.1119/1.3471291

Parkinson, C. N., & Osborn, R. C. (1957). *Parkinson's law, and other studies in administration.* Houghton Mifflin.

Pascarella, E. T., & Terenzini, P. T. (1991). *How college affects students: Findings and insights from 20 years of research.* Jossey-Bass.

Patterson, N. D., Alexander, M., Miller, V., & McPhail, B. (2006). The effects of undergraduate mathematics course redesign on student achievement. In S. Alatorre, J. L. Cortina, M. Sáiz & A. Méndez (Eds.), *Proceedings of the 28th North American Chapter of the International Group for the Psychology of Mathematics Education.* (pp. 888–896). Universidad Pedagógica Nacional.

Pope, D., & Anderson, H. (2000). Reducing the Costs of Laboratory Instruction through the Use of On-Line Laboratory Instruction. *MRS Proceedings, 632,* HH7.1.

Powell, R. M., Anderson, H., Spiegel, J. V. d., & Pope, D. P. (2002). Using web-based technology in laboratory instruction to reduce costs. *Computer Applications in Engineering Education 10*(4), 204–214. https://doi.org/10.1002/cae.10029

Rosenbaum, J., Deil-Amen, R., & Person, A. (2006). *After admission: From college access to college success.* Russell Sage Foundation.

Roth, M. (2014). *Beyond the university—Why liberal education matters* [Video]. https://www.youtube.com/watch?v=JD3PUVWpMds

Ryan, C. L., & Bauman, K. (2016). *Educational attainment in the United States: 2015.* https://vtechworks.lib.vt.edu/handle/10919/83682

Smith, K. L. (1990). Collaborative and interactive writing for increasing communication skills. *Hispania, 73*(1), 77–87. https://www.learntechlib.org/p/142356/

Smith, M. J. (2017). *Toward efficacy: Examining the reported impact of quality enhancement plans on student learning in postsecondary contexts* [doctoral dissertation]. College of William and Mary. W&M ScholarWorks. http://doi.org/10.21220/W4694T

Snyder, B. R. (1970). *The hidden curriculum.* Alfred A. Knopf.

Southern New Hampshire University. (n.d.) *Unlocking talent and opportunity: 2018–2023 strategic plan.* https://snhu-externalaffairs.app.box.com/s/7k526w442reszti50fdtceyrre2f1il8

Southern New Hampshire University. (2020). *About SNHU: University mission.* https://www.snhu.edu/about-us

Stewart, K., & Kilmartin, C. (2014). Connecting the dots: The decline in meaningful learning. *Journal of Faculty Development, 28*(2), 53–61.

Theobald, E. J., Hill, M. J., Tran E,, Agrawal, S., Arroyo, E. N., Behling, S., Chambwe, N., Cintrón, D. L., Cooper, J. D., Dunster, G., Grummer, J. A., Hennessey, K., Hsiao, J., Iranon, N., Jones II, L., Jordt, H., Keller, M., Lacey, M. E., Littlefield, C.E., . . . Freeman, S. (2020). Active learning narrows achievement gaps for underrepresented students in undergraduate science, technology, engineering, and math. *Proceedings of the National Academy of Sciences, 24*(12), 6476–6483. https://doi.org/10.1073/pnas.1916903117

Twigg, C. A. (2015). Improving learning and reducing costs: Fifteen years of course redesign. *Change: The Magazine of Higher Learning, 47*(6), 6–13. https://doi.org/10.1080/00091383.2015.1089753

University of Central Florida. (n.d.) *Business school for the 21st century.* https://business.ucf.edu/

University of Central Florida. (2016). *UCF collective impact: Five-year institutionalization plan.* https://www.ucf.edu/strategic-plan/files/2017/11/UCF-Collective-Impact-Five-Year-Institutionalization-Plan.pdf

University of Central Florida. (2020). *What's next: Integrative learning for professional and civic preparation.* https://undergrad.ucf.edu/whatsnext/about/qep/

University of Central Oklahoma. (2016). *STLR: Student Transformative Learning Record @ UCO—Faculty video* [Video]. https://www.youtube.com/watch?v=t42EDXgmaMc

University of Maryland. (2020). *Improve my teaching.* https://tltc.umd.edu/improve-my-teaching

Veney, R. M., & Sugimoto, L. H. (2017). *Transforming higher education: The guided pathways approach.* https://er.educause.edu/articles/2017/6/transforming-higher-education-the-guided-pathways-approach

Waldrop, J. B., & Bowdon, M. A. (Eds.). (2015). *Best practices for flipping the college classroom.* Routledge.

Weick, K. (1976). Educational organizations as loosely coupled systems. *Administrative Science Quarterly, XXI*, 1–19. https://doi.org/ 10.2307/2391875

Weinbaum, A., Rodriguez, C. & Bauer-Maglin, N. (2013a). *Rethinking community college for the 21st century.* https://guttman.cuny.edu/wp-content/uploads/2015/05/NCCCaseStudylowres.pdf

Weinbaum, A., Rodriguez, C. & Bauer-Maglin, N. (2013b). *Instructional teams at Guttman community college: Building a learning community of students, faculty, and staff.* http://guttman.cuny.edu/wp-content/uploads/2014/08/ITReportFinal.pdf

Wergin, J. (2005). Higher education: Waking up to the importance of accreditation—Ramifications of proposed 2005 extension of the higher education act. *Change: The Magazine of Higher Learning, 37*(3), 35–41.

Wiley, D. (2018). *When is an OER an OER?* https://opencontent.org/blog/archives/5463

Wilson, J., & Jennings, W. (2000). Studio courses: How information technology is changing the way we teach, on campus and off. *Proceedings of the IEEE, 88*(1), 72–80. https://doi.org/10.1109/5.811603

Wright, J., Millar, S., Kosciuk, S., Penberthy, D., Wampold, B., & Williams, P. (1998). A novel strategy for assessing the effects of curriculum reform on student competence. *Journal of Chemical Education, 75*(8), 986–992. https://doi.org/10.1007/s10956-005-4425-3

ABOUT THE AUTHOR

Stephen C. Ehrmann has received two national awards for his contributions to distance education research. He has served as vice provost for teaching and learning at The George Washington University; associate director for Research and Evaluation at the Kirwan Center for Academic Innovation at the University System of Maryland; vice president of the nonprofit Teaching Learning and Technology Group; director of the Flashlight Program for the Evaluation of Educational Uses of Technology; senior program officer for interactive technologies with the Annenberg/CPB Projects; program officer with the Fund for the Improvement of Postsecondary Education (FIPSE); and director of educational research and assistance at The Evergreen State College. He might be best known as the coauthor of the 1996 article, "Implementing the Seven Principles: Technology as Lever" (American Association for Higher Education, 1996) He earned a PhD in management and higher education from MIT.

INDEX

Also available from Stylus

The Small College Imperative

Models for Sustainable Futures

Mary B. Marcy

Foreword by Richard Ekman

"Mary B. Marcy's *Small College Imperative* is an urgent reminder that the all too familiar status quo approach in no longer viable and offers a timely blueprint for institutional transformation: five basic business and educational models for small colleges, institutional examples under each model, and risk evaluations for each. Higher education's challenging 'new normal' environment calls for decision-making at a pace heretofore unknown within the academy. Consequently her imperative is a clarion call for an immediate and rigorous analysis of sustainable institutional mission, market, and outcome expectations." —***Doug Orr***, *AGB Senior Fellow and Consultant, and President Emeritus, Warren Wilson College*

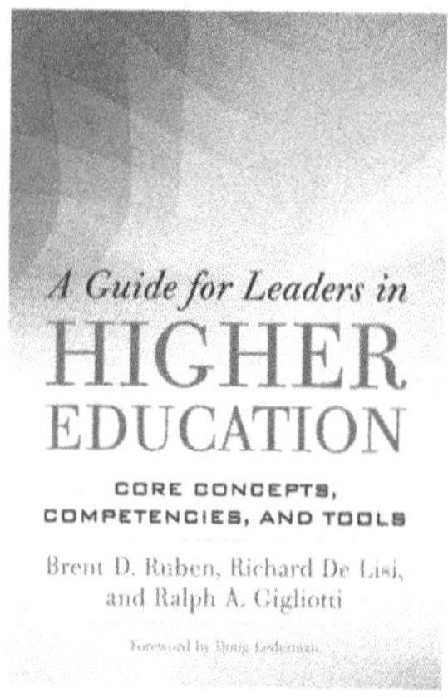

A Guide for Leaders in Higher Education

Core Concepts, Competencies, and Tools

Brent D. Ruben, Richard De Lisi, and Ralph A. Gigliotti

Foreword by Doug Lederman

"The work is both frank and optimistic, a common characteristic of Brent Ruben, a practiced author in reference works for higher education leaders. The Strengths, Weaknesses, Opportunities, and Threats analysis that constitutes the foreword sets a tone that pervades this book: challenges abound in the current landscape of American higher education, but informed and prepared leaders can respond to these challenges and achieve excellence.

"A *Guide for Leaders in Higher Education* succeeds in providing accessible and useful resources to individuals across different leadership roles. . . . As a midpoint between textbook and reference work, it is successful at both and provides a clear and unbiased background to issues facing current leaders."—***Reflective Teaching***

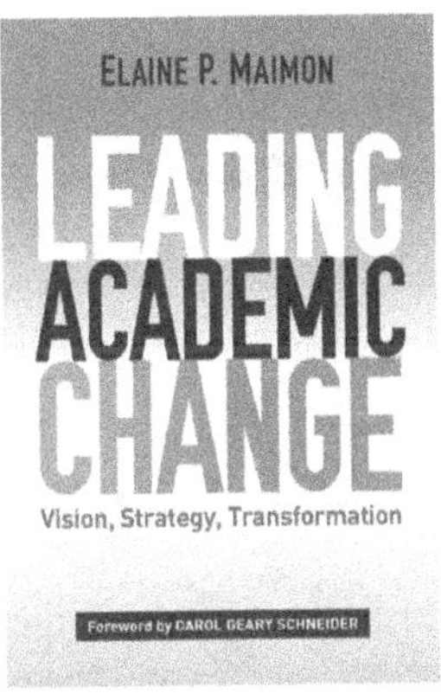

Leading Academic Change

Vision, Strategy, Transformation

Elaine P. Maimon

Foreword by Carol Geary Schneider

"College students were far more uniform in age, race, and socioeconomic background a few decades ago than they are now, yet colleges and universities have often failed to design programs of study that work for these students. *Leading Academic Change* outlines the steps to take toward change on behalf of the new majority students, the non-White, low-income, working, second language, or adult learners who often find themselves in very unfamiliar territory in college classrooms.

"This book is, above all, a call to give all students our very best, both in our classrooms and at our institutions. It is also a well-timed reminder that change is inevitable and that equity can be a means to achieving educational quality."—***Reflective Teaching***

Practical Wisdom

Thinking Differently About College and University Governance

Peter D. Eckel and Cathy A. Trower

Foreword by Richard Chait

"As colleges and universities face increased scrutiny and mounting pressures, effective board governance has moved from a luxury to a necessity; if our institutions are to succeed in this environment, they need effective leadership from their boards. Few are equipped to provide it. What a gift to have the wisdom of two distinguished leaders at our disposal during this critical time for higher education. Their extensive experience working with presidents and boards is displayed on every page of this book. Observations and suggestions are organized into clear and accessible essays that will prove equally valuable for public and private boards, presidents, and leaders. During a time of tumult and change, the wise counsel of Practical Wisdom serves as an essential guide to effective governance."—***Mary B. Marcy***, *President, Dominican University of California*

22883 Quicksilver Drive
Sterling, VA 20166-2019

Subscribe to our e-mail alerts: www.Styluspub.com